Theology after Wittgenstein

Theology
after Wittgenstein

Fergus Kerr

Basil Blackwell

British Library Cataloguing in Publication Data
Kerr, Fergus.
  Theology after Wittgenstein.
  1. Wittgenstein, Ludwig
  I. Title
  192   B3376.W564

  ISBN 0–631–14688–1
  ISBN 0–631–16186–4 (Pbk)
Library of Congress Cataloging in Publication Data
Kerr, Fergus.
  Theology after Wittgenstein.

  Bibliography: p.
  Includes index.
  1. Wittgenstein, Ludwig, 1889–1951—Contributions to
theology. 2. Theology—Methodology—History—20th
century. I. Title.
B3376.W564K44 1986 203'.01   85–30810
ISBN 0–631–14688–1
ISBN 0–631–16186–4 (pbk.)

Typeset by Cambrian Typesetters, Frimley, Surrey
Printed in Great Britain by Page Bros, Norwich

Contents

Preface   vii
Biographical Note   ix
Abbreviations   xi

PART ONE   Stories of the Soul

1   The Modern Philosophy of the Self   3
2   Wittgenstein's Religious Point of View   28

PART TWO   Changing the Subject

3   The Solipsist in the Flyglass   55
4   The Private Object in the Mind's Eye   77
5   Suspicions of Idealism   101
6   Assurances of Realism   121

PART THREE   Theology without the Mental Ego

7   Wittgenstein's Theological Investigations   145
8   Questions in the Philosophy of Theology   168

Bibliography   191
Index   199

self = autonomous + rational consciousness

Preface

indifference to community
antipathy to the body

W. clears the ground for a non-metaphysical way of thinking

The purpose of this book is to show students of theology that they have much more to gain from reading Wittgenstein's later writings than is commonly supposed, and, secondly, that they are in a good position to understand them.

I start, in chapter 1, with some examples of the innocent way in which modern Christian theology in the West often works with a picture of the self as an autonomous and rational consciousness, which turns out, in chapter 2, to be Wittgenstein's quarry. Excavating St Augustine's egocentric story of how an infant learns to speak, Wittgenstein strives to uncover the indifference to community and the antipathy to the body which constitute the metaphysical way of thinking that has interacted with Christian theology from the start.

In chapters 3 and 4 I try, by quoting freely, to lure the suspicious theologian into understanding how Wittgenstein wants to change the position of the subject. In chapters 5 and 6, on idealism and realism respectively, I go on to suggest how, by subverting this famous dilemma, he clears the ground for a non-metaphysical way of thinking.

For a modern philosopher, Wittgenstein wrote a great deal about religion, much more than I explore here. In chapter 7, however, I identify some of the overtly theological topics in his later writings. Finally, in chapter 8, I sketch a few theological questions that may look rather different in the light of understanding Wittgenstein.

My debts are many: I have tried to record them as I go along, but I owe far more than my references might suggest to the weird and wonderful works of Stanley Cavell, from which I have received endless delight and illumination.

Nobody writing about Wittgenstein could fail to express gratitude to his literary executors, G. E. M. Anscombe, Rush Rhees and G. H. von Wright, for making so much of the *Nachlass* available. I have sometimes departed from the official translations, to bring out a nuance, and occasionally to make what seems to me to be a correction.

I have some longstanding debts: to Donald MacKinnon, who introduced me to philosophy at Aberdeen between 1950 and 1952; to Cornelius Ernst, who got me to read Wittgenstein, together with Aristotle and Thomas Aquinas, at Hawkesyard in 1957–60; and to Adolf Darlap, who helped me to understand Heidegger (much easier than understanding Wittgenstein), in Munich between 1964 and 1965.

I have other more recently incurred debts. But for the initiative of Julia Mosse I should not have written this book at all. I have been discussing Wittgenstein for many years with students whose primary interest seldom lay in philosophy. I am grateful for their doggedness in unravelling this or that remark when I was willing to give up. I wish to thank Christopher Blaschak, Tony Crowley, Michael Daly, David Foster, Birgit Kremmers, Gilbert Markus and Nicholas O'Sullivan, as well as Selwyn Gross and Gareth Moore, who also read drafts of the book. I am particularly grateful to Timothy Ashplant and Timothy Radcliffe, who read the final draft and suggested improvements which I have tried to incorporate. But even if my thesis is wrong, in detail or completely, I have quoted so much from Wittgenstein himself that readers new to his work will surely be attracted to explore further, to reach their own conclusions.

Biographical Note

Ludwig Wittgenstein, born in Vienna on 26 April 1889 and baptized into the Roman Catholic Church, was the youngest of the eight children of a wealthy industrialist. He was educated at home and at school in Linz, and later took up mechanical engineering, studying in Berlin and Manchester, where he spent three years between 1908 and 1911. An interest in mathematics led him to study the philosophy of mathematics, and he worked for five terms in Cambridge with Bertrand Russell in 1912–13.

When war broke out he joined the Austrian army, serving on the Russian and then the Italian fronts, before becoming a prisoner of war. His *Logisch-Philosophische Abhandlung*, completed in August 1918, appeared in 1921, and again in 1922, with C. K. Ogden's translation, under the more familiar title of *Tractatus Logico-Philosophicus*.

Having trained as a teacher, he worked in remote village schools in Lower Austria for the six years 1920–6. He then spent two years in Vienna, supervising the building of a mansion for his sister.

Drawn back to philosophy, particularly by discussions with members of the so-called Vienna Circle, who had founded logical positivism partly on a deep misunderstanding of the *Tractatus*, he returned to Cambridge early in 1929 as a research student. He submitted the *Tractatus* and received his PhD in June 1929. From 1930 he lectured in philosophy at Cambridge, succeeding G. E. Moore as Professor of Philosophy in 1939.

During the 1939–45 war he worked as a porter at Guy's Hospital in London and then as a laboratory assistant in the Royal Victoria Infirmary in Newcastle upon Tyne. In 1949 he was found to have cancer. During his last years he continued to write copiously, as he had done since 1929, although he published nothing. He died at the home of his doctor in Cambridge on 29 April 1951.

His *Philosophical Investigations*, with facing English translation by G. E. M. Anscombe, appeared in 1953. His papers are kept in the Wren Library, Trinity College, Cambridge: photocopied and microfilmed sets may also be consulted in many libraries throughout the world. Much has been published since his death, including such major texts as *Remarks on the Foundations of Mathematics* (1956, revised 1978), *The Blue and Brown Books* (1958), *Zettel* (1967) and *On Certainty* (1969).

Abbreviations

The following abbreviations are used to refer to the major works of Wittgenstein and to editions of his lecture notes etc. compiled by others.

BB   *The Blue and Brown Books*, Blackwell, Oxford, 1958.

CV   *Culture and Value*, ed. G. H. von Wright in collaboration with Heikki Nyman, trans. Peter Winch, Blackwell, Oxford, 1980.

LC   *Lectures and Conversations on Aesthetics, Psychology and Religious Belief*, ed. C. Barrett, Blackwell, Oxford, 1966.

LW   *Last Writings on the Philosophy of Psychology*, vol. I, ed. G. H. von Wright and Heikki Nyman, trans. C. G. Luckhardt and Maximilian A. E. Auc, Blackwell, Oxford, 1982.

NB   *Notebooks 1914–1916*, ed. G. H. von Wright and G. E. M. Anscombe, trans. G. E. M. Anscombe, Blackwell, Oxford, 1961.

NL   'Notes for lectures on "Private Experience" and "Sense Data" ', ed. Rush Rhees, *Philosophical Review*, 77 (1968), pp. 275–320; reprinted in *The Private Language Argument*, ed. O. R. Jones, Macmillan, London, 1971, pp. 232–75.

OC   *On Certainty*, ed. by G. E. M. Anscombe and G. H. von Wright, trans. Denis Paul and G. E. M. Anscombe, Blackwell, Oxford, 1969.

PG   *Philosophical Grammar*, ed. Rush Rhees, trans. A. J. P. Kenny, Blackwell, Oxford, 1974.

PI   *Philosophical Investigations*, ed. G. E. M. Anscombe and R. Rhees, trans. G. E. M. Anscombe, Blackwell, Oxford, 1953.

PR   *Philosophical Remarks*, ed. R. Rhees, trans. R. Hargreaves and R. White, Blackwell, Oxford, 1975.

RC   *Remarks on Colour*, ed. G. E. M. Anscombe, trans. L. L. McAlister and M. Schättle, Blackwell, Oxford, 1977.

RFGB   *Remarks on Frazer's Golden Bough*, ed. Rush Rhees, trans. ?
          Miles and R. Rhees, Brynmill, Retford, 1979.
RFM   *Remarks on the Foundations of Mathematics*, ed. G. H. von
          Wright, R. Rhees, G. E. M. Anscombe, trans. G. E. M. Ansco?
          revised edition, Blackwell, Oxford, 1978.
RPP I   *Remarks on the Philosophy of Psychology*, vol. I, ed. G. E. ?
          Anscombe and G. H. von Wright, trans. G. E. M. Anscombe,
          Blackwell, Oxford, 1980.
RPP II   *Remarks on the Philosophy of Psychology*, vol. II, ed. G. H.
          Wright and Heikki Nyman, trans. C. G. Luckhardt and M. A?
          Aue, Blackwell, Oxford, 1980.
RW   *Recollections of Wittgenstein*, ed. Rush Rhees, Oxford Unive?
          Press, Oxford, 1984.
TLP   *Tractatus Logico-Philosophicus*, trans. D. F. Pears and B. F.
          McGuinness, Routledge & Kegan Paul, London, 1961.
WLAA   *Wittgenstein's Lectures Cambridge 1932–1935*, ed. Alice Amb?
          Blackwell, Oxford, 1979.
WLDL   *Wittgenstein's Lectures Cambridge 1930–1932*, ed. Desmond
          Blackwell, Oxford, 1980.
WLFM   *Wittgenstein's Lectures on the Foundations of Mathematics*
          Cambridge 1939, ed. Cora Diamond, Harvester Press, Hasso?
          1976.
Z   *Zettel*, ed. G. E. M. Anscombe and G. H. von Wright, trans.
          G. E. M. Anscombe, Blackwell, Oxford, 1967.

Wittgenstein usually divided his writing into numbered 'remarks', but
not always. Citations of his work will thus sometimes follow the usual
page-reference form (e.g. *BB*, p. 11); but where only a number is given,
the reference is to a remark rather than a page (e.g. *PI* 46). The first part
of *PI* is numbered by remarks, the second part, by pages. Sometimes,
however, the reference is to the part of the book as well as the remark
(e.g. *RC* III, 295).

In memory of George Gordon Kerr
1892–1967

PART ONE

Stories of the Soul

CHAPTER 1

The Modern Philosophy of the Self

It is very *remarkable* that we should be inclined to think of civilization — houses, streets, cars etc. – as distancing man from his source, from what is sublime, infinite and so on. Our civilized environment, along with the trees and plants in it, then seems as though it were cheaply wrapped in cellophane and isolated from everything great, from God, as it were. That is a remarkable picture that forces itself on us.

(CV, p. 50)

THE TURN TO THE SUBJECT

According to some theologians, the metaphysical load that Christian practice and discourse carry needs little exploration. They would say, for example, that confessing the doctrine of the Trinity or the resurrection of Christ is much more important than worrying about the consequences for theological work of the ancient controversy between realism and idealism. They would say, even after thinking about it, that the epistemological bias of the age need not interfere with biblical exegesis or systematic theology.

To disabuse them would be a difficult task. I would say only that, if theologians proceed in the belief that they need neither examine nor even acknowledge their inherited metaphysical commitments, they will simply remain prisoners of whatever philosophical school was in the ascendant 30 years earlier, when they were first-year students; or, more likely, 350 years earlier, which takes us neatly to René Descartes (1596–1650) and his famous turn to the first-person perspective: 'I think, therefore I am'.

The modern conception of the self sprang from explicitly theological concerns. The *Meditations*, which Descartes published in 1641, bore the subtitle: 'in which are demonstrated the existence of God and the immortality of the soul'. This work, dedicated to the Paris theology faculty, started the turn to the self. In the First Meditation, trying to get at what must be regarded as absolutely certain and indubitable, Descartes articulates the thought that one may be completely deceived about everything:

I will suppose therefore that not God, who is supremely good and the source of truth, but rather some malicious demon of the utmost power and cunning has employed all his energies in order to deceive me. I shall think that the sky, the air, the earth, colours, shapes, sounds and all external things are merely the delusions of dreams which he has devised to ensnare my judgement. I shall consider myself as not having hands or eyes, or flesh, or blood or senses, but as falsely believing that I have all these things.[1]

In the Second Meditation the famous conclusion follows:

In that case I too undoubtedly exist, if he is deceiving me; and let him deceive me as much as he can, he will never bring it about that I am nothing so long as I think that I am something. So after considering everything very thoroughly, I must finally conclude that this proposition, *I am, I exist*, is necessarily true whenever it is put forward by me or conceived in my mind.[2]

Descartes then seeks an understanding of what this 'I' is, the existence of which he has shown. He finds that he has to break with his inherited ideas – for example, 'that I was nourished, that I moved about, and that I engaged in sense-perception and thinking; and these actions I attributed to the soul'. Instead of that account of the soul, which would have made good sense to Thomas Aquinas or Aristotle, and is very much what Wittgenstein retrieves, Descartes systematically thinks away every attribute of the soul until he reaches bedrock:

At last I have discovered it – thought; this alone is inseparable from me ... I am, then, in the strict sense only a thing that thinks; that is, I am a mind, or intelligence, or intellect, or reason ... a thinking thing.[3]

I can make this thought-experiment, thinks Descartes: I can 'peel off' everything, my previous beliefs, my senses, my body, my confidence even that the external world really exists, and I shall find, in the end, that I am *essentially* a thinking thing.

As he says, he no longer thinks of himself as a man or even as a rational animal; he has redefined what it is to be human in terms of

[1] *Philosophical Writings*, vol. II, p. 15.
[2] Ibid., p. 17.
[3] Ibid., p. 18.

consciousness, and his perspective is completely *egocentric*. Thus the Cartesian 'I', as a thing that thinks, comes into the philosophical tradition.

Theology and spirituality, certainly in the Roman Catholic tradition, has been permeated with Cartesian assumptions about the self. The key figure, in transmitting the paradigm, is no doubt Malebranche (1638–1715). It is Kant (1724–1804), however, in his heroic efforts to reconcile the rationalism of the Enlightenment with his Lutheran inheritance, who has produced the most influential variation on the Cartesian paradigm – memorably described by Iris Murdoch:

> How recognizable, how familiar to us, is the man so beautifully portrayed in the *Grundlegung*, who confronted even with Christ turns away to consider the judgement of his own conscience and to hear the voice of his own reason. Stripped of the exiguous metaphysical background which Kant was prepared to allow him, this man is with us still, free, independent, lonely, powerful, rational, responsible, brave, the hero of so many novels and books of moral philosophy.[4]

As the remainder of this chapter will show, the picture of the self-conscious and self-reliant, self-transparent and all-responsible individual which Descartes and Kant between them imposed upon modern philosophy may easily be identified, in various guises, in the work of many modern theologians. It is a picture of the self that many modern philosophers, Wittgenstein certainly among them, have striven to revise, incorporate into a larger design, or simply obliterate.

THE DIAPHANOUS SELF

William James (1842–1910) was one of the philosophers to whom Wittgenstein often referred. His *Principles of Psychology*, published in 1890, is alluded to more frequently than any other text in the whole course of Wittgenstein's *Philosophical Investigations*. To see where the story of the Cartesian self had reached towards the end of the nineteenth century, it is instructive to note a comment that James offers on a sentence by G. E. Moore (1873–1958), who was to become one of Wittgenstein's life-long friends.

[4] *The Sovereignty of the Good*, p. 80.

James writes as follows:

> we are supposed by almost every one to have an immediate consciousness of consciousness itself. When the world of outer fact ceases to be materially present, and we merely recall it in memory, or fancy it, the consciousness is believed to stand out and to be felt as a kind of palpable inner flowing, which, once known in this sort of experience, may equally be detected in presentations of the outer world.[5]

James then cites this remark by G. E. Moore:

> The moment we try to fix our attention upon consciousness and to see *what*, distinctly, it is, it seems to vanish. It seems as if we had before us a mere emptiness. When we try to introspect the sensation of blue, all we can see is the blue; the other element is as if it were diaphanous. Yet it *can* be distinguished, if we look attentively enough, and know that there is something to look for.[6]

The first person plural should not mislead us: Moore is attempting to perform a very Cartesian act of self-discovery. He is trying to discover, by introspection, what the sensation of blue is – but 'that which makes the sensation of blue a mental fact seems to escape us: it seems, if I may use a metaphor, to be transparent – we look through it and see nothing but the blue'.[7] But what the metaphor suggests, if I am not mistaken, is the possibility that one is somehow able to stand back from one's body, so to speak, to look through it at the world beyond. We look through our eyes as through a window, which, by being transparent, is all but invisible.

William James certainly detected the implications:

> I believe that 'consciousness', when once it has evaporated to this estate of pure diaphaneity, is on the point of disappearing altogether. ... Those who still cling to it are clinging to a mere echo, the faint rumour left behind by the disappearing 'soul' upon the air of philosophy.[8]

It is a conclusion, as he recognizes, that many of his readers would

---

[5] *Radical Empiricism*, p. 25.
[6] *Philosophical Studies*, p. 25.
[7] Ibid., p. 20.
[8] *Radical Empiricism*, p. 4.

resist. He formulates their objection in words that would make sense to many people today:

> 'All very pretty as a piece of ingenuity', they will say, 'but our consciousness itself intuitively contradicts you. We, for our part, *know* that we are conscious. We *feel* our thought, flowing as a life within us, in absolute contrast with the objects which it so unremittingly escorts. We cannot be faithless to this immediate intuition.

James goes on, in his characteristically bluff and boisterous fashion, to declare that the stream of consciousness, which he too is aware of having, consists chiefly of the stream of his breathing:

> The 'I think' which Kant said must be able to accompany all my objects, is the 'I breathe' which actually does accompany them.[9]

So much, in outline, for the state of the question at the beginning of the twentieth century. Clearly, if William James's account of the self as a fictitious entity that has been philosophically generated out of the sensation of one's breathing is the alternative on offer, people with theological interests are going to opt for something more like Moore's vision of consciousness as an elusive diaphaneity. The question is, however, whether such a sublime philosophy of consciousness has much to do with the men and women that we are.

THEOLOGIANS IN THE CARTESIAN ERA

It is not difficult to find theologians who acknowledge the great significance for theological reflection of the Cartesian emphasis on the individual. As recently as 1967, for example, Karl Rahner reaffirmed that there must be no going back on 'the transcendental–anthropological turn in philosophy since Descartes'.[10] Modern philosophy has proved bad for rethinking Christian doctrine, so Rahner says, because it has developed into 'a philosophy of the autonomous subject', who is closed against the transcendental experience in which dependence on God becomes evident. The modern self is ill at ease in Christianity because of this failure to evince a sense of creatureliness. It appears to be a matter of moral blindness. But what if the difficulty arises at an earlier stage? What if the

[9] Ibid., p. 22.
[10] *Theological Investigations*, vol. IX, p. 38.

problem lies with the very idea of the Rahnerian subject? What if the transcendental experience that Rahner wants for the self only obscures and excludes the membership of a community and a tradition that gives rise to subjectivity in the first place?

My argument in this book is that, far from still having to incorporate Cartesian assumptions about the self, as Rahner supposed, modern theology is already saturated with them. It should be noted at once, however, that Rahner's belief that theology is belatedly still absorbing modern philosophy finds no echo in such an equally distinguished theologian as Eberhard Jüngel. In great detail, he argues that Descartes' attempt to demonstrate the necessity of God's existence by way of establishing the subject's self-certainty has resulted in the 'death of God' crisis.[11] Far from having yet to accept the turn to consciousness, theology has already been nearly ruined by it. The perspective within which Jüngel pursues his theological reflections is, then, resolutely anti-Cartesian.

Thus, while both vigorously asserting the importance of the anthropocentric turn, Rahner and Jüngel could not be further apart in their assessment of its significance for theology. Jüngel, to my mind, has by far the more plausible story to tell, but he seems to me greatly to exaggerate the ease with which the Cartesian legacy may be detected and disowned. He writes as if *naming* the problem were sufficient to *overcome* it. My contention, by contrast, is that such a powerfully attractive set of metaphysical preconceptions cannot be so swiftly dismissed. Theology (not alone in this) is surely much too deeply coloured by varieties of the philosophy of the self-conscious and autonomous individual. Besides, as we shall see, the idea of the detached ego itself springs from decidedly religious roots. In any case, since it is far from being simply wrong, the critique that is required is more a matter of making different connections than one of wholesale rejection.

Karl Barth, as one would expect, has provided the most substantial modern critique of theological anthropology.[12] But he had already come to grips in an interesting way with the Cartesian picture of the self.

There are two points to note. First, according to Barth, the Cartesian proof of the existence of God spirals back into the Cartesian metaphysics of the self:

This idea of divinity is innate in man. Man can produce it at will from the treasury or deficiency of his mind. It is made up of a series of pre-eminent attributes which are relatively and primarily attributes

[11] *God as the Mystery of the World*, pp. 111–26.
[12] *Church Dogmatics*, vol. III, part 2, p. 46.

of the human mind, and in which the latter sees its own
characteristics – temporality, finitude, limited knowledge and ability
and creative power – transcended in the absolute, contemplating
itself in the mirror of its possible infinitude, and yet remaining all the
time within itself even though allowing its prospect of itself to be
infinitely expanded by this speculative extension and deepening. By
transcending myself, I never come upon an absolute being confronting
and transcendent to me, but only again and again upon my own
being. And by proving the existence of a being whom I have conjured
up only by means of my own self-transcendence, I shall again and
again succeed only in proving my own existence.[13]

This might have been composed as a criticism of Rahner's trans-
cendentalism, although Barth could hardly have heard of it at this time.
In the Cartesian proof of God's existence, it is a certain conception of the
human being's capacity for self-transcendence that Barth finds endlessly
reflected.

Secondly, and even more instructively, Barth finds it necessary to
attack the Cartesian emphasis on the thinking self when he discusses the
right use of imagination in learning from Scripture.[14] The biblical
account of the creation is a saga that has a great deal to teach us:

We must dismiss and resist to the very last any idea of the inferiority or
untrustworthiness or even worthlessness of a 'non-historical' depiction and
narration of history. This is in fact only a ridiculous and middle-class habit
of the modern Western mind which is supremely phantastic in its chronic
lack of imaginative phantasy, and hopes to rid itself of its complexes
through suppression.[15]

As the original practitioner of 'narrative theology', Barth denounces the
rationalist epistemological bias that has affected so much biblical
exegesis since the Enlightenment:

But the human possibility of knowing is not exhausted by the ability
to perceive and comprehend. Imagination, too, belongs no less
legitimately in its way to the human possibility of knowing. A man
without imagination is more of an invalid than one who lacks a
leg.[16]

---

[13] Ibid., vol. III, part 1, p. 360.
[14] See D. F. Ford, 'Barth's interpretation of the Bible'.
[15] Barth, *Church Dogmatics*, vol. III, part 1, p. 81.
[16] Ibid, p. 91.

Theologians are thus well aware of the difficulties that the modern philosophy of the self has created. My suspicion, however, is that versions of the mental ego of Cartesianism are ensconced in a great deal of Christian thinking, and that many theologians regard this as inevitable and even desirable. The appeal of some theological writing also seems inexplicable unless it touches crypto-Cartesian assumptions which many readers share.

THE DEFICIENT ANGEL

Consider the work of Karl Rahner, whom nobody would dispute is by far the most influential Roman Catholic theologian of the day. The speed with which he charms the reader into his system, and the immediate rewards in theological assurance, conceal, from readers who are philosophically unwary, the problematic character of the first step. The obsession with epistemological preliminaries, which should at once indicate how Cartesian his theological constructions are likely to prove, only persuades students that they are on the right track. The presentation is usually so abstractly 'metaphysical', and the sentences so carapaced with qualifications, that the innocent eye runs swiftly over them in order to get to more familiar theological material.

In *Foundations of Christian Faith*, an acknowledged masterpiece of modern theology, Rahner begins by raising basic epistemological problems. To be sure, he expands the discussion to take in other dimensions of human life; but it is always as the cognitive subject that people first appear in Rahner's theology. Students alerted to the bias of the Cartesian legacy would suggest that language or action, conversation or collaboration, are more likely starting points, particularly if, like Rahner, you want to move towards a very strong ecclesiology. Yet consciousness, self-awareness in the cognitive act, is always his favoured way into theology.

'Everyone strives to tell someone else, particularly someone he loves, what he is suffering': this innocuous observation is Rahner's example to illustrate the following somewhat more obscure proposition: 'The original self-presence of the subject in the actual realization of his existence strives to translate itself more and more into the conceptual, into the objectified, into language, into communication with another'.[17] When the sequence is repeated in the next sentence, suspicions are aroused: 'Consequently in this tension between original knowledge and

[17] *Foundations of Christian Faith*, p. 16.

the concept which always accompanies it there is a tendency towards greater conceptualization, towards language, towards communication.'

Rahner's natural assumption – that communication comes after language, and language comes after having concepts – is precisely what the Cartesian tradition has reinforced. His example suggests that, when I am in pain, I first have the thought that I am in pain, I then put it into words and finally I find someone to whom to communicate it. It is, of course, an entirely natural thing to think: this is often exactly how it happens. But if the picture is that I *always*, or even *normally*, have the thought before I put it into words, then something very like the Cartesian vision of my epistemological predicament begins to show through. It looks as if Rahner might be working on the double assumption that I am in a position to identify my sensations prior to my applying the customary labels to them, and secondly that what I reveal of them to someone else remains wholly at my command. The picture would thus be that I enjoy immediate non-linguistic knowledge of my own inner experiences, while what I am experiencing at any moment necessarily remains hidden from other people unless I deliberately choose to disclose it. On this account, to put it straight into the Wittgensteinian terms which we still have to see, the individual is supposed to be able to locate, by a private mental act of ostensive definition, some item of his own consciousness, while, for knowledge of other people's thoughts or feelings, he is supposed to depend entirely on inferences that he makes from their outward demeanour (see chapter 4).

Such suspicions may seem exaggerated, even to readers who have been alerted by Wittgensteinian considerations. It certainly does not follow inescapably, either from his preoccupation with epistemology or from the little remark about having a pain, that Rahner was a firm subscriber to the story of the soul as a solitary individual, with direct acquaintance with his own inner experiences and in command of divulging them. But consider Rahner's account, unfortunately bare of examples, of an ordinary case of knowing something:

> In the simple and original act of knowledge, whose attention is focused upon some object which encounters it, the knowing that is co-known and the knowing subject that is co-known are not the *objects* of the knowledge. Rather the consciousness of the act of knowing something and the subject's consciousness of itself, that is, the subject's presence to itself, are situated so to speak at the other pole of the single relationship between the knowing subject and the known object. This latter pole refers to the luminous realm, as it were, within which the individual object upon which attention is focused in a particular primary act of knowledge can become manifest.

This subjective consciousness of the knower always remains unthematic in the primary knowledge of an object presenting itself from without. It is something which goes on, so to speak, behind the back of the knower, who is looking away from himself and at the object.[18]

The subjective consciousness of the knower, which goes on behind his back when he is looking at something, admittedly laced in metaphor, cannot but arouse suspicion, even if the idea makes any sense at all. But it leads immediately to the heart of Rahner's conception of the self:

If we ask what the *a priori* structures of this self-possession are, then we must say that, without prejudice to the mediation of this self-possession by the experience of sense objects in time and space, this subject is fundamentally and by its very nature pure openness for absolutely everything, for being as such.[19]

Thus, without prejudice to the finitude of time and place, the Rahnerian self turns out to be nothing less than 'pure openness for absolutely everything'. Even to suspect that our openness is for a good deal less than absolutely everything is already to have passed beyond that suspicion, so Rahner goes on to claim. To recognize your limitations is already to have transcended them. This takes us to Rahner's central notion of 'transcendence' and, with some omissions, to this key paragraph:

a subject which knows itself to be finite . . . has already transcended its finiteness . . . In so far as he experiences himself as conditioned and limited by sense experience, and all too much conditioned and limited, he has nevertheless already transcended this sense experience. He has posited himself as the subject of a pre-apprehension which has no intrinsic limit, because even the suspicion of such an intrinsic limitation to the subject posits this pre-apprehension itself as going beyond the suspicion.[20]

Obviously much more of Rahner's text would need to be probed; I do not claim to have fully understood even the pages from which I have quoted. But his preoccupation with the cognitive subject is clear: other people remain marginal to his epistemology. The emphasis on the subject's capacity for self-consciousness and self-reflexiveness, and his openness for absolute being, is equally conspicuous. By our insatiable questioning we are, perhaps unwittingly, the products of a dynamic

[18] Ibid., p. 18.
[19] Ibid., pp. 19–20.
[20] Ibid., p. 20.

movement of ceaseless self-transcendence towards the steadily receding horizon which is the absolute: in effect, anonymously, the deity. To feel chafed by sense experience is already to be the subject with this capacity for the absolute.

The theological rewards of Rahner's account of the epistemological privileges of the subject are very great. When he comes to discuss arguments for the existence of God, for example, he is able to say that we already have in place all that is required to substantiate them:

> In all the so-called proofs for the existence of God the one and only thing which is being presented and represented in a reflexive and systematic conceptualization is something which has already taken place: in the fact that a person comes to the objective reality of his everyday life both in the involvement of action and in the intellectual activity of thought and comprehension, he is actualizing, as the condition which makes possible such involvement [*Zugriff*] and comprehension [*Begriff*], an unthematic and non-objective pre-apprehension [*Vorgriff*] of the inconceivable and incomprehensible single fullness of reality.[21]

Whenever we have to do with the world to which we belong, whether working on it or thinking about it, we are always carried by that prior grasp *of*, which is simultaneously a being gripped *by*, that absolute which is, however 'anonymously', the deity itself. This antecedent invasion by the absolute constitutes our very nature as rational and self-reflexive beings in the first place. Self-presence is necessarily, if often unwittingly, openness to the absolute. We only have to reflect on the subject's constitutive self-presence in any cognitive or volitional act to have proof of the existence of God.

Rahner is also able to put this conception of the subject as essentially openness to the absolute at the heart of his brilliant interpretation of Chalcedonian Christology. The doctrine of the Incarnation almost ceases to be a scandal, so natural does it come to seem that, in one special case, such a self-presence should be transparently, even diaphanously, open to the absolute in what one might call 'hypostatic union'.

The unattractively abstract jargon, admittedly much less offensive in German and to ears tuned to a different philosophical tradition, easily tempts the reader to skip the epistemological preliminaries to get on to Rahner's theology. To make proofs of God's existence redundant, to offer a coherent account of the doctrine of the Incarnation, and much else, could not fail to draw students into the Rahnerian system – but at

[21] Ibid., p. 69.

what price? And why does it seem so natural to pay it? Much more evidently needs to be said, but there surely is a prima facie case for suggesting that Rahner's most characteristic theological profundities are embedded in an extremely mentalist–individualist epistemology of unmistakably Cartesian provenance. Central to his whole theology, that is to say, is the possibility for the individual to occupy a standpoint beyond his immersion in the bodily, the historical and the institutional. Rahner's consistently individualist presentation of the self emphasizes cognition, self-reflexiveness and an unrestricted capacity to know. It rapidly leaves time and place behind. It is not surprising if this mentalist–individualist conception of the self seems difficult to reconcile with the insistence on hierarchy and tradition that marks Rahner's Roman Catholic ecclesiology.[22]

We are conditioned and limited by sense experience – 'all too much', as Rahner expresses it. But where should we be if we were not so conditioned and limited? What if our relation to our physical and social setting is a matter for gratitude and celebration, rather than resentment and frustration? The idea that it is by leaving the world that one finds oneself is an ancient and a very alluring one, but, without radical reflection on its ambiguities, is it the most productive way of regarding ourselves, particularly from a Christian theological perspective? However interesting the theological developments, what if Rahner's foundation lies in supposing that, as Cornelius Ernst once put it,[23] one is 'a more or less deficient angel'?

THE THEISTIC GAMBLER

Karl Rahner will never be a popular writer; but much more widely read theologians reveal even more deeply entrenched Cartesian assumptions – Teilhard de Chardin for instance.[24] But consider the following remark in a recent book by Hans Küng, probably the most widely read theological writer in the English-speaking world: 'The history of modern epistemology from Descartes, Hume and Kant to Popper and Lorenz has – it seems to me – made clear that the fact of any reality at all independent of

[22] See G. D. Kaufman, 'Is there any way from Athens to Jerusalem?'
[23] See the pregnant footnote in his introduction to Rahner, *Theological Investigations*, vol. I, p. xiii.
[24] See Anthony Kenny's review of *The Phenomenon of Man*: the prototype for detecting Cartesian psychology in modern theology, reprinted in *The Legacy of Wittgenstein*, chapter 8.

our consciousness can be accepted only in an act of trust'.[25] He is arguing that, since we have nothing better than such an act of trust at the basis of our belief in the existence of *anything* outside our own minds, it is not very strange for us to have nothing better than an act of trust on which to found our belief in the existence of God. In fact, it is the line that he takes in his earlier massive book on God (*Does God Exist?*).

Here, after much else, we are offered a brilliant account of the radical scepticism introduced by Descartes and, according to Küng, carried further by Pascal. He might seem to be preparing the way to deflect it. He refers to Wittgenstein and to a galaxy of other philosophers in the Anglo-American tradition, but he shows no sign of understanding the deeply anti-Cartesian campaign which they have been conducting for the past 50 years. Anyone familiar with Wittgenstein's imaginative explorations of the charms of scepticism, as Küng is supposed to be, would expect a rehearsal of the anti-sceptical arguments at this point. But Küng tells us, as the book unfolds, that the alternative to radical scepticism in its most nihilistic Nietzschean form (everything is illusory) is simply the gamble that reality does really exist: 'Every human being decides for himself his *fundamental attitude* to reality: that basic approach which embraces, colours, characterizes his whole experience, behaviour, action'.[26] Innocent of all anti-Cartesian suspicions, he goes for individual decisions as establishing the foundations for belief in the reality of anything outside one's mind: It is up to me to choose the basic attitude I adopt towards this radically dubious reality with which I am surrounded. I simply *decide* to trust the reality of other people and all the rest of the rich tapestry of life.

Küng alludes to Kierkegaard and indeed to Ignatius Loyola, but this liberty that the individual has to choose his reaction to reality is expounded mainly with reference to recent Anglo-American philosophers, whose writings have encouraged Küng to think that it is all a matter of the individual's decision. From Popper he has learnt that 'all rational thinking rests on a choice, a resolution, a decision, an attitude'. From Carnap he has learnt that the principles and rules of argument in an artificial language are a matter of 'free choice'. From Wittgenstein he has learnt, even more amazingly, 'that the rules of language may be chosen with complete freedom'.[27] This would be laughable if the case were not being built up with such earnestness and apparent learning. All along the line, culling phrases from one supposed authority after another

[25] *Eternal Life?*, p. 275.
[26] *Does God Exist?*, p. 432
[27] Ibid., p. 461.

that would knock out the adversary, Küng insists that the individual is at liberty to choose his beliefs about the intelligibility, and even about the reality, of the world around him. The argument comes to a head in these words: 'as there is no logically conclusive proof for the reality of reality, neither is there one for the reality of God'.[28] Belief in the existence of God is a 'basic decision', a creative option one might say, on analogy with the *Urentscheidung* in favour of the reality of the external world. In other words: there is nothing irrational about believing in the existence of God – after all, we have nothing stronger than *belief* in the existence of *anything* outside our own minds.

The self is pictured as having to confront that which surrounds it and then decide whether it is as it seems, or even whether it is there at all. A viewpoint seems to be available from which one is able to survey the passing show and impose a pattern upon it. The individual seems to be free to put what construction he will upon the surrounding world. The supposition is always that one is able to view the world from somewhere else – as if one were God, perhaps.[29]

A MODERN PERSON

The idea of the self as being in a position to decide how to take the world reappears in the writings of Don Cupitt, another widely read theologian. In *Taking Leave of God*, for example, he writes as follows:

> the principles of spirituality cannot be imposed on us from without and cannot depend at all upon any external circumstances. On the contrary, the principles of spirituality must be fully internalized a priori principles, freely adopted and self-imposed. A modern person must not any more surrender the apex of his self-consciousness to a god. It must remain his own.[30]

While one shares Cupitt's detestation of a morality or a religion imposed by intimidation or spiritual terrorism, it looks very much as if we are again presented with the self-conscious individual who is apparently able and willing to provide himself with principles of spirituality from his own inner resources. Indeed, the apex of his self-consciousness, wherever that is supposed to be, has to be entirely independent of all external circumstances as well as of every god. As

[28] Ibid., p. 574.
[29] For more detail see my 'Küng's case for God'.
[30] *Taking Leave of God*, p. 9.

Cupitt says, in the book's opening words, 'Modern people increasingly demand autonomy, the power of legislating for oneself . . . they want to live their own lives, which means making one's own rules, steering a course through life of one's own choice, thinking for oneself, freely expressing oneself and choosing one's own destiny'.

Now, obviously, it is a good thing to think for oneself, to have the freedom to express oneself, and the like. The central values of the Enlightenment, which Cupitt so vigorously defends, have yet to take root in most of the social systems across the world, including many supposedly Christian countries. But does the rhetoric not outrun the case? What is meant by 'making one's own rules'? The difficult and precious responsibility of trying to think for oneself, have an informed conscience, etc., is presented as if one had the power to invent one's own standards of right and wrong. Everyone wants to be captain or his or her own soul: 'I must be autonomous in the sense of being able to make my own rules and impose them upon myself', as Cupitt says. And, again in the preface to *Taking Leave of God*, 'each chooses his own ethic'.

There is much more in this vein of heady individualist libertarianism. But there is all the difference in the world between making the rules one's own, critically and responsibly, and making one's own rules: a distinction that Cupitt blurs all the time, apparently without noticing. Much of the time what he says is no more than any sensible parent's advice in a society like ours – attempting to get a child to think for itself, to be reasonably suspicious of the moral standards that it finds around it, and so on. Certainly everybody needs to have the courage to be critical of the decrees of any authority, political or religious, that demands unthinking loyalty and mindless obedience. But again and again, in the midst of much common sense, Cupitt's rhetoric conjures up a more exciting and dramatic portrait of the Modern Person who creates his own moral rules, which, happily – but also just as it happens – coincide with those adopted by like-minded individuals so that it becomes possible, as he says, to form 'a liberal democratic republic, the best kind of society'.

Don Cupitt's theological writings are haunted by the figure of this self-conscious autonomous individual to whom it falls in radical freedom to choose his own moral world. The Cartesian ego has received a Kantian twist. But this lonely agent of ultimate choice is plainly the alter ego of the epistemological subject who can view everything from a standpoint outside history and community. The solitary individual with the God's-eye view turns out, unsurprisingly, to be the creator of his own moral universe. The person at the centre of modern theology has acquired the attributes of the God of classical theology. Far from still having to get theology to make more room for the modern philosophy of the self, it is time to recognize that philosophy today (in Wittgenstein especially) is striving to rid itself of a certain displaced theology. The worldless ego is remarkably like a substitute for the deity in the game of creation. It is, at any rate, bizarre to be writing theology with such deference for the self as deity, transcending and creating the world, just when philosophers have developed strategies to extirpate this alienated theology from philosophy.

Ironically enough, in more recent speculations, Don Cupitt has appealed to Wittgenstein's work in support of his radical voluntarism: 'Everywhere he is a thoroughgoing constructivist and voluntarist: logical necessity is created by the rules governing language. If he is a non-realist about religion, he is also a non-realist about everything else'.[31] This is a highly disputable reading of Wittgenstein which I attempt to refute in chapter 5. The only point to be made at this stage is that Cupitt's emphasis on the will of the autonomous self is entirely consonant with Küng's picture of the individual who is required to gamble on the reality of the world outside his head.

THE HIDDEN SELF

What a hydra-headed creature it is! The self who is free to survey the world from no point of view within the world often turns out to be the self who is totally impenetrable to anyone else – in this being once again rather like the hidden God of classical theism.

Consider the following thought from Schubert Ogden's attempt to conceive divine action on analogy with human action:

> Behind all its public acts of word and deed there are the self's own private purposes or projects, which are themselves matters of action or decision. Indeed, it is only because the self first acts to constitute itself, to respond to its world, and to decide its own inner being, that it 'acts' at all in the more ordinary meaning of the word; all its outer acts of word and deed are but ways of expressing and implementing the inner decisions whereby it constitutes itself as a self.[32]

To speak of one's private purposes and inner decisions as lying 'behind' one's words and deeds is a perfectly good figure of speech. On the other hand, if our words and deeds, thus our speaking and acting, are 'but' ways

[31] *The Sea of Faith*, p. 222.
[32] *The Reality of God*, p. 177.

of expressing and implementing the inner goings-on and private states of consciousness by which one is constituted, a dualism of inner and outer, and of private and public, seems to threaten the integrity of the common space constituted by language and our other institutions. It is no great surprise, therefore, to find Ogden continuing as follows:

> the primary meaning of God's action is the act whereby, in each new present, he constitutes himself as God by participating fully and completely in the world of his creatures . . . his relation to his creatures and theirs to him is direct and immediate. The closest analogy . . . is our relation to our own bodily states, especially the states of our brains. Whereas we can act on other persons and be acted on by them only through highly indirect means such as spoken words and bodily actions, the interaction that takes place between our selves or minds and our own brain cells is much more intimate and direct.[33]

As a self, then, I can exercise a more direct effect on my brain than I can on other persons. But how does the mind direct the brain? Leaving aside Ogden's non-classical, Whiteheadian doctrine of God, is his conception of the self not very curious? These speculations about the relation of God to the world surely rely on an account of the mind–body question which makes the obscure even more obscure.

It would be difficult to find a better case for Wittgensteinian treatment. We are being asked to think that the self which acts in an 'intimate and direct' manner on its brain interacts with other selves 'only through highly indirect means such as spoken words and bodily actions'. One human being has no access to another except by resorting to the circuitous devices of gesture and speech: a poor relation compared with the immediate access that the self has to its own brain! I have nothing better than language and the expressiveness of my own body with which to communicate with other people, while I have a direct view of my inner experiences, if not even of my brain processes.

THE DIMENSIONLESS PINPOINT

Timothy O'Connell, in an important and ambitious recent attempt to reconstruct moral theology as a discipline, obviously requires some working model of the moral agent. Amazingly, he comes out with this beautiful portrait of the self-disembodying Cartesian ego:

[33] Ibid., pp. 177–8.

> In an appropriate if homely image, then, people might be compared to onions . . . At the outermost layer, as it were, we find their environment, their world, the things they own. Moving inward we find their actions, their behaviour, the things they do. And then the body, that which is the 'belonging' of a person and yet also *is* the person. Going deeper we discover moods, emotions, feelings. Deeper still are the convictions by which they define themselves. And at the very centre, in that dimensionless pinpoint around which everything else revolves, is the person himself or herself – the I.[34]

At least when Descartes peeled off he discovered a thinking thing, rather than 'a dimensionless pinpoint'. The essence of the person is now within an ace of vanishing. In the crucible of O'Connell's homely negative anthropology, in fact, we find the residue of the *actus purus* of apophatic theology: God, once again.

Once again, as it turns out, the disembodied self has problems with relating to people (as one onion to another). It is even difficult to say what we mean by the expression 'human person':

> personhood is the one thing about human beings which we cannot actually see. In a process of reflection I seek to discover myself. I hold up to the eye of my mind the experiences that I have. But who looks at these experiences? I do, the person that I am . . . Repeatedly I attempt to gaze upon the very centre of myself. But I always fail. For the real person that I am always remains the viewer, and can never become the viewed.[35]

What I see, in my own case as well as in meeting other people, is never anything but actions behind which I have to 'posit' a 'moreness' which is 'the human person'. It certainly seems that, when I meet a human being in ordinary circumstances, I have to hazard the opinion that he has a soul (see *PI*, p. 178).

Very much the same philosophy of the self reappears in a recent attempt by Peter Chirico to make sense of the notion of the infallibility of the Church. Laying his epistemological foundations necessarily with great care, he comes out with the following two remarks. First: 'No man can be more certain of anything than he is of his own self-awareness. The standard or limit of human certitude and human infallibility is that consciousness which one has of oneself'.[36] The name of Descartes is never mentioned in Chirico's book, but that first sentence might have been drawn straight from the Second Meditation.

[34] *Principles for a Catholic Morality*, p. 59.
[35] Ibid., p. 59; see also Stanley Hauerwas, *The Peaceable Kingdom*, pp. 40–1.
[36] *Infallibility*, p. 58.

The second remark comes in the context of explaining why Christ, after the resurrection, is 'unrecognizable as risen in our experience'. The Church, so Chirico says, 'cannot identify the risen Christ present in its experience because the risen condition and mode of operation makes Christ inaccessible to human awareness'. Making a move very like Hans Küng's, Chirico argues that there is nothing all that strange about our being unable to recognize the risen Christ because, after all,

> We never recognize or see another being in itself; we only recognize directly the effects of its activity towards us, activity that occasions the actualization of our experiential continua in a way we can consciously detect and isolate. Hence, for example, we identify the change in us as caused by the visible appearance, the barking, and the furry softness of the dog that enters the room.[37]

Thus, when the doggy contour, the canine yelp, the hairy surface and so on variously impinge upon my senses, I put two and two together and judge that it must be that cur from down the street. That is hardly a caricature. Chirico's highly sophisticated attempt to rehabilitate one of the most contentious bits of Roman Catholic dogma is founded on the crudest epistemological dogmas of the Cartesian/empiricist tradition.

THE GODLIKE OTHER

Gordon Kaufman, finally, in his attempt to work out a notion of 'transcendence without mythology', provides a good example with which to break off this catalogue, for two reasons. His theory also trades on a radically Cartesian conception of the self – but, after criticism, he has disowned it. Thus, he not only shows once again the powerful imaginative hold that the modern philosophy of the subject has in theology, but also that, perhaps a little unusually, a theologian can learn to acknowledge his metaphysical prejudice and disclaim it.

Consider the following account of our relationship to one another:

> What one directly experiences of the other are, strictly speaking, the external physical sights and sounds he makes, not the deciding, acting, purposing centre of the self – though we have no doubt these externalities are not *merely* physical phenomena, but are the outward and visible expression of inner thought, purpose, intention.[38]

[37] Ibid., p. 76.
[38] *God the Problem*, pp. 63–4.

So far so good, one may be inclined to say: this is, after all, 'strictly speaking'. But is it not already a highly artificial sense of 'experiencing' someone's presence to suggest that it is 'the external physical sights and sounds he makes' that one 'directly experiences'? Is it not when someone's behaviour is unintelligible that one is left with bare physical sights and sounds? But the passage goes on as follows:

> In our interaction with other persons we presuppose a reality (the active centre of the self) *beyond* that which we immediately perceive . . . It is in the act of communication that we discover that the other is more than merely physical being, is a conscious self; it is in the experience of speaking and hearing that we come to know the *personal* hidden behind and in the merely physical. This is the most powerful experience we have of *transcendence of the given* on the finite level, the awareness of genuine activity and reality *beyond* and *behind* what is directly open to our view.

We '*presuppose*' that there is more to the people around us than there is to rocks and cows, and it is in conversation with them that our hypothesis is tested and, no doubt usually, verified. In later criticism of such remarks as these Kaufman has acknowledged that his conception of transcendence here depended on a picture of the self as a reality that is radically private and normally concealed.[39] He has gone on to develop a conception of the self which involves the possibility of our deceiving one another, and the like, such that one has a certain inaccessibility to others, but, as he now allows, in a great deal of what an individual does and says his or her inner self is perfectly transparent. Accordingly, Kaufman has set about revising his theory of the hiddenness of God in terms of an avowedly non-Cartesian understanding of the self.

Of course, in this sample of theologians, drawn from the Roman Catholic, Anglican, Methodist and Mennonite traditions, the variations on the figure of the mentalist–individualist self would deserve examination. My concern is, however, with the common paradigm. One thing is beyond dispute: in each case the starting point is naturally assumed to be the individual. With Karl Rahner the emphasis is upon the subject in a cognitive situation: the capacity for self-presence in acts of knowledge is tacit apprehension of the absolute. With Hans Küng and Don Cupitt we have a very powerful picture of the self as isolated will and autonomous individual, left in radical freedom to bring a moral universe out of the surrounding chaos either by a gamble of faith or by a God-like act of

[39] Ibid., p. xiii, taking into account criticism by Michael McLain, 'On theological models'.

creation. With Schubert Ogden the self has retreated into the inviolable mystery of a private inner world from which messages emerge obliquely in signs. Timothy O'Connell's 'onion peel view of the self', as he calls it, strips off nature, culture, the body, desires and convictions, to lay bare one's identity in a dimensionless pinpoint. Peter Chirico holds out for good old-fashioned Cartesian epistemology in the purest form – nothing is more certainly known to me than the contents of my own mind, nothing else is ever directly accessible. Finally, Gordon Kaufman, until he thought better, supposed that it was only when the other opened his mouth and spoke that one realized that a person lay hidden within the middle-sized, lightly sweating and gently palpitating object on the other side of the dinner table.

In every case, though variously, and sometimes very significantly so, the model of the self is central to some important, sometimes radical and revisionary, theological proposal or programme. A certain philosophical psychology is put to work to sustain a theological construction. Time and again, however, the paradigm of the self turns out to have remarkably divine attributes. The philosophy of the self that possesses so many modern theologians is an inverted theology which philosophers today are working hard to destroy.

THE ABSOLUTE CONCEPTION OF REALITY

My claim is that the most illuminating exploration of the continuing power of the myth of the worldless (and often essentially wordless) ego is to be found in the later writings of Ludwig Wittgenstein. It will be helpful to approach them by way of a brief survey of more recent investigations of the question, from somewhat different angles. This will indicate how post-Wittgensteinian philosophers consider the Cartesian legacy.

Bernard Williams has suggested that, in its main thrust, the Cartesian project must be intuitively attractive to most people brought up in a culture such as ours, where paradigms of knowledge are tied to ideals of impartiality and objectivity. In the historical context of the rise of modern physics and natural science, Descartes strove to delineate what Williams calls 'the absolute conception of reality'.[40] The investigator, that is to say, tries to extricate himself from every contingent restriction upon the pursuit of knowledge. He aspires to be so liberated from bias in his outlook that he can attain a representation of the world exactly as it

---

[40] *Descartes: The Project of Pure Enquiry*, p. 65.

is, uncoloured by his prejudices. To enjoy such an objective picture of reality demands the elimination of the observer. The goal of natural science, for people in the Cartesian tradition, is to have a representation of reality that eschews all the properties that things have simply as a result of the presence of human beings among them. To want the absolute conception of reality is to aim at a description of things as they would be in our absence. This or something like it has been the spirit animating science since the seventeenth century. It would be returning to barbarism to surrender or even dilute such ideals of impartiality and objectivity.

For Descartes, however, the absolute conception of reality was tied up with the individual's certainty of his own existence as well as with the idea that God alone guaranteed the existence of reality outside the individual's consciousness. The great modern expression of the ideals of the new science was embedded in the epistemology of the disengaged ego as well as in natural theology. Thus, if certain metaphysical options have swayed theology, they have themselves a theological matrix. The eggshell clings to the thinking.

However well concealed it may be, these metaphysical aspirations still carry a powerful theological charge. As Paul Feyerabend has pointed out, the very idea of a personal experience that would be infallible, self-authenticated, unprejudiced etc., because it was the result of sloughing off all received opinion, tradition, authority etc., in fact the very idea with which Descartes opens the *Meditations*, is remarkably reminiscent of certain tendencies in the history of Christianity that would put the individual believer directly and inwardly into a relationship with God which excluded in advance all mediation by a historical community with authoritative tradition, rituals and the like.[41] The desire of philosophers like Russell and Moore, at the dawn of modern analytic philosophy in Cambridge, to get down to the primitive sense-data in order to find a level of experience that would supposedly be free of all interpretation, subjective distortion etc., is fundamentalism transposed into an adjacent discourse. I shall say a little more about logical atomism in chapter 3.

The drive for objectivity, then, brought with it the uncanny thought that the only perfect depiction of any reality would have to be from nobody's point of view – or, if there is any difference, from God's. Objectivity requires, as Thomas Nagel argues, 'departure from a specifically human or even mammalian viewpoint'.[42] A 'transcendence of

[41] *Problems of Empiricism*, p. 19.
[42] *Mortal Questions*, ch. 14.

the self' – his phrase – is required for an account of what is of interest simply in itself, independently of anybody's interest in it. As he says, 'the power of the impulse to transcend oneself and one's species is so great, and its rewards so substantial' that 'detachment from the contingent self' is bound to remain an ethical as well as a scientific obligation – again, if there is any difference. But it is not surprising that there has been an equally powerful drive to protect the inner reality of the subject, which is what makes Cartesian psychology appealing.

THE DRIVE TO SPIRITUAL REALITY

Charles Taylor has long been concerned with the same issue. He began with polemics against behaviourism and allied theories (not to mention the practices that they have legitimated), particularly in psychology.[43] His subsequent essays, recently collected, constitute a general critique of the drive in many (if not all) of the social sciences to exclude subjectivity.[44]

According to the absolute conception of reality, then, the subject is detached from the significance that things have for him personally, so that he attains a certain freedom to objectify, and thus to depict and control, them all, in various ways and with degrees of expected success. The appeal of this ideal, so Taylor says, derives from the obvious benefits of mastering one's natural and historical environment, not to mention one's personality and domestic circumstances. But there is more to it, he suggests. The ideal of the detached self, disengaged from personality and historical contingency, and thus free to see reality objectively, is, so he says, a new variant of that immemorial 'aspiration to rise above the merely human, to step outside the prison of the peculiarly human emotions, and to be free of the cares and the demands they make on us' – 'a novel variant of this very old aspiration to spiritual freedom'.[45] The drive to objectivity is thus 'of spiritual origin', or, at any rate, that helps to account for its attractions.

It is highly paradoxical, as Taylor goes on to say, because the ideals of our modern scientific culture are supposed to have left religion behind. Of course there is a great difference. In the modern case, it is the natural universe that is to be represented as independently as possible of all

[43] *The Explanation of Behaviour.*
[44] *Philosophical Papers*, vols. 1–2.
[45] Ibid., vol. 1, p. 112.

human interpretation. In the ancient case, the self wants to lose itself in dispassionate contemplation of the reality that subsists in itself. In both cases, however, the subject is required to transcend human emotions, cultural and historical particularity, and the like, in order to encounter, bare, that which is truly important. What Taylor claims, then, is that the motivating power of the secular and naturalistic drive to extend objective knowledge as far as possible, *and even farther*, receives its deepest energy from 'the traditional drive to spiritual purity'.[46]

Thus, for several modern philosophers (and my list could easily be extended), one of the deep questions on the agenda is, in one way or another, how to expose and explain the continuing psychological and imaginative appeal of a certain picture of the self's place in the world. Despite what is often supposed, even by themselves, philosophers are, at their best, no more interested in knockdown logical refutations of this or that thesis than they are in spinning airy speculations. They try, rather, to search out the obscure motivations in the recurrence in fresh guises of certain metaphysical prejudices which, although often 'refuted', retain their vitality and charm.

What I am suggesting in the rest of this book, at least as a way of getting into his later writings, is that Wittgenstein was attempting to free himself from something very like 'the absolute conception of reality'. Consider only this somewhat gnomic utterance from the *Tractatus*:

> Here it can be seen that solipsism, when its implications are followed out strictly, coincides with pure realism. The self of solipsism shrinks to a point without extension, and there remains the reality co-ordinated with it. (*TLP* 5.64)

As the self withdraws, the world in itself emerges. When subjectivity becomes so perfect that it vanishes into absolute privacy, reality remains in splendid objectivity. In the notes of 1916, from which this remark was extracted, Wittgenstein went on as follows:

> What has history to do with me? Mine is the first and only world!
> I want to report how *I* found the world.
> What others in the world have told me about the world is a very small and incidental part of my experience of the world. (*NB*, p. 82)

That sounds very much like an echo of Descartes' voice in the *Meditations*: what I have learnt from the community and the tradition,

---

[46] Ibid., p. 113.

from my companions and precursors, is a tiny and marginal factor in my *Welt-Erfahrung*. But, again in notes that did not survive into the *Tractatus*, Wittgenstein completed his day's reflections thus:

> The human body, however, my body in particular, is a part of the world among others, among beasts, plants, stones, etc., etc.
> Whoever realizes this will not want to procure a pre-eminent place for his own body or for the human body.
> He will regard humans and beasts quite naively as objects [*Dinge*] which are similar and which belong together. (*NB*, p. 82)

In the *Investigations*, however, the first move is to secure a focal significance for the human body, and thus to inaugurate a radical critique of 'the traditional drive to spiritual purity'.

CHAPTER 2

Wittgenstein's Religious
Point of View

That the feeling we have for our life is comparable to that of a being who
could choose his own standpoint in the world is, I believe, the basis of
the myth – or belief – that we choose our body before birth.

(*RFGB*, p. 11)

THE MARE'S NEST OF WITTGENSTEINIAN FIDEISM

Wittgenstein's connection with theology is commonly supposed to have
to do with 'Wittgensteinian fideism'. Since that is all that many
theologians know about him, this mare's nest requires to be examined
briefly.

The phrase seems to have been introduced into the philosophy of
religion by Kai Nielsen.[1] As an atheist he wants to go on arguing that
religion is a massive error. He therefore objects to the way that certain
Christian philosophers allegedly maintain that religion is a way of life
that is intelligible only to participants. On such a view, when an atheist
argues against the existence of God he could not know enough about the
matter to make sense, let alone engage in refutation of the hypothesis.
The concepts that are familiar in religion are supposedly available only to
those who share the 'form of life' in which they are employed. Religious
talk supposedly constitutes a distinctive and autonomous 'language-
game' which outsiders could not understand, let alone expose as
incoherent or erroneous.

This clearly counts as a form of fideism: unless you have the faith you
cannot take part in rational discussion of the Christian religion. The
appeal of some such view for believers who are weary of arguing is plain
enough. It also has a good deal of plausibility: those who argue for, as
well as those who argue against, the existence of God, frequently lead the
ordinary Christian to question whether they know what they are talking
about. But whether this variety of fideism is 'Wittgensteinian' is another
matter.

[1] 'Wittgensteinian fideism' is the title of his article published in *Philosophy* in 1967.

His name has been drawn into this kind of apologetics for two reasons. Religion is, firstly, thought to be the sort of thing that he meant by a 'form of life' – which therefore just 'has to be accepted' (*PI*, p. 226). Religious talk, secondly, is supposed to be a 'language-game', autonomous, with its own rules, intelligible only to the players. Wittgenstein may well have been some kind of fideist, but these cannot have been the reasons. The very idea that religion, or anything else on that grand scale, would count as a 'form of life' in Wittgenstein's sense, although it keeps cropping up, has to be excluded on textual grounds. Once that is made clear, the notion that a language-game is autonomous, in the sense required to generate 'Wittgensteinian fideism', proves equally empty. (It may nevertheless be an Aunt Sally which it is instructive for philosophers of religion to have in stock.)

Philosophers have certainly made heavy weather of Wittgenstein's phrase. For example: 'Neither Wittgenstein nor any of those influenced by him have given any clear indication of how a form of life is to be identified. It might perhaps be enlightening if applied to the study of geographically separate societies in some such field as social anthropology'.[2] That at least indicates the scale of the phenomenon to which the phrase 'form of life', for all its putative obscurity, is supposed to refer. Roger Trigg goes on: 'We have only to ask whether religion, Christianity or a particular Christian denomination such as Catholicism should be regarded as a form of life. There is no clear way of answering such a question . . .'.

The clearest way is to consult Wittgenstein's text. It soon emerges that, whatever he meant by forms of life, it was nothing on the scale that Trigg has suggested.

That would be an entirely natural meaning for the phrase 'form of life', but it is not what Wittgenstein meant by it, at any rate in the *Investigations*. Introducing it, he writes as follows:

> It is easy to imagine a language consisting only of orders and reports in battle. – Or a language consisting only of questions and expressions for answering yes and no. And innumerable others. – And to imagine a language means to imagine a form of life [*eine Lebensform*]. (*PI* 19)

Wittgenstein has already asked us to imagine a community in which giving and obeying orders would be the only 'system of communication' required: something much less than *we* call language (*PI* 2–3). It is

[2] Roger Trigg, *Reason and Commitment*, p. 72. An even grander view is assumed by Saul Kripke, *Wittgenstein on Rules*, pp. 96–8.

natural for us, when asked to imagine a language, to think of English or Japanese, which then easily brings to mind a whole way of life, a literature and so on. Indeed, at an earlier stage, Wittgenstein identified a language with a culture: 'We could easily imagine a language (and that means again a culture) in which there existed no common expression for light blue and dark blue' (*BB*, p. 134). He is considering how one colour might be distinguished from another in some radically different way from our actual practice. To imagine a language in which green and red were identified, and yellow and blue were similarly identified, would require us to imagine, for instance, a tribe with two castes: the patricians always in red and green clothes, the plebians always in blue and yellow. Each caste would have its colours. If the social distinction had bitten deeply enough into people's sensibilities they would simply perceive the colours differently from the way that we do. Asked to compare a piece of red cloth with a piece of green, one of these tribesmen would unhesitatingly say that they were the same colour – patrician.

The example needs more detail to be convincing, but the point I want to make is that, even here, it already suggests the sort of 'forms of life' that are in question.

In the second appearance of the expression 'form of life' in the *Investigations* it is equated with the kind of activity that customarily includes some speaking (*PI* 23): activities such as giving and obeying orders, describing, surmising, forming a hypothesis, telling a story, joking, counting, thanking, cursing, greeting and praying. Wittgenstein is evidently concerned with very elementary patterns of social interaction, not all of which are easily found in every society (perhaps some tribes have not got to the stage of forming a hypothesis, perhaps some have gone past praying), but which are the kind of activities out of which human life is formed, no matter what language is spoken or what the social structure is. To imagine a language is to imagine an activity such as commanding and obeying. Language is the conversation that is interwoven with the characteristic activities of human life. According to Norman Malcolm, a good example of a form of life would be the complex of gestures, facial expressions, words and activities, that we call pitying and comforting an injured man.[3] To wonder whether such a vast and internally diverse phenomenon as religion or Catholicism would count seems superfluous.

Oddly enough, Malcolm is largely responsible for the talk about religion as a form of life:

[3] *Knowledge and Certainty*, p. 119.

I do not wish to give the impression that Wittgenstein accepted any religious faith – he certainly did not – or that he was a religious person. But I think that there was in him, in some sense, the *possibility* of religion. I believe that he looked on religion as a 'form of life' (to use an expression from the *Investigations*) in which he did not participate, but with which he was sympathetic and which greatly interested him.[4]

Indeed, this idea has evidently grown on Malcolm:

Religion is a form of life; it is language embedded in action – what Wittgenstein calls a 'language-game'. Science is another. Neither stands in need of justification, the one no more than the other.[5]

That is a perfect example of Wittgensteinian fideism. 'Religion' – like 'science' – is 'language' embedded in 'action', and neither stands in need of 'justification'.

But if Malcolm's original insight is correct – that comforting a wounded creature is a good example of what Wittgenstein meant by a form of life – it is impossible to apply the expression to any phenomenon on the scale of 'religion' – which must include innumerable language-laced activities. As a very specific exchange that normally involves talking, comforting someone cannot be isolated, either empirically or conceptually, from encouraging him, explaining, promising, calling a doctor and many other different but obviously related activities. The notion that any language-game functions in isolation from others has no basis in Wittgenstein's work. On the contrary: the famous and beautiful comparison between our language and a medieval city shows how far from his mind such a notion was (*PI* 18).[6]

It is sad that Wittgenstein's name is now associated, perhaps irreversibly, with a position in the philosophy of religion that rests upon radical misconceptions of two of his most inventively liberating expressions (about which more will be said in chapter 3). For one thing, it deters theologians from reading his work.[7]

---

[4] *Ludwig Wittgenstein: A Memoir*, 1958, p. 72; 1984, p. 60.

[5] *Thought and Knowledge*, p. 212.

[6] Interestingly different from Descartes' admiration for planned towns, *Discourse on Method*, 2, in *Philosophical Writings*.

[7] The best introductions to this whole debate, both with good bibliographies, are Alan Keightley, *Wittgenstein, Grammar and God*, and Patrick Sherry, *Religion, Truth and Language-Games*. See also Nicholas Lash, 'How large is a "language game"?'.

WITTGENSTEIN'S PERSONAL RELIGION

Norman Malcolm, as we have seen, felt confident enough about the matter to deny that Wittgenstein was a religious man. Georg von Wright spoke somewhat more cautiously: 'I do not know whether he can be said to have been "religious" in any but a trivial sense of the word. Certainly he did not have a Christian faith. But neither was his view of life un-Christian, pagan, as was Goethe's'.[8] G. E. M. Anscombe, more bluntly, once declared that nobody understood Wittgenstein's views on religion.[9] She has reported that he once said of his later work: 'Its advantage is that if you believe, say, Spinoza or Kant, this interferes with what you believe in religion; but if you believe me, nothing of the sort'[10] The authority of these three eminent philosophers, all of whom were among his friends, is not to be gainsaid. Faced with the considerable number of profound and often anguished remarks about religious matters extracted from the *Nachlass* and included in *Culture and Value*, Norman Malcolm has modified his judgement.[11] We also have to take account of notes made by M. O'C. Drury, a friend of long standing with whom Wittgenstein had theological discussions for 20 years.[12]

Drury remembered the following three remarks, all made in 1949, while Wittgenstein was living in Dublin, working on the second part of the *Investigations*.

First:

> I would like it if some day you were able to read what I am writing now. My type of thinking is not wanted in this present age, I have to swim so strongly against the tide. Perhaps in a hundred years people will really want what I am writing. (*RW*, p. 160)

This remark concurs with many others. As to what he meant, some measure of agreement exists. The judgement of David Pears is representative: 'All his philosophy expresses his strong feeling that the great danger to which modern thought is exposed is domination by science,

---

[8] Malcolm, *Memoir*, p. 18.

[9] Hallett, *Companion to Wittgenstein's 'Philosophical Investigations'*, p. 426.

[10] 'Misinformation: What Wittgenstein really said', *The Tablet*, 1954.

[11] *Memoir*, 1984, pp. 82–3.

[12] Drury, who arrived from Dublin when the dying Wittgenstein was already unconscious, took the responsibility for asking a Dominican priest, Fr Conrad Pepler, then of Blackfriars, Oxford, to say the customary prayers – 'But I have been troubled ever since as to whether what we did then was right' (*RW*, p. 171).

and the consequent distortion of the mind's view of itself'.[13] Our understanding of ourselves as subjects has been deeply affected by the drive to objectivity that appeared in a new form in the seventeenth century, to put it in Charles Taylor's terms.

The second remark is as follows:

> It is impossible for me to say in my book one word about all that music has meant in my life. How then can I hope to be understood? (*RW*, p. 160)

The book that became the *Investigations* is baffling indeed, but few readers can have suspected that this might have anything to do with the importance of *music*.

The third remark Drury noted is equally enigmatic:

> I am not a religious man but I cannot help seeing every problem from a religious point of view. (*RW*, p. 79)

It is clear that Drury took this remark to apply to the problems about which Wittgenstein was writing in his philosophical work at the time. (To judge by the memoirs that have appeared, Wittgenstein was not a man whom one could easily ask to explain his more gnomic utterances.) In some sense, then, every problem traversed in the course of his writing was envisaged from a religious point of view – whatever we are to make of that astonishing claim.

There are thus dimensions to his work which were visible to himself but which have not become accessible to many readers. After decades of academic exegesis, often of high quality and great penetration, how much evidence is there (Drury asks) that people have found the absence of anything about music a likely reason for not understanding the tenor of the *Investigations*? And how many of the commentators read the book in the light of the claim that the problems are all being regarded from a religious point of view?

Drury records a conversation, again in 1949, when he outlined Origen's doctrine of apocatastasis (that ultimately all rational and moral agents, angels and human beings, will have the grace of salvation): 'This was a conception that appealed to me – but it was at once condemned as heretical' (*RW*, p. 161). Wittgenstein was pleased to hear that his friend was reading some of the early Church

---

[13] *Wittgenstein*, p. 183.

Fathers, but Drury's Origenist sympathies ran into the following response:

> Of course it was rejected. It would make nonsense of everything else. If what we do now is to make no difference in the end, then all the seriousness of life is done away with. Your religious ideas have always seemed to me more Greek than biblical. Whereas my thoughts are one hundred per cent Hebraic.

On a somewhat later occasion Wittgenstein asked Drury which was his favourite gospel, apparently only in order to disclose that his own was St Matthew's: 'Matthew seems to me to contain everything' (*RW*, p. 164). He went on to say that he could not make headway with the Fourth Gospel.

Again in 1949, walking in Phoenix Park, Drury said that he regretted not having lived a religious life, and they agreed that his having met Wittgenstein (in 1929), which diverted him from ordination, was perhaps to blame. Drury quotes Wittgenstein as then saying:

> I believe it is right to try experiments in religion. To find out, by trying, what helps one and what doesn't. When I was a prisoner of war in Italy [in 1918–19, near Monte Cassino], I was very glad when we were compelled to attend mass. Now why don't you see if starting the day by going to mass each morning doesn't help you to begin the day in a good frame of mind? I don't mean for one moment that you should become a Roman Catholic. (*RW*, p. 165)

Drury had, as it turned out, too much loyalty to the Church of Ireland tradition in which he had been brought up to be able to follow out this extraordinary suggestion – but he seems to have regarded it as a perfectly reasonable one for Wittgenstein to make.

It is not easy to evaluate any of these remarks. In that last exchange it appears that living a religious life would be bound up with going to church services. Many years before, perhaps in 1930, when Wittgenstein had given Drury a copy of Samuel Johnson's *Prayers*, they talked about the ancient liturgies, particularly the collects in the Latin mass. When Drury said that it was surely important that priests be ordained to carry on the tradition, Wittgenstein replied:

> At first sight it would seem a wonderful idea that there should be in every village someone who stood for these things. But it hasn't worked out that way at all. For all you and I can tell, the religion of

the future will be without any priests or ministers. I think one of the things you and I have to learn is that we have to live without the consolation of belonging to a Church. (*RW*, p. 114)

He suggested that Drury might join the Quakers, but visited him the following morning especially to withdraw the suggestion: 'As if nowadays any one organization was better than another.'

In about 1935, Wittgenstein spent Easter with Drury's family in Devon. He was pleased to be included in the ceremony of receiving a chocolate egg, and said how much he liked keeping up such old customs. When Drury said that he missed taking part in the Holy Week liturgy Wittgenstein replied:

> But Drury, when I wanted to dissuade you from becoming a parson I didn't mean that you should as the same time cease to attend your church services. That wasn't the idea at all. Though it may be that you have to learn that these ceremonies haven't the importance you once attached to them – but that doesn't mean that they have no importance. (*RW*, p. 129)

He went on to remark that often, as he develops, 'a man's expression of his religion becomes much drier'. He cited the case of his Protestant aunt, whose only religious observance was to keep Good Friday 'in complete silence and complete abstinence'.

There is no reason to expect a great philosopher to have clear and consistent ideas about religion any more than about literature or politics. On all these topics, as *Culture and Value* and the memoirs of friends testify, Wittgenstein had thoughts that were deep, together with others that seem tentative and even, to my mind, quite idiotic.[14] The charge that Drury's religious ideas were too 'Greek', while his own were purely 'Hebraic', which may in any case have been a joke, could be no more than a conventional view about the Hellenization of Christianity. On the other hand, in the early 1930s particularly, if the notes in *Culture and Value* are anything to go by, Wittgenstein had a strong sense of his Jewishness. The attitude to liturgy recalls Seamus Heaney's remark

---

[14] Consider the following remarks, all in *CV*: 'Rousseau's character has something Jewish about it', p. 20. 'The people now making speeches against producing the bomb [in 1946] are undoubtedly the *scum* of the intellectuals, but even that does not prove beyond question that what they abominate is to be welcomed', p. 49. 'If Christianity is the truth then all the philosophy that is written about it is false', p. 83.

about 'the necessities that crave expression after the ritual of church going has passed away'.[15] But there is much else, as the reader will easily find, particularly in the notes from 1937 onwards, that demonstrates the depth and persistence of Wittgenstein's thoughts about religion. While one cannot dispute Georg von Wright's judgement that he did not have a Christian faith, many passages in *Culture and Value* disclose a sympathetic and penetrating under-standing of the matter that few Christians, never mind professed non-believers, could match.

SAYING NO MORE THAN WE KNOW

So far we have seen little with any obvious bearing on the question of how the problems discussed in the *Investigations*, or anywhere else in the later writings, may be considered 'from a religious point of view'. Drury's theory must now be explained.[16]

In 1948, again walking in Dublin's Phoenix Park, Drury and Wittgenstein discussed philosophers (rather unusually, it seems). Wittgenstein said that Kant and Berkeley were 'deep thinkers'. He felt that he would not get far with Hegel because he seemed 'to be always wanting to say that things which look different are really the same' (*RW*, p. 157). It is not clear how much of Hegel's work he had ever read, but he placed himself at the opposite pole: 'my interest is in showing that things which look the same are really different'. He was thinking, as a motto for his book, of the phrase 'I'll teach you differences'.[17] When Drury remarked that Kant's fundamental ideas did not come to him until he was middle-aged, Wittgenstein commented: 'My fundamental ideas came to me very early in life' (*RW*, p. 158). Drury, unfortunately, instead of asking him to explain this remark, seems to have gone on asking his opinion of the great thinkers of the past.

On reflection, however, Drury concluded that, from the *Tractatus* to his last writings, Wittgenstein was out to do what he had said to Ludwig von Ficker, probably in 1919, when he was trying to get him to publish the *Tractatus*:

> I am pinning my hopes on you. And it will probably be helpful for you if I write a few words about my book: For you won't – I really

---

[15] *Preoccupations*, p. 151.

[16] Drury, 'Letters to a student of philosophy'.

[17] Shakespeare, *King Lear*, Act 1, scene 4, Kent (in disguise) to the Steward.

believe – get too much out of reading it. Because you won't understand it; the content will seem quite strange to you. In reality, it isn't strange to you, for the point of the book is ethical. I once wanted to give a few words in the foreword which now actually are not in it, which, however, I'll write to you now because they might be a key for you: I wanted to write that my work consists of two parts: of the one which is here, and of everything which I have *not* written. And precisely this second part is the important one. For the Ethical is delimited from within, as it were, by my book; and I'm convinced that, *strictly* speaking, it can ONLY be delimited in this way. In brief, I think: All of that which *many* are *babbling* today, I have defined in my book by remaining silent about it. Therefore the book will, unless I'm quite wrong, have much to say which you want to say yourself, but perhaps you won't notice that it is said in it.[18]

The book is offered, then, as an ascetical exercise in learning to acknowledge what may be said in order to respect that which is unsayable. Ficker was editor of one of the most adventurous cultural journals in the German-speaking world of the time: he had published Trakl's expressionist poetry and the work of Theodor Haecker, who was introducing Kierkegaard to a wider public. Such was the context in which the young Wittgenstein thought that the *Tractatus* would be at home.[19]

People want to say things about ethical and religious matters which simply cannot be said. The drawing, from inside, of the limits of what we may say requires a renunciation of a very powerful desire in our nature. From start to finish, so Drury suggests, Wittgenstein understood his work as a discipline of reticence: the ethical dimension is 'the simple demand that we should at all times and in all places say no more than we really know'.[20] Wittgenstein's 'critique of language' (*TLP* 4.0031) is a radicalization of Kant's critique of reason. Reminding us that Wittgenstein spoke of Kant's depth, Drury insists on the comparison, citing in particular this remark by Kant: 'The critique of pure reason is a preservative against a malady which has its source in our rational nature. The malady is the opposite of the love of home (homesickness) which

---

[18] 'Letters to Ludwig von Ficker', translated by Bruce Gillette, in Luckhardt, *Sources and Perspectives*, p. 94.

[19] See Allan Janik, 'Wittgenstein, Ficker, and *Der Brenner*', in Luckhardt, *Sources and Perspectives*: an important investigation of the still largely unexplored background to the *Tractatus*.

[20] Drury, 'Letters to a student of philosophy', p. 84.

binds us to our fatherland. It is a longing to pass out beyond our immediate confines and to relate ourselves to other worlds.'[21]

In effect, according to Drury, the religious point of view from which the problems in the later writings are all envisaged is the same as the ethical dimension of the *Tractatus*: 'The whole sense of the book might be summed up in the following words: what can be said at all can be said clearly, and what we cannot talk about we must pass over in silence' (*TLP*, p. 3). The failure of the metaphysical constructions which we are naturally inclined to raise leaves us with the chastening knowledge that our desire to go beyond the confines of language has to be satisfied in some other way than our *saying* anything. 'The work of philosophy', so Drury concludes, 'is to show once and for all and conclusively that what at first begins as the desire for a metaphysical theory is really something deeper, something which can only be satisfied by other than speculative constructions'.[22]

I would not say that Drury had got all this wrong: there surely are deep continuities throughout the whole of Wittgenstein's work.[23] Yet, as far as I can see, this proposal sheds very little light on how we are to read the endless remarks on philosophical psychology with which Wittgenstein, almost obsessively, occupied his last years.

AUGUSTINE'S ENTRY INTO THE CONVERSATION

'Anything your reader can do for himself,' Wittgenstein noted in 1948, 'leave to him' (*CV*, p. 77). Perhaps one clue to understanding what is going on in the *Investigations* lies in the quotation from St Augustine's *Confessions* with which the book opens.

How to start the book had preoccupied Wittgenstein for many years. At one time, prompted apparently by Goethe's admonition that people should get out into the open air and learn from there, he thought of beginning with a description of nature (*CV*, p. 11, in 1931). It is difficult to imagine what that would have been like. In the event he stuck to a somewhat earlier idea: 'I should like to start with the original data of philosophy, written and spoken sentences, with books as it were' (*CV*, p. 8).

The book with which he finally began might be described as the autobiography of the Western Christian soul. According to Drury, he

---

[21] Ibid., p. 83; the reference, which Drury does not give, is to *Reflexionen*, in the Berlin edition, vol. XVIII, p. 79.

[22] Ibid., p. 84.

[23] See Peter Winch's introduction to *Studies in the Philosophy of Wittgenstein*.

thought Augustine's *Confessions* possibly the most serious book ever written (*RW*, p. 90). Norman Malcolm explains the choice thus: 'He revered the writings of St Augustine. He told me he decided to begin his *Investigations* with a quotation from the latter's *Confessions*, not because he could not find the conception expressed in that quotation stated as well by other philosophers, but because the conception *must* be important if so great a mind held it.'[24]

He must certainly have valued the book's immensely powerful analysis of the emotional reaches of Christian experience. He may well have learned from the style: 'The philosophical sections of St Augustine's *Confessions*', so von Wright thinks, 'show a striking resemblance to Wittgenstein's own way of doing philosophy'.[25] Above all he must have known that, in electing to start his book with a conception expressed by Augustine, he was invoking the decisive representative of that interweaving of metaphysical anthropology with Christian faith that remains the background of modern Western thought. That Augustine is the dominant figure in Western Christianity is indisputable: Thomas Aquinas and Martin Luther bear witness to that, however differently they strove to revise him. But whether Wittgenstein fully recognized it or not, and his remark to Drury about the difference between Greek and Hebraic ideas perhaps suggests that he did, he was intervening in a centuries-long tradition that has shaped our self-understanding.

What he found in Augustine was a primitive conception of how language works (*PI* 2). In effect, Augustine's story of how he learned to speak secretes the myth that the infant arrives like an immigrant in a strange land, already able to speak but completely ignorant of the alien language (*PI* 32).

It is important to put Augustine's account back into its context in the *Confessions*. Consider first this passage:

> Gradually I realized where I was, and I decided to display my wishes to those who might fulfil them, and I could not, because my wishes were inside and they were outside, and powerless to get inside my mind by any of their senses. So I shook my limbs and varied my voice, the few signs like my wishes that I could manage, as well as I could, but they were really not very similar.[26]

This account has great intuitive appeal. It turns on a pre-philosophical

[24] Malcolm, *Memoir*, 1984, p. 59.
[25] Ibid., p. 19.
[26] *Confessions*, Book I, chapter 6.

picture of the relationship between what lies 'inside' the individual mind and what stands 'outside'. I cannot show other people the thoughts and wants that I have in my mind, and they are impotent to get inside my mind with any of their senses. The epistemological predicament of the infant Augustine is clear.

The text goes on to describe the frustrated infant's rage at not being able to translate his thoughts and wants into signals that his elders understand. Augustine toys for a moment, then, with the possibility that he existed before he was dropped into their company:

> Tell me, my God, did my being an infant succeed some previous existence of mine that was past? Or was that what I passed in my mother's womb? For I have heard something about that, and I have seen pregnant women. But, my delight, my God, what preceded *that*? *Was* I anywhere, or anyone?

Obviously Augustine does not succumb to the heretical anthropology, attributed to Origen, among others, according to which people are angelic beings who have been exiled for a time into the degradation of flesh. Later, in *The City of God* (XI, 23), he attacked Origen's doctrine of the fall of pre-existing souls, on the grounds (in effect) that it belonged with the Neoplatonism of Plotinus from which Augustine had escaped into Catholic Christianity.[27] But in the *Confessions* at least, for all the authorial intentions that dominate the text, the suppressed metaphysical longings often show through the fabric in a figure of speech or a tone of voice or a plaintive question – 'Was I anywhere, or anybody?'. Augustine repeatedly casts himself as the prodigal son in the parable, but the far country in which he squandered his property in loose living is identified with the temporality of the human condition. Knowledge of God is to be sought in the recesses of the individual's memory. Subdued versions of the Platonic doctrine of reminiscence and of the pre-existence of the soul echo throughout some of the most memorable passages in the book. To open the *Confessions* is at once to be under the spell of the theological story of the soul that has decisively affected Christian spirituality and hence the Cartesian and modern philosophy of the self.[28]

Presumably Wittgenstein expected us to re-read the whole of the first book of the *Confessions*, but it will be enough for my purposes to set the passage that he quotes into its immediate context:

[27] See R. J. O'Connell, *Saint Augustine's Early Theory of Man*.
[28] See J. M. Cameron, 'Autobiography and philosophical perplexity', and Martin Warner, 'Philosophical autobiography: St Augustine and John Stuart Mill'.

I was no longer a speechless infant, I was a talking boy. I remember this, and I afterwards saw how I learned to speak. For the grown-ups did not teach me, by offering me words, according to a standard method of teaching, as they were soon to do with the alphabet. With the mind that you gave me, my God, I decided to exhibit the thoughts of my heart so that my will might be obeyed, and by dint of grunting and various sounds and movements of my limbs I did so, but I was powerless to show all that I wanted, or to do it by all the means that I desired. I thought it over . . .[29]

Pensabam memoria, pensively weighing up his epistemological predicament the infant Augustine performed the following remarkable feat, as described in the passage with which Wittgenstein opens the *Investigations*:

When [my elders] named some object, and accordingly moved towards something, I saw this and I grasped that the thing was called by the sound they uttered when they meant to point it out. Their intention was shown by their bodily movements, as it were the natural language of all peoples: the expression of the face, the play of the eyes, the movement of other parts of the body, and the tone of voice which expresses our state of mind in seeking, having, rejecting, or avoiding something. Thus, as I heard words repeatedly used in their proper places in various sentences, I gradually learnt to understand what objects they signified; and after I had trained my mouth to form these signs, I used them to express my own desires.

The egocentric perspective needs no demonstration. Language is assumed to be necessary neither for framing one's thoughts nor for identifying one's desires. Prior to, and independently of, all ability to talk, one is supposed to be already aware of one's mental states and acts. The self is pictured as 'inside', fluttering with its limbs, spluttering out words, striving with gruntings, and so on, to get its mind understood by the surrounding company. One has to be taught to read and write, but we apparently learn to speak by a sort of pulling ourselves up by our bootstraps. The infant is pictured as knowing from the outset what he thinks and wants: the problem is to master his limbs, lips, and so on, to get others to understand.

It is important to notice that Wittgenstein never says that Augustine's story is entirely wrong. Indeed, the passage contains the solution as well as the problem to which he wants to direct attention. In the end it is to the common human way of acting that he refers us (*PI* 206) – which is surely Augustine's natural language: the expressiveness of the face and

[29] *Confessions*, Book I, chapter 8.

eyes, of voice and gesture. But before retrieving this understanding of how bodily our intersubjectivity always is, Wittgenstein wants to trace the genealogy and the ramifications of the conception of the self that dominates the forefront of this text. For this picture of how an infant learns to speak, and hence the idea of language and communication, and so of how one human being is related to another, seems very much tied up with the idea of the self-transparent and autonomous subject which we encountered in chapter 1.

Thus, by opening the *Investigations* with this passage from Augustine's *Confessions*, Wittgenstein was placing his explorations of the epistemological predicament of the self in the context of a narrative which, as it interweaves biblical language with metaphysical dualism, autobiography with doxology, establishes the sense of the 'I' in the sight of God which remains the paradigm for the self even where the theology has been abandoned. One of the most familiar versions of this conception of the self is associated with the name of Descartes. As Wittgenstein said, he could have found it in many other philosophers: he might have been thinking of the author of the *Tractatus*. Finally, however, he chose to direct his readers to the greatest autobiography in the Christian tradition. To probe the epistemological predicament of the soul in the *Confessions* was to open up a seam in the theological anthropology that has shaped Christian self-understanding since the fifth century. It is difficult to believe that Wittgenstein did not know what he was doing.

EPISTEMOLOGICAL SOLITUDE

By starting with Augustine's story of how the little soul gets into the conversation Wittgenstein set out on his criss-crossing traversal of the deeply appealing conception of meaning as a private mental activity: 'Nothing is more wrong-headed', so he wrote in the concluding remark in the *Investigations*, 'than calling meaning a mental activity' (*PI* 693). That is to say: to think of meaning as some essentially occult state or act inside one's consciousness, radically inaccessible to anyone else, is, residually, and all the more insiduously for that, to succumb to the appealing thought that the self is concealed inside the man.

Hardly any modern philosopher would suppose that the soul is a self-conscious entity lodged in the flesh (although what many non-philosophers would say in reflective moments may be judged by the number of books on the occult so widely offered for sale). In the 'written and spoken sentences' of many of his contemporaries, however,

Wittgenstein detected arguments and assumptions that fed parasitically on the continuing vitality of the ancient religious myth of the soul. In a lecture given in the early 1930s he spoke of trying to convince the class of 'just the opposite of Descartes' emphasis on *I*' (*WLAA*, p. 63). That word 'I', that is to say, was already on the list of words that needed to be brought back from their metaphysical application to their home in everyday conversation (*PI* 116). From the first-person perspective it is very easy to generate a sense of oneself as a thinking thing which shows obvious kinship with the portrait of the infant Augustine's travails.

However, a philosophical account of the self set forth in a textbook easily becomes a topic for analysis and refutation. The Cartesian (or any other) conception of the 'I' might seem so innocent in a philosophical text that its more insidious attractions escape notice. Wittgenstein preferred for the most part to leave aside the standard texts, and seldom named his contemporaries when he stalked them. This was not because he had not read them:[30] he wanted to show how the picture of the self that appears in the standard texts infiltrates reflection far beyond their confines. He strove to examine what, in reflective moments, almost anyone in the Western tradition would naturally be inclined to say.

The agenda was set pretty clearly in a lecture in 1930, according to student notes.

> This simile of 'inside' or 'outside' the mind is pernicious. It is derived from 'in the head' when we think of ourselves as looking out from our heads and of thinking as something going on 'in our head'. But then we forget the picture and go on using language derived from it. Similarly, man's spirit was pictured as his breath, then the picture was forgotten but the language derived from it retained. We can only safely use such language if we consciously remember the picture when we use it. (*WLDL*, p. 25)

Thus, the inclination to think of meaning, or any other mental or spiritual activity, as something that is radically private, 'in our head', is explicitly related to the ancient religious myth of the soul. The lecture goes on immediately to discuss whether we could read one another's thoughts without having to resort to 'mere' language:

> Would it be possible to communicate more directly by a process of 'thought-reading'? What would we mean by 'reading thought'?

[30] Von Wright's remark (Malcolm, *Memoir*, 1958, p. 20) that he had 'done no systematic reading in the classics of philosophy' has led people to think that Wittgenstein had read almost no philosophy.

> Language is not an indirect method of communication, to be contrasted with 'direct' thought-reading. Thought-reading could only take place through the interpretation of symbols and so would be on the same level as language. It would not get rid of the symbolic process. The idea of reading a thought more directly is derived from the idea that thought is a hidden process which it is the aim of the philosopher to penetrate. But there is no more direct way of reading thought than through language. Thought is not something hidden; it lies open to us. (*WLDL*, pp. 25–6)

In effect, souls dream of being wordlessly transparent to one another. The picture of ourselves as isolated entities 'looking out from our heads' goes with a longing to communicate in some more direct way than by using symbols.

The 'epistemological solitude'[31] to which the soul is mythically condemned (or, if you prefer, delivered), reappears explicitly in Wittgenstein's later writings – for instance, in the *Investigations*: 'A man's thinking goes on within his consciousness in a seclusion in comparison with which any physical seclusion is an exhibition to public view' (*PI*, p. 222). He wants to expose the temptation to think of 'the total solitude of the spirit within itself' (*RPP* I, 578). The idea that the soul is more secluded than any hermit – because 'it is given to man to converse with himself in total seclusion' (*RPP* I, 577) – is clearly traced to religious origins, as Wittgenstein's irony here shows.

Connected with the fascinations of epistemological solitude, there is a certain frustration with the limitations upon human knowledge altogether. Discussing Bertrand Russell's claim that we have no direct acquaintance with an infinite series but only knowledge of it by description,[32] Wittgenstein notes that it creates the illusion that 'our problem is to find an indirect method of knowing something which the infinite Being or God knows already in its entirety' (*WLAA*, p. 193). He rephrases the point a little later: 'It does not matter that we have to resort to a series of dodges to get some approximation to the result, for this is only because we are finite creatures and the difficulty is purely psychological' (*WLAA*, p. 196). We are easily tempted into contrasting human ways of knowing with putative divine ways. It is a theme that reappears in the *Investigations*:

[31] J. M. Cameron's phrase.
[32] In 'Knowledge by acquaintance and knowledge by description', Russell introduced a distinction which soon led him to say that, since we have knowledge only of that of which we are directly aware, namely sense-data, we have no knowledge by acquaintance of persons.

Here again we get the same thing as in set theory: the form of expression we use seems to have been designed for a god, who knows what we cannot know; he sees the whole of each of those infinite series and he sees into human consciousness. For us, of course, these forms of expression are like pontificals which we may put on, but cannot do much with, since we lack the effective power that would give these vestments meaning and purpose. In the actual use of expressions we make detours, we go by side-roads. We see the straight highway before us, but of course we cannot use it, because it is permanently closed. (*PI* 426)

Compared with a god's way of knowing either mathematical truths or people's mental states, our mere human forms of knowing such matters seem hopelessly inadequate and indirect. We may put on the sacred vestments but we lack the mana to work the magic. We dream of the direct route to the centre of the mystery but we are never allowed to take it. The knowledge that is accessible to the gods is offered to mere human beings only in the materiality of signs.

Wittgenstein's wry, self-mocking remarks are intended to provoke us into reflecting on the limits of our knowledge, and why we find these limits so chafing and restrictive. Why do we have to, or want to, devalue human ways of knowing in comparison with the unmediated knowledge that a god must presumably have?

In questioning the validity of this (often hidden) object of comparison, Wittgenstein invites us to remember ourselves as we really are. Once and for all, that is to say, we need to give up comparing ourselves with ethereal beings that enjoy unmediated communion with one another.

THE METAPHYSICALLY GENERATED BODY

The longing for unrestricted incorporeal freedom lies deep, if not in human nature, then certainly in the culture to which we belong. The craving to burst out of the bonds of body and of time may well be exactly what it takes to free animals of our kind into the space of culture and history; but it is an ambivalent gift. If we never learn to own our finitude we remain tormented by a powerful inability ever to be satisfied by *anything*. The desire to transcend the present, whatever it may be, comes out in the whole variety of ways in which human beings have made the world inhabitable. But the thought of the transcendent spirit inevitably brings with it a certain notion of the body as weighing down and trammelling it. From this it has been easy to conceive the body as little more than a corpse that requires to be animated: the face becomes a veil, a mask that needs to be manipulated from behind, while the production of meaning retreats from the materiality of signs into the recesses of the invisible mind. In effect, a metaphysically generated concept of the human body, derived from the thought of the immateriality and invisibility of the soul, displaces our experience of the whole living man or woman. This picture of the body gets in the way of our conversation with one another. The body become a site for occult spiritual goings-on – which turn out in the end to be how the individual enjoys a private view either of the divine or, perhaps more commonly, of himself.

There is no sense in regretting the history of the metaphysically generated body, but the time has long since come to try to deconstruct it. The latest form of this metaphysical reduction of the human being is no doubt, as Charles Taylor suggests, the drive in many of the social sciences to extend the objectifying way of conceiving things to our own case.[33] Behaviour as such is supposed to lack significance, in such a way that when it does appear significant it has to be because it is the outwardly observable effect of certain internal mental goings-on. The mind retreats from the face, just as the immaterial soul once disappeared behind the body. The idea of the mind as radically private and inaccessible to outsiders then becomes inescapable.

What this amounts to, in the end, is the devaluation of intrinsically expressive behaviour. The rumour spreads that we are an assembly of zombies. The difficulties that are certainly present in everyday conversation are exploited to strengthen the belief that people's minds and selves are essentially hidden – as hidden as the mind and nature of God. An 'objectifying' scientific conception of human behaviour turns into a highly 'subjectivist' religious or theological one. Either way, the soul withdraws, leaving nothing but a quantity of matter for others to measure. The mind retreats inwards, out of the public world, and this undermines confidence in direct openness to the world itself. Before we know where we are, then, we find ourselves with problems about how we could ever have knowledge of anything outside our own self-certain solitary minds. The metaphysically generated body turns out to hide a paranoid–schizoid soul.

If anything is more powerful psychologically and imaginatively than this myth of the solitary worldless 'I', it must be nostalgia for an eternally present state of total intimacy between one soul and another, unhampered

---

[33] See especially 'Interpretation and the sciences of man', *Philosophical Papers*, vol. 2, chapter 1.

and uninterrupted by exigencies of space and time, body and history. The only thing that might be better would perhaps be the soul's possession of its own pure diaphaneity.

If it is at this deep level of our mythological inheritance that Wittgenstein conducts his explorations of what we are naturally inclined to say in certain moments of self-reflection, then it is not hard to understand what he meant when he told Drury that he saw all the problems in his later writings 'from a religious point of view'. His obsession with the philosophy of psychology brought him back again and again to the theological conception of the self which has dominated the Western tradition for centuries. But what he sought to illuminate cannot be separated from how he tried to do it, which brings me to mention the methods he developed to make us more vigilant as regards some of the things we are so naturally inclined to say when we have to think about our place in the world.

WITTGENSTEIN'S SPIRITUAL EXERCISES

The development of Wittgenstein's style deserves much more extended treatment than I can offer here. The *Tractatus*, with its elegant structure of numbered propositions – 'By the way, the decimals will have to be printed along with the sentences because they alone give the book lucidity and clarity and it would be an incomprehensible jumble without this numeration'[34] – certainly differs profoundly from the *Investigations*. It is possible to trace the transition, even from the published work. The text, dating from 1930, which appeared as *Philosophical Remarks*, admits the authorial first person singular, while the argument unrolls in more substantial paragraphs of apparently consequential assertion. The material of 1932–4, from which a somewhat idiosyncratic selection has been published as *Philosophical Grammar*, is divided into conventional chapters and thus has the makings of something more like a standard textbook than anything else that Wittgenstein attempted. He also allowed Friedrich Waismann to draft a kind of handbook to the new way of doing philosophy.[35]

The texts known as the *Blue Book* and the *Brown Book*, dictated in English in 1933–5, display the later style for the first time: Wittgenstein

[34] Wittgenstein to Ficker, 5 December 1919, in Luckhardt, p. 97.
[35] The book reached the galley-proof stage by 1939, but Wittgenstein's approval, perhaps never unequivocal, had turned to outrage: much rewritten, it appeared after Waismann's death as *The Principles of Linguistic Philosophy*.

thinks aloud, argues with himself, changes the subject apparently at random, suppresses connections, and so on. He had only to cut up these texts, mix the fragments even more disconcertingly, interject more jokes, question marks and exclamations, and finally rearrange everything as cunningly as possible to slow the reader down', or to get him to give up in despair, and he had invented the method of the *Investigations* and the later writings in general.

There is no doubt that he strove to get his writing read slowly:

> Sometimes a sentence can be understood only if it is read at the *right tempo*. My sentences are all supposed to be read *slowly*. (CV, p. 57)

That remark, noted in 1947, was exemplified the following year:

> I really want my copious punctuation marks to slow down the speed of reading. Because I should like to be read slowly. (As I myself read.) (CV, p. 68)

That saying *shows* what he meant. People accustomed to scanning the newspapers, or who are philosophically trained to scent fallacies, have great difficulty in learning to read Wittgenstein's later writings. (Experience of amateur dramatics, or of reading poetry, would be a help.) Indeed, in 1933–4, when he was still searching for his later style, he made this astonishing remark:

> I think I summed up my attitude to philosophy when I said: philosophy ought really to be written only as a *poetic composition* [*Philosophie dürfte man eigentlich nur DICHTEN*]. It must, as it seems to me, be possible to gather from this how far my thinking belongs to the present, future or past. For I was thereby also revealing myself as someone who cannot quite do what he would like to be able to do. (CV, p. 24)

To say that philosophy should really be 'composed', like poetry or a work of fiction, even if he at once allows that he cannot bring this off to his satisfaction, is certainly to reveal how far his thinking was from his contemporaries in Vienna or at Cambridge.

The desire to slow the reader down to the point even of having to read the text aloud, preferably in a group, so that the countless little 'dialogues' with which the text is punctuated may be 'performed', is of great philosophical importance. The 'raw material' for 'philosophical treatment' being 'what we are tempted to say' (*PI* 254), it is vital to bring the temptation out into the open. The intuitive appeal of the temptation has first to be exposed, often against a strong desire to trivialize or deny it. Patience, not incisiveness, is required: 'In philosophizing we may not *terminate* a disease of thought. It must run its natural course, and *slow* cure is all important' (Z 382).

What we are tempted to say, in reflective moments, has to be compared with what is actually possible for us to say – a boundary that we often find it hard to acknowledge:

> One cannot guess how a word functions. One has to *look at* its use and learn from that. But the difficulty is to remove the prejudice which stands in the way of doing this. It is not a *stupid* prejudice. (*PI* 340)

That is to say, we are reluctant to believe that we can, and have to, learn from what we find ourselves saying. That seems to mean that, in philosophy, we talk only about talk, whereas we expected to get on to something more important than mere words; we expected to get beyond language. The inveterate desire to transcend mere language prejudices us against attending to what are after all only fluttering limbs and gruntings. Students, even of philosophy, not to mention theologians, often give up the struggle to read Wittgenstein because it is hard to see what he is doing. As he said at the beginning of a course of lectures in 1934, 'What we say will be easy, but to know why we say it will be very difficult' (*WLAA*, p. 77)

It is not a *stupid* prejudice that stands in the way of our listening to what we say. If we cannot take what we say as seriously as Wittgenstein requires, may not this resistance be for the following reason?

> We are tempted to think that the action of language consists of two parts; an inorganic part, the handling of signs, and an organic part, which we may call understanding these signs, meaning them, interpreting them, thinking. (*BB*, p. 3)

What if this exclusion of the materiality of signs from the constitution of meaning is one more version of the myth of the mind as a ghostly presence hidden inside the body? What if we find it hard to learn what we are able to say from our signs simply because we do not want to do so? What if despising signs for their inert and inorganic materiality is to collude, however unwittingly, in centuries of discrimination against the mundane realities of how human beings live in community with one another?

To see what is obvious is difficult because we so much want to see something beyond it. What Wittgenstein offers, as he says, 'are really remarks on the natural history of human beings' – not contributions to science, 'but observations which escape remark only because they are always before our eyes' (*PI* 415). It is not a matter of having special instruction in abstruse disciplines like formal logic. What makes the thing hard to understand is simply the difference between understanding it as it is and as we want it to be: 'Because of this the very things which are most obvious may become the hardest of all to understand. What has to be overcome is a difficulty having to do with the will, rather than with the intellect' (*CV*, p. 17).

Descartes, of course, used other pronouns in most of his writing. For the *Meditations* he adopted, or created, the autobiographical style for very Wittgensteinian reasons: offering himself as a paradigm for the difficult transition from medieval ways of thinking into the modernity of anti-Aristotelian philosophy of science.[36] He wanted to subvert people's prejudices by taking them, rhetorically, into his confidence: he too had been benighted. The reader is also supposed to 'give months, or at least weeks, to [thinking over the matter of which the First Meditation treats], before going further'.[37] As an alumnus of the most celebrated Jesuit academy in France, Descartes clearly had in mind the *Spiritual Exercises* of St Ignatius Loyola (1491–1556), which, by then, had been established for half a century as the method by which the individual might discover his illusions and work his way into the light.

Certainly, as early as 1931, Wittgenstein knew what he was aiming at: 'I ought to be no more than a mirror, in which my reader can see his own thinking with all its deformities so that, helped in this way, he can put it right' (*CV*, p. 18). Philosophers have sometimes been content to refute other people's views, views to which they themselves have felt no attraction. But Wittgenstein sought to find at the back of his mind, as it were, the motivation for the views that he criticized. He wanted to draw his readers into the most sympathetic understanding of the appeal of the ways of thinking against which he was arguing: 'You must not try to avoid a philosophical problem by appealing to common sense; instead, present it as it arises with most power. You must allow youself to be dragged into the mire, and get out of it' (*WLAA*, pp. 108–9). The problem was to create a style of writing that would enable others to discover and acknowledge the power of the mythology in their own

---

[36] M. D. Wilson, *Descartes*, p. 4.
[37] Ibid., p. 5.

thinking, for, as he said, 'I should not like my writing to spare other people the trouble of thinking. But, if possible, to stimulate someone to thoughts of his own' (*PI*, p. x).

Wittgenstein set out to design a set of practical exercises to curb his reader's inclination to frame the familiar in an alienating picture and thus to lose his place in the world. For this, he developed a self-interrogative style: 'Nearly all my writings are private conversations with myself' (*CV*, p. 77). Indeed, F. R. Leavis quotes this remark by a no doubt exasperated fellow don at Cambridge: 'Wittgenstein can take all the sides himself; he answers before you've said it – you can't get in' (*RW*, p. 51). Whatever discussion with him was like, his later writing is a conversation that exercises the reader, often against his will, in an exploration of what, in reflective moments, we may say about ourselves. It is an exploration of the limits of self-knowledge, and it requires an exorcising of certain self-images.

In a remarkable passage, written in 1932–4, on the philosophy of mathematics, he compared himself with Freud:

> A mathematician is bound to be horrified by my mathematical comments, since he has always been trained to avoid indulging in thoughts and doubts of the kind I develop. He has learned to regard them as something contemptible and, to use an analogy from psychoanalysis (this paragraph is reminiscent of Freud), he has acquired a revulsion from them as infantile. That is to say, I trot out all the problems that education represses without solving. I say to those repressed doubts: you are quite correct, go on asking, demand clarification. (*PG*, pp. 381–2)

Thus, one thing that philosophical work involves is giving voice to thoughts and doubts that our culture has taught us to repress. Wittgenstein's later writing, with its incessant questions, deliberate mistakes, imaginative fantasies, provocative allusions, and so on, sets out to lure the reader into consenting to say something that sounds perfectly acceptable until its teasing out in the text arouses suspicion about its very particular historical provenance. Much that we are 'naturally' inclined to think, that is to say, turns out to be historically contingent and far from inevitable. 'My aim', as he said, 'is to teach you to pass from a piece of disguised nonsense to something that is patent nonsense' (*PI* 464). The hard part is to acknowledge that the nonsense lurks at the back of one's own mind.

No doubt it is a pleasure to uncover some piece of nonsense in someone else's thoughts, but that was not Wittgenstein's intention:

> The results of philosophy are the disclosure of one or another piece of plain
> nonsense and bumps that the understanding has received in colliding with
> the limit of language. These bumps let us see the value of the disclosure.
> (*PI* 119)

The value of exposing our metaphysical illusions may be judged, that is
to say, by the bruises that reaching the limit of language leaves upon the
thinker.

It may never be possible to settle what Wittgenstein meant when he
spoke of the religious point of view from which he regarded the problems
that he discussed so persistently and imaginatively in the later writings. A
non-metaphysical understanding of the place of the self in nature and
history would certainly encourage resistance to the antipathy to the body
which is so characteristic of one ancient and powerful religious tradition;
and renouncing a certain nostalgia for spiritual purity might clear the
way for another look at the Christian religion.

PART TWO

Changing the Subject

CHAPTER 3

The Solipsist in the Flyglass

'But I *am* in a favoured position, I am the centre of the world.' Suppose I saw myself in the mirror saying this and pointing to myself. Would it still be all right?

(NL, p. 256)

THE EGO IS MENTAL

The first part of the *Investigations* concludes (if that is the correct word) with an exclamation and a schoolboyish joke:

And nothing is more wrong-headed than calling meaning [*Meinen*] a mental activity! Unless, that is, one is setting out to produce confusion. (It would also be possible to speak of an activity of butter when it rises in price, and if no problems are produced by this it is harmless.) (*PI* 693)

But clearly there is a way of talking about meaning which is harmful. When butter rises in price you may speak of an activity on the part of the butter, provided that this figure of speech does not create confusion. To speak of meaning or intending or believing or supposing as acts that take place in the realm of the mind is to get everything the wrong way round. It is perverse – *verkehrt* – to think of meaning as a mental activity because it only entrenches us in a bewildering picture of the world.

In the *Blue Book*, an earlier version of much the same material, Wittgenstein concluded with a comment on the use of the word 'I' which he expected by this point to release the reader from supposing that 'that which has pains or sees or thinks is of a mental nature' (*BB*, p. 74). To hold that 'the ego is mental' (*BB*, p. 73) is to place oneself in the long and intuitively appealing tradition of isolating the spiritual from the physical: the tradition which Wittgenstein was out to question, at least on the reading that I am proposing. That he had Descartes in mind, as he reached these two conclusions, is surely obvious.

People who would at once deny that they believe in the self as an immaterial entity that floats free of space and time, may well continue to harbour the myth in more subtle and recondite forms. To overcome their resistance against owning that some such picture might dictate some of their thoughts and actions demands slow initiation into habits of vigilance as regards the kind of thing they (we) are naturally inclined to say. Those who have taken the mentalist–individualist turn in their epistemology are strongly tempted to picture the self very much as the autonomous bearer of mental or spiritual properties. The social and historical surroundings in which the individual has any thoughts or feelings in the first place are unconsciously played down.

The text from Augustine's *Confessions* with which Wittgenstein opens the *Investigations* registers a strong sense of how the self-transparent little soul looks out from its head, hears the adults making various noises, watches them (through its eyes) as they lumber towards some item of middle-sized dry goods, and then suddenly, on its own, makes the connection, in its own mind, between the sounds the adults emit and the objects that they touch.[1] Augustine pictures his infant self as already aware of its own identity (what is going on inside its own mind) and of what is going on around it (outside its mind), prior to and independently of its mastering the arts of speech. The text offers 'a particular picture of the essence of human language' (*PI* 1). It is important to notice, however, from the outset, that the 'words name objects' doctrine of language which Wittgenstein at once extracts from the text is interwoven with the idea that meaning is always in the head: the last remark in the *Investigations* has to be allowed to illuminate the first one. As Waismann wrote, recapitulating the idea:

> What we object to is the idea of the contents of different people's minds as shut off from each other by insurmountable barriers, so that what is experienced is eternally private and inexpressible – the idea that we are, so to speak, imprisoned behind bars through which only words can escape, as though it were a defect in language that it consists wholly of words.[2]

That is the idea, among others of course, of which Wittgenstein strove to unravel the ramifications in the metaphysically structured tradition which we have inherited. Augustine's reference to his elders and to their bodily movements as the natural language of all peoples already reminds us of the community and of the expressiveness of the body – but, so

---

[1] It is not clear whether Wittgenstein knew how much more complicated Augustine's theory of language was: whether, for example, he had read the *De Magistro*. See Patrick Bearsley, 'Augustine and Wittgenstein on language'.

[2] Waismann, *Principles*, p. 248.

Wittgenstein thinks, we badly need the reminder. Indeed, the only problem that he has with Augustine's story is that what is presented as secondary and marginal to self-understanding needs to be acknowledged as vital and fundamental. He wants only to draw attention to what Augustine's picture leaves in the background.

In the Augustine passage, then, we find a certain paradigm of the working of language: 'These words, it seems to me, give us a particular picture of the essence of human language' (*PI* 1). Perhaps the qualification 'it seems to me' allows for the possibility that it is only the post-Cartesian reader who would find questionable the model of the nature of language in this text. At any rate, the picture of language as essentially the association of words with items in the world occludes the community with the natural expressiveness of people's bodies. Perhaps it is only if we are already strongly tempted to treat the self as a solitary intellect locked within a space that is inaccessible to anyone else that language looks intuitively like a system of referring to things.

THE HERMIT IN THE HEAD GOES SHOPPING

That words label things, and that sentences describe states of affairs, seem very natural ideas: 'The cat sits on the mat'. But this thought, which Wittgenstein extracts from Augustine's picture of the essence of language, does not stand up to examination. The simplest situation one can imagine immediately shows how interwoven naming is with other activities:

> Now think of the following use of language: I send someone shopping. I give him a slip marked 'five red apples'. He takes the slip to the shopkeeper, who opens the drawer marked 'apples'; then he looks up the word 'red' in a table and finds a colour sample opposite it; then he says the series of cardinal numbers – I assume that he knows them by heart – up to the word 'five' and for each number he takes an apple of the same colour as the sample out of the drawer. It is in this and similar ways that one operates with words. (*PI* 1)

Wittgenstein exaggerates the shopkeeper's actions grotesquely, but his point is that linking objects with words goes with being already able to do a good deal else (cf. *PI* 30). Within the very first paragraph of the *Investigations*, then, he moves meanings out of the infant Augustine's head to retrieve them in a mundane transaction in the village store. From the outset he reminds us of the obvious: the locus of meanings is not the epistemological solitude of the individual consciousness but the practical exchanges that constitute the public world which we inhabit together. He has sketched a scene that apparently accords with the doctrine that words stand for things, and it simply shows that the point of language lies elsewhere – in what people do together. The picture of the infant hermit in the head who is desperately trying to make the noises that label the goods in his ambience is deflated as soon as we recall what happens when someone goes shopping. The 'essence' of human language is the round of collaborative activity that generates the human way of life.

Wittgenstein has no more to show us: we might as well stop reading at this point if we want only to hear the result of his work. For most of his readers, however, it would be premature to go no further. We should not have begun to fathom the implications of this simple demonstration of the obvious. 'The philosophical problem is: how can we tell the truth and *pacify* [*beruhigen*] these strong prejudices in doing so' (*RFM* IV, 34). The difficult and interesting part is to draw out the prejudices and deal with them. To remind us that we do things with words, rather than simply associate them with objects, shifts the locus of meanings from the ego's mental enclosure to the social world where people sell apples, but it remains natural to suppose that the shopkeeper's reactions must be founded upon his having a mental picture of what each word represents:

> But how does [the shopkeeper] know where and how he is to look up the word 'red' and what he is to do with the word 'five'? (*PI* 1)

After all, when asked what it means to set up a connection in a child's mind between a word and an object, 'one very likely thinks first of all that a picture of the object comes before the child's mind [*vor die Seele tritt*] when it hears the word' (*PI* 6). There is surely some internal consultation before the individual reacts – which may, with practice, become instantaneous.

Wittgenstein insists that the intelligent actions that a man performs do not have to be preceded every time by a parade of mental images, but he also writes as follows:

> There really are cases when the sense of what one wants to say hovers [*vorschwebt*] in the mind much more clearly than one can express in words. (This happens to me very often.) It is as though one saw a dream picture quite clearly before one's mind's eye [*vor sich*], but could not describe it to someone else so that he might see it too. (*CV*, p. 79)

The idea that words stand for things goes very naturally with the feeling that one always has a mental image of a thing before mentioning it. There is no question of trying to stop our talk about seeing things in the mind's eye. Wittgenstein wants us to be wary of this way of talking only because it invites us to regard a great deal of human behaviour as lacking in significance, as merely automatic or mechanical reaction, unless it is preceded or accompanied by an appropriate parade of mental pictures.

Wittgenstein rebuffs his mentalist–individualist alter ego who wants to get the focus back on the shopkeeper's private mental acts:

> Well, I assume that he *acts* [*handelt*] as I have described. Explanations come to an end somewhere. – But what is the meaning of the word 'five'? – No such thing was in question here, only how the word 'five' is used. (*PI* 1)

The scene in the shop, this everyday episode of trading, is already, as described, an intelligible instance of intelligent behaviour: there is no need to postulate some special 'consciousness' on anyone's part. (Perhaps Wittgenstein drags out the shopkeeper's actions precisely to mock the idea that he needs to behave 'consciously'.) Counting is a technique: the 'meaning' of the word 'five' is the use to which it is put in the appropriate setting – there need be no mental picture of the numeral in the shopkeeper's head.

RUSSELL'S LITTLE MORTAL ABSOLUTES

The ego in its own private mental space is, however, not so easily demythologized. It reigned in the philosophy of Bertrand Russell and G. E. Moore with which the young Wittgenstein was confronted when he spent five terms at Cambridge in 1912–13. That philosophy, with which Wittgenstein was identified for a time, was called logical atomism.

The history of the origins of analytic philosophy has hardly yet begun to be written: even less has it been placed in a wider intellectual context.[3] But the Cambridge of Russell and Moore interests the literary as well as the philosophical historian. D. H. Lawrence's judgement of Russell's philosophical inclinations at this period is, to my mind, quite relevant.

Their common interest lay in opposition to the First World War. The two men first met early in 1915. Lawrence was soon planning lectures in

---

[3] But see Thomas Baldwin, 'Moore's rejection of idealism', and Peter Hylton, 'The nature of the proposition and the revolt against idealism', both in *Philsophy in History*.

London together with Russell – 'he on Ethics, I on Immortality'.[4] Within
a month, Lawrence was writing as follows:

> What ails Russell is, in matters of life and emotion, the inexperience of
> youth. He is, vitally, emotionally, much too inexperienced in personal
> contact and conflict, for a man of his age and calibre. It isn't that life has
> been too much for him, but too little.[5]

Soon afterwards after a visit to Russell's circle in Cambridge, he wrote:

> What does Russell really want? He wants to keep his own established ego,
> his finite and ready-defined self intact, free from contact and connection.
> He wants to be ultimately a free agent. That is what they all want,
> ultimately . . . so that in their own souls they can be independent little gods,
> referred nowhere and to nothing, little mortal Absolutes, secure from
> question.[6]

Lawrence's perceptions were remarkable. He sensed that, for Russell
and the tradition he represented, knowledge had to be founded on
something better than the mere human body. Russell's notion of the self
was an ego 'free from contact and connection', as it were the dream-wish
of people who wanted to be 'little mortal Absolutes',
    Russell's circle, according to J. M. Keynes, had much the same effect
on Wittgenstein as it had on Lawrence (they never met):

> We were not aware that civilization was a thin and precarious crust erected
> by the personality and will of a very few, and only maintained by rules and
> conventions skilfully put across and guilefully preserved. We had no
> respect for traditional wisdom or the restraints of custom. We lacked
> reverence, as Lawrence observed and as Ludwig with justice also used to
> say – for everything and everyone.[7]

LOGICAL ATOMISM

Russell's philosophy at this time, as has been said, went by the name of
logical atomism. He distinguished it against what he regarded as the two
dominant philosophical movements of the day (1914): the classical

---

[4] *Collected Letters*, vol. 1, p. 350.
[5] Ibid., p.351. At the time Russell was aged 43 and Lawrence, 29.
[6] Ibid., p. 360.
[7] Keynes, 'My early beliefs', p. 99.

tradition (F. H. Bradley, in effect Hegelianism), and evolutionism (Nietzsche, Bergson and the American pragmatists, such as William James). The course of lectures which he gave early in 1918 under the title of 'The Philosophy of Logical Atomism' was, according to the preface, 'very largely concerned with explaining certain ideas which I learnt from my friend and former pupil Ludwig Wittgenstein'.[8]

Russell writes as follows:

> The logic which I shall advocate is atomistic, as opposed to the monistic logic of the people who more or less follow Hegel. When I say that my logic is atomistic, I mean that I share the common-sense belief that there are many separate things; I do not regard the apparent multiplicity of the world as consisting merely in phases and unreal divisions of a single indivisible Reality.[9]

For Russell, as opposed to Hegel (or so he thinks), the world is 'a collection of hard units, whether atoms or souls, each completely self-subsistent'. The sort of thing he had in mind for his atoms would be 'predicates or relations and so on', together with 'such things as little patches of colour or sounds, momentary things'.[10]

In effect, he was reacting against the Hegelian emphasis on the priority of the system over the constituents. Propositions are true if they cohere with other propositions, and only the whole set would be completely true. Since we could never master the whole set, or have a complete description of reality, we have to be content with saying things that are at best only partly true. Against some such view (I do not claim to have made it intelligible) Moore and Russell strove to prove that every proposition could be analysed into its elements, which would be indivisible and irreducible atomic units of meaning. These in turn would refer directly to the fundamental entities out of which states of affairs in the world are composed – or something along these lines.

Little patches of colour held a privileged position: they typified the simple objects of direct acquaintance out of which states of affairs are composed, and hence sentences about them.

The attraction of the theory lies in showing how our knowledge of the world is pinned to objects with which we are each individually and directly acquainted. Put thus baldly, it may seem an idea that nobody could take seriously for long. Yet the idea that the universe is the result of

[8] *Logic and Knowledge*, p. 177.
[9] Ibid., p. 178.
[10] Ibid., p. 179.

collisions between eternal and indestructible elements is surely one that has fascinated thinkers for many centuries.

The desire to bring the passing show to a halt, to secure it to immovable objects, lies deep in the metaphysical tradition. For Plato, knowledge (as opposed to belief) lies in cognitive encounters with immaterial, super-sensible, eternal objects.[11] Whether it is Plato's forms or the colour patches of Russell's atomism, there is a powerful inclination to get up or down to something simple and ultimate: that which defies all further analysis, something self-sufficient and elemental. Whether it is the building blocks out of which knowledge is constructed or the eternal paradigms with which the mind has to conform, we evidently have a profound craving to secure ourselves to such foundations.

WITTGENSTEIN'S SIMPLE THINGS

Wittgenstein was to publish his own philosophy in the *Tractatus*, and whether it counts as logical atomism is a disputed question.[12] But in June 1915, in the intervals of soldiering in Galicia, when Lawrence and Russell were planning their joint lectures during country weekends, he was already questioning the motivation of logical atomism.

'Are spatial objects composed of simple parts', he asks himself: 'in analysing them, does one arrive at parts that cannot be further analysed, or is this not the case?' (*NB*, p. 62). Speaking with the voice of 20 years later, he observes: 'But this is surely clear: the propositions which are the only ones that humanity uses will have sense just as they are and do not wait upon a future analysis in order to acquire a sense.' That anticipates disavowals made in the *Investigations* (cf. *PI* 91 and 98). In the *Notebooks* he continues as follows:

> Now, however, it seems to be a legitimate question: Are – e.g. – spatial objects composed of simple parts; in analysing them, does one arrive at parts that cannot be further analysed, or is this not the case?
> — But what kind of question is this? —
> *Is it*, A PRIORI, *clear that in analysing we must arrive at simple*

---

[11] According to the conventional view, but see Richard Sorabji, 'Myths about non-propositional thought', in *Language and Logos*, esp. p. 299 footnote.

[12] The *Tractatus* can certainly be expounded without making much of logical atomism: see G. E. M. Anscombe, *An Introduction*, and H. O. Mounce, *Wittgenstein's Tractatus*; but see also James Griffin, *Wittgenstein's Logical Atomism*.

components – is this, e.g., *involved in the concept of analysis* – , or is
analysis *ad infinitum* possible? –
Or is there in the end even a third possibility? (*NB,* p. 62)

At the very moment that Russell was preparing lectures to expound it,
Wittgenstein had already committed his doubts about the whole idea of
logical atomism to his private notebook. But, no doubt because he was
caught up in the excitement of composing the *Tractatus,* he at once
repressed these doubts, as the following remarkable passage shows:

> *And it keeps on* forcing itself upon us that there is some simple indivisible,
> an element of being, in brief a thing [*etwas Einfaches, Unzerlegbares . . .*
> *ein Element des Seins, kurz ein Ding*].
> It does not go against our feeling, that *we* cannot analyse PROPOSITIONS
> so far as to mention the elements by name; no, we feel that the WORLD
> must consist of elements. (*NB,* p. 62)

It is thus a matter of our 'feeling'. There is something compulsive about
it. It forces itself on us that there is something simple, something
unanalysable and irreducible, something 'atomic', at the bottom of
everything. It does not dispel this feeling if we reflect that, with the
inadequate means at our disposal, we poor humans are not able to take
what we say to pieces in such a way as to lay bare the elements of which
the world is composed. It is natural to suppose that our analysis must fail
to get down to bedrock, but we continue to feel that 'the WORLD must
consist of elements':

> And it appears as if that were identical with the proposition that the world
> must be what it is, it must be definite. Or in other words, what vacillates is
> our determinations, not the world. It looks as if to deny things were as
> much as to say that the world can, as it were, be indefinite in some such
> sense as that in which our knowledge is uncertain and indefinite. (*NB,*
> p. 62)

It is intolerable to think that the world is as indeterminate, as shaky in its
foundations, as our knowledge, which (it is supposed) is 'uncertain and
indefinite'. The foundation of knowledge must be laid upon rock solid
entities: 'The demand for simple things *is* the demand for definiteness of
sense' (*NB,* p. 63).
    Much more would need to be said to make the logical atomist
programme intelligible. My purpose is served if Wittgenstein's notes
reveal a sense of the apparently reasonable, and yet obscurely menacing,

'requirement', as he later put it, 'to see to the bottom of things' (*PI* 89 and 107).

WITTGENSTEIN'S FORMS OF LIFE

The demand for simple elements was eventually transformed into attention to our 'forms of life'. Consider first this remarkable passage, written in 1947, which, whether deliberately or not, echoes phrases just quoted from the *Notebooks*:

> Instead of the unanalysable, specific, indefinable: the fact that we act in such-and-such ways, e.g. *punish* certain actions, *establish* the state of affairs thus and so, *give orders*, render accounts, describe colours, take an interest in others' feelings. What has to be accepted, the given – it might be said – are facts of living [*Tatsachen des Lebens*]. (*RPP* I, 630)

The demand for something 'atomic' is thus met by returning to 'facts of living', or 'forms of life', *Lebensformen*, the variant in this passage which Wittgenstein preferred when he pruned it (too severely, one might think!) for the second part of the *Investigations* (*PI*, p. 226).

This passage is decisive for Wittgenstein's idea of forms of life. The focus is clearly on the endless multiplicity of small scale and ubiquitous social practices such as punishing, noting, commanding, telling, etc. The 'given', in other words, is no longer atomic elements of being, whatever they might be, but *Tatsachen des Lebens*, a phrase which recalls the opening of the *Tractatus*:

> The world is everything that is the case.
> The world is the totality of facts [*Tatsachen*], not of things.
> . . .
> The facts in logical space are the world. (*TLP* 1–1.13)

The world of the *Tractatus*, identified with 'the facts in logical space', becomes the world of the *Investigations*, the given, now discovered to be 'facts of living'.

The metaphysical requirement of hitting upon atomic elements becomes a vision of 'life as a weave':

> How could one describe the human way of behaving [*die menschliche Handlungsweise*]? Surely only by sketching the actions of a variety of human beings as they interweave. What determines our judgement, our concepts and reactions, is not what *one* man is doing *now*, an individual

action, but the whole hurly-burly [*das ganze Gewimmel*] of human actions, the background against which we see any action. (*Z* 567–9)

The change of metaphor tells it all. The prejudice in favour of a crystal-clear analysis of reality (cf. *PI* 108) has given way to seeing life as an immensely intricate carpet, and, if that is still too static an image, as a teeming swarm. Indeed, it is not the hard units but the background that now comes to seem irreducible:

> Perhaps what is inexpressible (what I find mysterious and am not able to express) is the background against which whatever I could express has its meaning. (*CV*, p. 16)

The background, which is, so to speak, the swarming carpet of human activity, cannot be captured in any representation. The ineffable is the whole hurly-burly; the whole hurly-burly is the ineffable.

The distance that this takes us from logical atomism, or any other expression of the metaphysical desire for secure foundations, is obvious. The post-Cartesian preoccupation has been with the individual subject of mental states and events, with the focus (as in Augustine's story) on what exists or transpires 'inside' the individual's consciousness. It is surely no accident that the little story with which Wittgenstein first confronts Augustine's picture of the egocentric predicament takes us out shopping. From the outset we are reminded that we are agents in practical intercourse with one another – not solitary observers gazing upwards to the celestial realm of the eternal forms, or inwards at the show in the mental theatre. What constitutes us as human beings is the regular and patterned reactions that we have to one another. It is in our dealings with each other – in how we *act* – that human life is founded: Wittgenstein's word *handeln*, conveniently enough, means dealing and trading as well as acting and doing. When the shopkeeper acts as he does in the story he necessarily acts with his customer: it is an exchange, a collaboration. Community is built into human action from the beginning.

Starting out, then, from something like Russell's anti-Hegelian atomism Wittgenstein moved gradually in the direction of a certain 'holism'; towards a rediscovery of 'the whole [*das Ganze*], consisting of language and the activities with which it is interwoven' (*PI* 7).

MARXIST CONNECTIONS

How consciously Wittgenstein reversed the anti-Hegelian atomism of the founding fathers of analytic philosophy it is hard to judge. Certainly, in the years when he was gestating the later work, several of his friends had strongly Marxist sympathies: Roy Pascal,[13] George Thomson,[14] and Nicholas Bachtin,[15] for example. Thomson doubts that Wittgenstein had read any of the Marxist classics, but says that he was 'deeply influenced' by Marxism, though 'only indirectly'.[16] Bachtin was the friend with whom he re-read the *Tractatus*, during which he realized that his new thoughts could be seen in the right light only by contrast with and against the background of the logical atomist way of thinking (*PI*, p. x).

In the preface to the *Investigations*, Wittgenstein names only two friends who helped him to recognize 'grave mistakes' in the *Tractatus*. The first of these is F. P. Ramsey, whose criticism helped 'to a degree which I myself am hardly able to estimate'.[17] Even more than to this 'always certain and forcible' criticism, however, Wittgenstein says that, 'for the most consequential ideas of this book', he is indebted to the criticism which was 'for many years unceasingly practised on [his] thoughts' by his colleague Piero Sraffa, who lived in the same college quadrangle at Cambridge.[18]

It is unusual for a philosopher to say that he is indebted for his richest ideas to a non-philosopher. Unfortunately, though typically, we are left with no explanation of this cryptic remark. The only piece of evidence is the anecdote about how, when Wittgenstein was expounding how a proposition must have the same logical form as what it describes, Sraffa made a gesture, familiar to Neapolitans as meaning something like disgust or contempt, of brushing the underneath of his chin with an

[13] His wife, Fania Pascal, has published reminiscences of Wittgenstein in which, among much else of interest, she suggests that he chose to live in England because he found Cambridge undergraduates the most apt interlocutors to test and perfect his thoughts: 'In them, sons of the English middle class, were combined the two features Wittgenstein required at that time in a disciple: childlike innocence and first-class brains' (*RW*, p. 26).

[14] Starting in 1941 with *Aeschylus and Athens*, George Thomson has published several important Marxist studies of ancient Greek civilization.

[15] Younger brother of Mikhail Bakhtin (1895–1975), whose works on Dostoevsky, Rabelais, Freud, literary theory and philosophy of language, make him one of the major thinkers of the century. See Terry Eagleton, 'Wittgenstein's friends'.

[16] George Thomson, 'Wittgenstein: some personal recollections', p. 86.

[17] Ramsey (1903–30), whose younger brother Michael will be better known to theologians, visited Wittgenstein several times during his years as a schoolmaster in Austria.

[18] Sraffa (1898–1983), an economist, was a friend of Antonio Gramsci, the Marxist theoretician imprisoned by Mussolini in 1926: by 1931 he was listed as an influence whom Wittgenstein recognized (*CV*, p. 19).

outward sweep of the finger-tips of one hand, and enquired: 'What is the logical form of *that*?'.[19] It makes sense that Wittgenstein might have been liberated from the prejudice that the function of language is primarily to depict states of affairs by some such joking gesture, into recognizing language as the conversation in which human beings deal with each other and their surroundings. But Sraffa's memories of their many lengthy conversations would have been of much deeper philosophical interest than most of the reminiscences now published.

In the early 1930s Sraffa undertook the definitive edition of Ricardo which was to be his life's work: if this return to classical political economy may be taken as a rejection of marginalist economic theory, it may offer an illuminating parallel to Wittgenstein's reorientation of *his* work (cf. *PI* 108: 'One might say: the axis of reference of our examination must be rotated, but about the fixed point of our real need.')[20] In these years Bukharin, a great critic of marginalist economics, lectured in London:[21] it is unlikely that Sraffa heard nothing of what he said. Among other things, Bukharin criticized the *Tractatus* for leaving out 'the real subject, i.e. social and historical man', in favour of a mere 'stenographer'. He also insisted that 'epistemological Robinson Crusoes are just as much out of place as Robinson Crusoes were in the "atomistic" social science of the eighteenth century', and he suggested that epistemology – 'How is *cognition* possible?' – should yield to 'praxeology' – 'How is *action* possible?'. It is difficult not to believe that Sraffa passed such ideas on.

Wittgenstein's Marxist friends must all have been excited by the appearance at last, in 1932, of *The German Ideology*, the first mature exposition of the materialist theory of history, written jointly by Marx and Engels in 1845–6 but for which they never found a publisher. It is hard to believe that Sraffa did not procure a copy. In any case, a few key passages appeared in English in 1938, edited by Roy Pascal. One way or another Wittgenstein surely received stimulus from this direction: Sraffa must have done more than make Neapolitan gestures during these years.

---

[19] Malcolm, *Memoir*, 1984, p. 58; cf. von Wright: 'He said that his discussions with Sraffa made him feel like a tree from which all the branches had been cut', ibid., pp. 14–15.

[20] S. M. Easton, *Humanist Marxism*, p. 131.

[21] N I. Bukharin, 'Theory and practice', in *Science at the Cross Roads*, esp. pp. 1–7. Editor of *Pravda* until 1929 and shot during the 1938 purges, Bukharin was a member of the Soviet delegation to the Second International Congress of the History of Science and Technology, held in London, 29 June–3 July 1931. It was an important event in the history of British historiography.

I am not saying that Wittgenstein was a Marxist, or that he had studied the Marxist theory of historical materialism, or that he would have accepted it if he had: the comparisons that have been undertaken all show that he was not a Marxist.[22] But such passages as I now quote from *The German Ideology* clearly have affinities with his later philosophy:

> The production of ideas, of conceptions, of consciousness, is at first directly interwoven with the material activity and the material intercourse of men – the language of real life.

> The 'mind' is from the outset afflicted with the curse of being 'burdened' with matter, which here makes its appearance in the form of agitated layers of air, sounds, in short, of language. Language is as old as consciousness, language *is* practical, real consciousness that exists for other men as well, and only therefore does it also exist for me . . . Consciousness is, therefore, from the beginning a social product . . .

> My relation to my surroundings is my consciousness

> One of the most difficult tasks confronting philosophers is to descend from the world of thought to the actual world.

> The philosophers have only to dissolve their language into the ordinary language, from which it is abstracted, in order to recognize it as the distorted language of the actual world, and to realize that neither thoughts nor language in themselves form a realm of their own, that they are only *manifestations* of actual life.[23]

Wittgenstein's strategies for returning the solitary ego to the forms of life in which alone any human being is alive and at home certainly work in favour of the Marxist thesis that it is from labour, and not from consciousness or even language, that structures of meaning arise.[24] Three weeks before his death, indeed, in his last outburst of writing, he committed himself to the following remark:

> I want to regard man here as an animal; as a primitive being to which one grants instinct but not ratiocination. As a creature in a primitive state. Any

[22] Besides Easton, see David Rubinstein, *Marx and Wittgenstein*. It may be noted that Wittgenstein's closest friend at the time, Francis Skinner (1912–41), volunteered for the International Brigade during the Spanish Civil War but a physical disability prevented his being accepted (*RW*, p. 24).

[23] Marx and Engels, *Collected Works*, vol. 5, pp. 36, 43, 44 footnote, 446 and 447.

[24] Len Doyal and Roger Harris, 'The practical foundations of human understanding', *New Left Review*.

logic good enough for a primitive means of communication needs no apology from us. Language did not emerge from some kind of ratiocination. (*OC* 475)

THE KIND OF CREATURE WE ARE

It is neither objective metaphysical realities (whether forms or atoms) nor subjective states of consciousness (raw feels, mental pictures, innate ideas) but *Lebensformen* that are 'the given'. What is given is the human world: neither meanings in the head, accessible by introspection, nor essences in the objects around us, yielding to analysis, but the order that human beings establish by their being together.[25]

The great metaphysical search for something ultimate brings us back to where we started, to see it for the first time. The order without which our lives would be impossible comes neither from our apprehending and copying transcendental forms that exist in some higher world nor from exhibiting the ideas before the mind's eye. However deeply inclined we may be to suppose that the stability there is to our way of life, and thus to our structures of knowledge and so on, must be grounded in (say) the unchanging realities that underlie the flux of experience, perhaps certain non-observable entities occupying a realm that escapes the ravages of change and the vicissitudes of history, Wittgenstein wants us to acknowledge that the stability there is, such as it is, is already given in the customs and practices of everyday human intercourse. The given cannot be explored or explained any more deeply because it is the foundation of every kind of exploration and explanation. If you like: the given cannot be discovered except by showing how it makes possible all that we do and suffer. I discover myself, not in some pre-linguistic inner space of self-presence, but in the network of multifarious social and historical relationships in which I am willy-nilly involved.

The example of shopping for apples shows, as it is teased out, that the idea that naming things is the basic function of language only surrounds language with such a fog that the phenomena themselves cannot be properly seen (*PI* 5). What intuitively seems to be the essence of language only prevents us from seeing how conversation actually takes place.

One way of loosening the grip of the fascination with naming is to recall some of the forms of language which a child is taught to employ when it is being drawn into the conversation of the community.

[25] Derek Bolton, *An Approach to Wittgenstein's Philosophy*, but esp. 'Life-form and idealism', pp. 269–275.

Augustine's picture is immediately transformed. We have only to remember how children are trained to perform certain actions, to participate in certain activities, to make habitual use of certain words as they do so, and so on, to realize that it all depends on their *reacting* to others (*PI* 6). Augustine's picture of the mental ego watching its elders so that it can train its lips and limbs to make the signals and sounds that will communicate what it has been thinking and feeling all along, soon collapses. It loses its plausibility as soon as we recall how an infant is incorporated into the community, in response to endless verbal and non-verbal encouragement. Wittgenstein reminds us of the games that parents and teachers use to extend children's linguistic skills: 'Language-games [*Sprachspiele*]', as one might call them (*PI* 7).

However, this does not dispel the attractions of the feeling that *pointing* – 'ostensive definition' (*PI* 6) – is the ultimate foundation of meaning. Pointing to objects is undoubtedly an important part of training a child to speak, but the pointing usually occurs in the *use* of words (*PI* 9). The first 60 or so remarks in the *Investigations*, although at one level a satire on logical atomism which can be appreciated only by its former partisans, may also be read, more accessibly, as an exploration of the temptation to equate meaning with pointing to objects.

There is nothing to say what the words designate except the kind of use to which people put them (*PI* 10). You may equate the use of a word with the word's referring to an object, but the kind of reference is already agreed (10). To say that all words signify something is so far to say nothing (13). Designating is most straightforwardly understood as labelling (15). Wittgenstein draws in meaning (*bedeuten*, 19; *meinen*, 20), then reporting (*Meldung*, 21) and asserting (*Behauptung*, 21–2). He then comes back to the tempting thought that learning to speak just is, essentially, learning to name objects: people, shapes, colours, pains, moods, numbers, etc. (26). We first name things and then we are able to talk about them, or refer to them in conversation (27). Designating objects, whether ideas in one's head or the middle-sized dry goods in the environment, seems singularly fundamental to the conduct of human life.

But it is impossible to isolate naming, or any of its surrogates, from a cluster of other activities, at least so as to hold it up as what alone makes the other activities possible (*PI* 23). It is a mistake even to think of talking about a thing as a unitary phenomenon (27). Think only of a few exclamations – 'Water!' for example. You might be labelling it, or pointing it out, if you were among people, or extraterrestrial visitors, who did not know yet what this colourless runny substance was. You might also be trying to get a simple dictionary together if you had come upon a tribe with an unknown language. You might be appealing for help if a lady had swooned. You might be celebrating the results of digging a hole. (You might be a diviner.) You might just have noticed that the dam had burst. Of course the name of the substance in question comes into it, but what matters is being acquainted with the innumerable different situations in which the word is *used*.

You can explain things by pointing, but this is because you have been brought up to ask 'What is that called?', or some similar question (*PI* 27). Definition is an extremely common activity, at least in our culture, but it cannot be isolated from further verbal explanations, before or afterwards: 'So one might say: the ostensive definition explains the use – the meaning – of the word when it is already clear what role the word is supposed to be playing in the language in the first place' (30). You have to be master of a fair number of other skills before you are able to ask a thing's name (31).

Far from being something almost natural and spontaneous, naming turns out to be quite a sophisticated achievement. It is natural in the sense that it depends on certain physical capacities to handle things, focus the eyes, repeat an action, distinguish one thing from another, and the like. Such biological desires and powers are cultivated and reinforced by practice, so they become 'second nature' to any creature with (more or less) our physical and psychological constitution; but it takes a great deal of education – rousing the infant's interest, teaching it to discriminate among its perceptions etc. Augustine's picture presents the infant self as already understanding what naming, referring, meaning etc. are all about – as if the infant knew that already, in its head. But it is not so natural to designate objects. Wittgenstein plays with the prejudice in favour of the natural priority of naming in order to get at the roots of the metaphysically generated conception of meaning as an internal mental activity.

Other themes are infiltrated, but Wittgenstein's first concern in the *Investigations* is to get the reader thinking about the fancied priority of naming, and about the deeper motivation for the desire to put such emphasis on designation. Consider this remark:

> Someone coming into a strange country will sometimes learn the language of the inhabitants from ostensive definitions that they will give him; and he will often have to *guess* the meaning of these definitions; and will guess sometimes right, sometimes wrong.
> And now, I think, we can say: Augustine describes the learning of human language as if the child came into a strange country and did not understand

the language of the country; that is, as if it already had a language, only not this one. Or again: as if the child could already *think*, only not yet speak. And 'think' would here mean something like 'talk to itself'. (*PI* 32)

In effect, the soul is in exile, alone among creatures whose language is barbarous. It is as if one belonged to another world, with one's own private language. The picture also suggests that thinking is conversing with oneself, interior soliloquy.

This picture of the solitary self-communing self, radically independent of relationships with anyone or anything else in this world, overwhelms many people with its plausibility at certain points in their lives, perhaps when they badly misunderstand someone or feel totally misunderstood, or when they have a mental illness. The metaphysics of solipsism may well feed on the realities of madness. But this picture of the soul in exile in this world clearly also has deep religious roots. That is to say, if we probe what we are naturally inclined to say about the fundamental importance of naming, we begin to perceive the residual effects of an ancient myth of the soul that gets in the way of our finding each other – or ourselves. This is what Wittgenstein is trying to bring out.

But the mentalist–individualist voice is not easily silenced:

> Suppose, however, someone were to object: 'It is not true that you must already be master of a language-game in order to understand an ostensive definition: all you need – of course! – is to know or guess what the person giving the explanation is pointing to. (*PI* 33)

It still seems possible to hold that one is able to mean something, prior to being initiated into any linguistic operation, just by concentrating one's attention on it. Few would say in so many words that the individual's consciousness is entirely independent of the context of social practices of which Wittgenstein has reminded us. Nevertheless, animosity against the 'system' often revives the dream of being an entirely free agent in a situation without bounds or bonds. To suggest that the thoughts and feelings a person has 'inside' depend on the character of the physical and cultural setting which he inhabits is a proposal that easily arouses resistance. Our mental and spiritual states, we are inclined to insist, are constituted by certain internal private phenomena. Feelings of this kind express themselves in such protests as these:

> But it is just the queer thing about *intention*, about the mental process, that the existence of a custom, of a technique, is not necessary to it . . . (*PI* 205)

But you surely cannot deny that, for example, in remembering, an inner process takes place . . . (*PI* 305)

Isn't it very odd that I should be unable to think that it will soon stop raining – even without the institution of language and all its surroundings? (*PI* 540)

The function of such exclamations, which punctuate the *Investigations*, is to bring out how intuitively appealing the mentalist–individualist prejudices are: I can surely *think* 'Rain soon stop', in my own pidgin mentalese, without all this business about being initiated into the linguistic practices of the people around me!

Naming objects, or designating states of affairs, seems to be the one fundamental mental act that the solitary observer in the midst of the passing show is able to perform independently of any institution – on his own, as it were. The inclination to regard ostensive definition as the fundamental act of meaning suggests that we thereby pass beyond the confines of language and get in touch with reality itself. It seems possible for the mind to conduct its most important business without being beset by custom and technique, community and surroundings. That there is a certain 'theology of the self' in this inclination – 'the urge to fly above location in culture, to reject the trammels of the historically given, to be masterless and immediate' – is surely obvious.[26]

My mind cannot have moments of self-transparence, any more than I can designate objects in the world around me, unless I have been brought up in a tradition which is sustained by the very many other practices besides these two relatively sophisticated ones. The designation of objects, whether in the private seclusion of one's consciousness or by pointing out into the external world, far from being the privileged and foundational experience which the narcissistic metaphysics of subjectivity inclines to suppose, comes very late in the course of anyone's education. The craving for unmediated encounter either with my own states of consciousness or with the objects that confront me has to be resisted.

Such a conclusion is, of course, quite banal. After all:

What we are supplying are really remarks on the natural history of human beings; we are not contributing curiosities, however, but observations which no one has doubted, and which escape remark only because they are always before our eyes. (*PI* 415)

[26] David Martin, *Tracts against the Times*, p. 155.

Wittgenstein's observations are intended to be incontestable. If we do not agree with what he says about what we say he will try again, or perhaps drop that particular remark. He is ready to learn that prejudice blocks his own view of what is obvious. But the deeper point is to understand why he makes such obvious remarks.

What he is attempting is well described by Norman Malcolm:

> he is trying to get his reader to think of how the words are tied up with human life, with patterns of response, in thought and action. His conceptual studies are a kind of anthropology. His descriptions of the human forms of life on which our concepts are based make us aware of the kind of creature we are.[27]

What he seeks to show is that, however intuitively appealing the thought may be, I do not have some natural way of being in touch with external reality (say by pointing or meaning), or any equally natural way of being directly in touch with my own inner life (by introspection), as if such possibilities were independent of my membership of a lifelong *conversation*. He is not interested in the thesis that 'Man thinks' (*RPP* II, 14); his radically anti-Cartesian ambition is to show how hope, belief etc. are embedded in human life, 'in all of the situations and reactions which constitute human life' (*RPP* II, 16). He is interested in *behaviour* – but he is using the word 'behaviour' in a rather special sense: 'for it includes in its meaning the external circumstances – of the behaviour in a narrower sense' (*RPP* I, 314).

The 'foundations' upon which I exist as a self-conscious and autonomous being are the innumerable practices that collectively establish the tradition which is my native element. There is nothing deeper – there need be nothing deeper – than the unending 'game' which is 'the whole that consists of the language and the activities with which it is interwoven' (*PI* 7).

There could be no more radical attack on the dominance of the modern philosophy of the self-conscious individual. If I cannot even grasp some object in the world, or indulge in a moment's self-presence, without relying upon an initiation into countless practices that remain essentially social and collaborative, then every dream (or nightmare) of having some totally private experience of the world, or some perfect access to oneself, simply collapses. If the act of pointing can be variously interpreted in every case (*PI* 28), there can be no primordial act of designating that would secure an unambiguous extra-linguistic 'meaning'.

[27] *Thought and Knowledge*, p. 149.

There is no 'inner experience' which does not have conceptual links with other people's experience; the surroundings give it its significance (*PI* 580–3).

'What has to be accepted', as Wittgenstein said, 'is *forms of life*' (*PI*, p. 226). The implications, for the philosophy of the self, have been beautifully spelled out by Stanley Cavell:

> The extent to which we understand one another or ourselves is the same as the extent to which we share or understand forms of life, share and know, for example, what it is to take turns, or take chances, or know that some things we have lost we cannot look for but can nevertheless sometimes find or recover; share the sense of what is fun and what loss feels like, and take comfort from the same things and take confidence or offence in similar ways. That we do more or less share such forms rests upon nothing deeper; nothing *ensures* that we will, and there is no foundation, logical or philosophical, which explains the fact that we do, which provides the real forms of which our lives, and language, are distortions.[28]

But this is a hard conclusion to accept. Philosophy, as Cavell says elsewhere, 'concerns those necessities we cannot, being human, fail to know. Except that nothing is more human than to deny them'.[29] That is to say: we have a very strong desire to deny that we depend so radically on our forms of life. In the end, as Wittgenstein surely knew, we are captivated by that love of self which Augustine called *amor sui*: the desire to believe that we are indeed 'little mortal Absolutes', to recall Lawrence's phrase.

But if Wittgenstein was eventually able to find the roots of the myth of the isolated worldless 'I' in a tradition of writing that stretches back through Descartes to Augustine and beyond, he was not really out to rewrite the history of philosophy or even put an end to it. His innovation was to find the myth in the back of his own mind. His originality as a philosopher is to have written a text that enables the reader, with patience and luck, to become suspicious of the power the myth still wields. Even with some preliminary guidance, however, readers often find Wittgenstein's later writing intolerably difficult. 'The solipsist flutters and flutters in the flyglass, strikes against the wall, flutters further' (*NL*, p. 256).[30] The only consolation is that if the reader is not

[28] *Themes out of School*, pp. 223–4.
[29] *Must We Mean What We Say?*, p. 96.
[30] A flyglass is a stoppered bottle with a hole bored near the bottom, sitting in a saucer of beer; a rustic device Wittgenstein must have seen in villages in Lower Austria. Lured by the fumes, the fly finally crawls into the bottle and keeps vainly flying upwards to escape. cf. *PI* 309.

bewildered and even angered by the *Investigations* he will never get anything out of the book. (This may, of course, be because he is already free of the metaphysically generated pictures that so regularly dominate our reflective moments: Wittgenstein's cannot be the only available therapy.)

From Socrates onwards, of course, philosophers have worked hard, on and off, to bring us to an understanding of our place in the scheme of things. But to see what is obvious, particularly about ourselves, against the power of the fantasies, requires practice and discipline. Wittgenstein strives to voice our deepest metaphysical inclinations in order to permit, again in Cavell's words, 'an acknowledgement of human limitations which does not leave us chafed by our own skin'.[31]

Our metaphysical inclinations are difficult to acknowledge. The quotations from Augustine's *Confessions* with which the *Investigations* opens inaugurates an examination of the picture of meaning as an occult adventure that goes on in secret behind one's high brow. Again and again Wittgenstein reminds the reader that all meaning, even the very gesture of pointing something out, must have conceptual links with the whole system of the human way of doing things together. There is nothing inside one's head that does not owe its existence to one's collaboration in a historical community. It is established practices, customary reactions and interactions, and so on, that constitute the element in which one's consciousness is created and sustained: my sense of myself, not to mention the contents of my mind and memory, depend essentially on my being with others, my being in touch with others, of my physical and psychological kind. If Wittgenstein is right, the congruence of our reactions over a wide range of matters is the only foundation that we have or need – and these reactions are interwoven with language. Nothing is more foundational to the whole human enterprise than the community that we create in our natural reactions to one another as they have been cultivated and elaborated in a very contingent historical tradition. 'Commanding, questioning, recounting, chatting, are as much a part of our natural history as walking, eating, drinking, playing' (*PI* 25).

Such admissions of the banal and mundane, however, seem to leave out all that is great and important: the little mortal Absolute strikes back.

---

[31] *Must We Mean What We Say?*, p. 61.

CHAPTER 4

The Private Object in the Mind's Eye

There may be nothing at all going on in your mind, and still you may not talk like a parrot.

(*WLAA*, p. 78)

THOUGHT AS A GASEOUS MEDIUM

A move in chess, though it no doubt involves thoughts and feelings on the player's part, is a move in chess only because of the circumstances (*PI* 33). Wittgenstein's constant theme is that, for our inner life, we are radically dependent on customs, uses, institutions (*PI* 199). But what he rather abusively introduces as 'the conception of thought as a gaseous medium' (*PI* 109), recurs monotonously to tempt us out of the common forms of life that constitute our existence:

One is constantly tempted into wanting to explain a procedure with symbols by some special psychological occurrence; as if the mind 'could do much more in these matters' than signs can. (*PG*, p. 99)

The feeling returns insistently that, with allowance for the social and historical factors duly made, the individual consciousness can after all do the most amazing things. *Thinking* is surely something unique (*PI* 95): it is surrounded by a *halo* (*PI* 97). It seems to be something incorporeal, thus transcending our present limitations:

We are accustomed to thinking of [thinking] as something ethereal and unexplored, as if we were dealing with something whose exterior alone is known to us, and whose interior is yet unknown like our brain. (*PG*, p. 108)

The idea that thinking takes place in the mind, or that meaning is a mental activity, feeds on the picture of the mind as 'a cloudy gaseous medium in which many things can happen which cannot occur in a different sphere, and from which many things can be expected that are otherwise not possible' (*PG*, p. 100).

Paradoxically enough, for a metaphysician, the idea that thinking takes place in the head is the root of a great deal of misunderstanding:

> One of the most dangerous ideas philosophically is, oddly enough, that we think with, or in, our heads.
> The idea of thinking as an occurrence in the head, in a completely enclosed space, makes thinking something occult. (*PG*, p. 106; *Z* 605–6)

The danger is, of course, that it sets up the mentalist–individualist paradigm of thinking which occludes the hurly-burly of manifestly intelligent dealing with the world and helps to perpetuate a certain ideology. Among other things, it creates apparently insuperable difficulties in our understanding one another.

THE PROBLEM OF OTHER MINDS

Doubts about how reliable our knowledge of other people's minds is have roots deep in ordinary everyday experience. Most of us have had the shock, at one time or another, of discovering that we had totally mistaken the expression on someone's face or the force of what that person had just said. A few failures to communicate with certain people soon lead us to treat them as if they were as unintelligible as creatures from an alien planet. Perfectly ordinary people develop a paranoid outlook. The solipsistic desire that nobody may really exist but myself only mirrors the fear that I matter to nobody. Retreat into private worlds often leads to confinement in public institutions for people whose eccentricity makes them increasingly anonymous.

Wittgenstein did not separate epistemology from real life:

> Everybody is mistrustful (or most people are), perhaps more so towards their relatives than towards others. Has this mistrust any basis? Yes and no. One can give reasons for it but they are not compelling. Why shouldn't a man suddenly become *much* more withdrawn? Or devoid of love? Don't people get like this even in the ordinary course of events? – Where, in such cases, is the line between will and ability? Is it that I *will* not communicate with anyone any more, or that I *cannot*? If so much can lose its attraction, why not everything? If people are wary even in ordinary life, why shouldn't they – *perhaps* suddenly – become *much* more wary? And *much* more inaccessible? (*CV*, p. 54)

That note, made in 1946, as he began to concentrate on the epistemo-logical problems that our understanding one another traditionally raises, indicates that he was well aware of much darker and more disturbing obstacles to mutual comprehension. That other people are radically untrustworthy, and that I dare not reveal any more of myself to them than I can help, are no doubt convictions that are all the more deeply grounded the more arbitrary and spy-ridden the political structure of one's environment. But, whatever the politics, the enigma of (certain) others, and one's own (relative) isolation in the world, are common enough realities.

Permanent scepticism about other people's thoughts and feelings seems logically demanded by the gaseous conception of the mind. We seem to have to strive all the time to get at a mental or spiritual reality that lies behind 'coarser and therefore – for us – readily visible accompaniments' (*PI* 153). If we were not so *human*, so it begins to seem, we could understand one another perfectly.

This conception may easily be documented from classical theological texts. Consider, for example, Thomas Aquinas's fascinating discussion of whether angels talk to each other.[1] If he was to say that they did, he had powerful objections to deal with. Gregory the Great says that bodiliness, *corpulentia*, does not conceal one mind from another at the general resurrection: the paradigm of luminous bodies diaphanously accessible to one another in an ecstasy of mutual self-transparence. It is even less likely, then, that one angel's mind is hidden from another's. Thus, since the purpose of speaking is to manifest to someone else what lies hidden in one's mind (cf. *PI* 304), it has to be concluded that, in spite of what the Bible says, angels do not talk to one another.

Secondly, we have to distinguish talking interiorly, when one addresses oneself, from talking outwardly, to other people. Exterior speaking requires some perceptible sign such as a word or a nod or some other bodily movement. Angels have no bodies, *ergo* . . . Thirdly, when I speak it is always to attract other people's attention to what I have to say – we human beings have to depend on physical signs for this, but, once again, angels have no such need.

Thomas, having to take account of Scripture, insists that angels do talk to one another, but the fascination of what he says lies in his assumptions about the nature of human language. Against the first objection, for instance, he argues that a human being's thoughts are hidden behind two barriers. In the first place, it is always up to the individual whether to

---

[1] *Summa Theologiae*, I, 107, 1.

disclose what he is thinking or feeling. We have to *decide*, on *every* occasion, whether to reveal our thoughts. Note that Thomas is not saying that, after a certain education, one can conceal one's feelings by putting on an expressionless face. The face is *always* under the control of the will. His assumption is that the face is naturally blank until the soul behind it deliberately allows itself to show through.

But there is a second problem. Our minds are concealed by the opacity of our bodies: even when you have chosen to show me, I can never see directly what you think or feel. It is beautifully put by Gregory the Great, as quoted by Aquinas: 'We stand, as it were, behind the wall of the body, sheltered from the eyes of others in the recesses of our mind; but when we wish to reveal ourselves we come forth, with speech as the gateway, in order to show our inner selves'.[2] But, since angels do not have this *grossities*, so the argument concludes, one knows the other's mind as soon as the latter wills to manifest it.

Here, with Thomas Aquinas, who strove to correct some of the anti-incarnational philosophy in Christian discourse, the systematic comparison of how angels communicate with one another with how human beings do the same openly devalues the latter, which comes to seem very clumsy, precarious and uncertain. With the passage from Gregory, the feeling of epistemological solitude is well established. We turn out to be a crowd of hobbled angels, each isolated 'behind the wall of the body', like a hermit in a moated grange. We have every reason to conceive ourselves as naturally unintelligible to each other.

Contrary to all this, Wittgenstein reminds us of the obvious fact that, a great deal of the time, we understand one another's intentions, hopes, fears etc., immediately and quite unreflectively. We do not have to wait for calculated displays of feeling, or strain to get past the body of our interlocutor to find his mind – at least *normally*. The problem is that what we have to do *sometimes* is presented as what we have to do *always*. But the feeling which epistemological scepticism about other people's minds expresses has roots in certain common enough experiences – perhaps, as John Wisdom suggests, in our infancy: 'an earlier time when there was something, namely the world of the grown-ups, knowledge of which we desperately desired and equally desperately dreaded'.[3]

Again and again the model of the parapet and its mysterious defender,

[2] *Morals on the Book of Job*, II, 8.
[3] *Philosophy and Psycho-Analysis*, p. 281, but also, on the whole question, his *Other Minds*: a classic.

to take Gregory the Great's version, dominates attempts to discuss the difficulties that one has in understanding other people. It is as if I watched certain privileged objects in my environment and had to infer or guess from their surfaces what was going on inside. I see many eyes but I cannot be certain that they are not all blind, never mind whether they are watching me. It is as if I were alone – eyed, perhaps, but never knowing for certain if I am feared or desired. The solipsist is surrounded by creatures whose kinship with himself he has to deduce by interpreting the noises they emit. It is when we yield imaginatively to the ambivalences of epistemological solitude that we begin to understand how deeply Wittgenstein's later writings disturb the metaphysically generated concept of the self.

THE PREDICAMENT OF PRIVATE WORLDS

One way of dealing with the soul is to eliminate it. This course is followed, for example, by Quine, one of the major figures in Anglo-American philosophy since the 1950s. Primarily a logician he is, like many logicians, also a master of rhetoric. His prose certainly exhibits a deflationary notion of the self.
   Consider the following account:

> I am a physical object sitting in a physical world. Some of the forces of this physical world impinge on my surface. Light rays strike my retinas; molecules bombard my eardrums and fingertips. I strike back, emanating concentric air waves. These waves take the form of a torrent of discourse about tables, people, molecules, light rays, retinas, air waves, prime numbers, infinite classes, joy and sorrow, good and evil.[4]

The deliberate way in which he interweaves references to people, feelings and values with the jargon of elementary physics and mathematics says far more than any arguments Quine has produced about this matter, here or anywhere else. He pictures himself in a sedentary posture, exposed to an assault by molecules which provokes him to retaliate, apparently by talking:

> My ability to strike back in this elaborate way consists of my having assimilated a good part of the culture of my community, and perhaps modified and elaborated it a bit on my account. All this training consisted

---

[4] *The Ways of Paradox*, p. 228.

in turn of an impinging of physical forces, largely other people's utterances, upon my surface . . . All I am or ever hope to be is due to irritations of my surface, together with such latent tendencies to response as may have been present in my original germ plasm. And all the lore of the ages is due to irritation of the surfaces of a succession of persons, together, again, with the internal initial conditions of the several individuals.

The soul for which such grand metaphysical privileges have been claimed is thus transformed by Quine's rhetoric into the effect of certain 'surface irritations'. He goes on to offer an associationist account of human learning and then defends the potentiality of language to be 'occasionally descriptive in a way that other quiverings of irritable protoplasm are not'. Finally, these particular quiverings eventually turn into science, when 'system' is introduced, together with 'an artificial proboscis of punch cards and quadrille paper' (a quintessentially Quinean conceit).[5]

Thus, one is the result of the mutually interacting surface irritations of a certain kind of physical object. But this needs to be contrasted with what Quine takes to be the alternative: the belief that the mind is a repository of mental entities.[6] Each sentence that one utters copies some pre-existing mental entity, a meaning. Meanings are all in the head. Thus it comes about that, as Quine says elsewhere, 'in mentalistic philosophy there is the familiar predicament of private worlds'.[7] The alternative locks each mind into its own private mental asylum and communication becomes almost impossible. It then becomes uncertain whether people have minds, let alone thoughts or feelings like one's own.

Quine's poetic conception of the soul as the effect of a kind of skin rash makes short work of the problem of epistemological solitude; but is there no way between these extremes?

THE ARGUMENT FROM ANALOGY

In the Second Meditation, Descartes makes the point that, if he happens to look out of a window on the street, what he sees are hats and cloaks that might cover ghosts or dummies that move mechanically, but he *judges* them to be human beings. John Stuart Mill rephrased the problem thus: 'By what evidence do I know, or by what considerations am I led to

---

[5] Ibid., p. 233.
[6] e.g., Ibid., pp. 221–7.
[7] *Word and Object*, p. 79.

believe, that there exist other sentient creatures; that the walking and speaking figures which I see and hear, have sensations and thoughts, or in other words, possess minds?'.[8] To this question he offered the following reply:

> I conclude that other human beings have feelings like me, because, first, they have bodies like me, which I know, in my own case, to be the antecedent condition of feelings; and because, secondly, they exhibit the acts, and other outward signs, which in my own case I know by experience to be caused by feelings.

The idea that I believe, or even know, that other people often have the same thoughts and feelings as I have, on the strength of inferences that I make from their outward behaviour, sounds plausible enough. It seems acceptable to start from one's own case. It seems all right also to say that one *believes*, on analogy with one's own case, that other people have thoughts and feelings, and that one believes this as the result of some kind of *inference* from such premises as their moving their bodies, and so on, all in the way that Mill indicates.

Much the same line is followed by William James:

> Why do I postulate your mind? Because I see your body acting in a certain way. Its gestures, facial movements, words and conduct generally, are 'expressive', so I deem it actuated as my own is, by an inner life like mine. This argument from analogy is my *reason*, whether an instinctive belief runs before it or not.[9]

But the argument is permeated by mentalist–individualist assumptions. My belief that you have a mind may be instinctive, but it is nevertheless some kind of 'belief'. My 'reason' for this 'postulate' results from my 'deeming', from what I see of your body, that it is actuated from within as mine is. On the basis of my observation of your face, actions, etc., and of my introspective awareness of my own mental properties, I elaborate a hypothesis that you too have these mental properties. But it is a matter of framing a hypothesis. We have, as A. J. Ayer says, defending the argument from analogy as the right answer to the problem, a 'theory' that other people have minds.[10] This theory 'has no serious rival' – but it is nevertheless a *theory*.

---

[8] *An Examination of Sir William Hamilton's Philosophy*, p. 243.
[9] *Radical Empiricism*. p. 42.
[10] *Central Questions*, p. 134.

That the argument always starts from the Cartesian first-person singular perspective needs no demonstration. The picture is very much of a self-enclosed *mind*, striving to bring the lumbering objects around it under a *theory*.

THE PRIVATE LANGUAGE FANTASY

If forced to choose between Quine's elimination of mental entities and some version of the argument from analogy, anyone with theological interests would naturally opt for the latter. Wittgenstein tries to remove the dilemma. The theory about other people's having minds, the same thoughts and feelings that I have, and so on, derives its plausibility from a fantasy about the ineffability of my primary sensations.

Let us acknowledge that no mental event on the scale (say) of intention is possible but for the existence of the customs of a community into which one has been initiated (*PI* 205): may we nevertheless have *sensations* that we can identify on our own? Surely, whatever we have to concede to the community, our sensations are always our own, inalienably and inimitably, radically *private*? Wittgenstein invites us to use our imagination:

> But could we also imagine a language in which a person could write down or give vocal expression to his inner experiences – his feelings, moods, and the rest – for his private use? – Well, can't we do so in our ordinary language? – But that is not what I mean. The individual words of this language are to refer to what can be known only to the person speaking; to his immediate private sensations. So another person cannot understand the language. (*PI* 243)

The language would thus be unintelligible, in principle, to anyone but me: its referents are my unmediated, and so uninterpreted and unlearnt, primary sensations. It is not a private code that I develop out of the common language in order to mark certain sensations in a secret diary. It is the language that I have for my inmost experience prior to, and independently of, my having to master the public tongue. (It is its creator's own language.)

This takes us back to the language that, as Augustine's story suggests (*PI* 32), the infant must already possess. It seems possible to locate a sensation from inside, by an inwardly directed act of pointing, whether or not one can apply the public term to it: 'It is as if when I uttered the word I cast a sidelong glance at the private sensation, as it were in order to say to myself: I know all right what I mean by it' (*PI* 274–5). Whatever about the initiation of babies into the public language, I surely reach a stage of self-consciousness when I can have direct acquaintance with the contents of my own mind, so the argument runs.

My sensations, not to mention my feelings, moods, etc., are tacitly pictured as objects that I am in a position to identify independently of my being able to describe them to other people. Scepticism about how reliable one's knowledge of other people's minds is, together with the complementary desire to preserve one's own solipsistic mystery, have roots that spread too deeply for easy philosophical excavation. One root, which Wittgenstein strives to uncover, is the ubiquitous paradigm of describing physical objects (*Z* 40). When we begin to reflect on it we are easily led to take the expression of sensation on the model of designating an object (*PI* 293). Subjectivity is turned into a kind of object:

> Where do we get the concept of the 'content' of an experience from? Well, the content of an experience is the private object, the sense-datum, the 'object' that I grasp immediately with the mental eye, ear, etc. The inner picture. (*RPP* I, 109)

But if it can be shown that the contents of a man's awareness are not necessarily to be conceived as private objects that hover before his mind's eye, it follows that we are not in the epistemological difficulty about understanding one another that the metaphysically constituted self has evidently to face. If my inner life is not a scene of private items that I alone am in a position to observe and, if I so will, to reveal, then we are released from the fear (or hope) that knowing what other people feel is always a precarious adventure of inference from their outward demeanour.

Having introduced the fantasy of a radically private language, Wittgenstein begins to explore its ramifications. How does this language 'refer' (*PI* 244) to 'private' (246) 'sensations' (261)?

How do we learn to name sensations? By saying that it is a matter of *learning* Wittgenstein reminds us of our dependence on the community, but his first point is that we did not learn to identify sensations as we learnt to identify physical objects, however tempting the analogy. An infant learns to *refer* to a sensation such as pain as a development of screaming or moaning with pain. The expression 'I am in pain' first appears in the conversation as a substitute for screaming or moaning. It then becomes available to function as a description of my pain, when I try to answer the doctor's questions or when I write the novel about the end of my love affair. The illusion that needs to be exposed is that saying

'I am in pain' starts out as a description of my inner state. That encourages the belief that I am always in a position to designate my sensations inwardly prior to coming out with any utterance. But if learning to describe sensations grows out of screaming or moaning and the like, no room exists for description to get in between the sensation and the expression of the sensation. 'How can I still [*denn*] go on wanting to insert language between the pain-expression and the pain?' (*PI* 245). I can go on trying to drive a wedge between a sensation and the primitive animal expression of that sensation only if I stick to the metaphysical prejudice that language is a device for naming objects. I then suppose myself able to treat my feelings as objects of private observation prior to my choosing to manifest them to the world. The desire for this gap is the desire to escape from the body (cf. *PI* 256).

But first – in what sense, in any case, are my sensations 'private'? Wittgenstein conducts the following argument with himself:

> Well, only I can know whether I am really in pain; another person can only surmise it. – In one way this is false, and in another nonsense. If we are using the word 'to know' as it is normally used (and how else are we to use it?), then other people very often know when I am in pain. – Yes, but all the same not with the certainty with which I know it myself! – It can't be said of me at all (except perhaps as a joke) that I *know* I am in pain. What is it supposed to mean – except perhaps that I *am* in pain?
> Other people cannot be said to learn of my sensations *only* from my behaviour, – for *I* cannot be said to learn of them. I *have* them. (*PI* 246)

To say that other people learn of my inner feelings *only* from my outward demeanour is to imply that I myself have some better way of knowing them – as if I were in a position to observe them directly, whereas you have to be content with making inferences from my always enigmatic face. This suggests that my behaviour, and that means my body, my gestures, and my words, are a second-best, radically ambiguous and defective way of letting other people see what I am feeling. The corollary is that my feelings lie transparently open to me, as objects before my mind's eye.

Intuitively appealing as all this is, says Wittgenstein, to people brought up on a metaphysically generated doctrine of the self, it is exactly the kind of nonsense that needs to be uncovered (*PI* 119). The fact is that other people usually know perfectly well when I am in pain, or elated or angry and so on. I have learnt how to conceal and to fake my feelings; but those are relatively sophisticated skills that depend on the existence of natural expressions of feeling.

It makes sense – it has a place in the conversation – to say that I may not know what you are feeling. It is because of this possibility that fears that we may never be absolutely certain about one another's inner feelings arise in the first instance. It seems then that I can only guess at someone else's feelings, with greater success as we get to know one another, but never with *absolute* certainty. We may then resign ourselves, with a certain pleasure, to this mitigated version of the doctrine that 'our lives are a congeries of solipsisms'.[11] But that once again overlooks the role of the body:

> 'I can only guess at someone else's feelings – does that really make sense when you see him badly wounded, for instance, and in dreadful pain? (*LW* 964)

I may not be able to judge how intense his pain is, or how complicated it is by sadomasochistic desires or anger at his stupidity in stepping in front of the bus – but I should be acting very abnormally if I *guessed*, or *inferred*, that he must have a certain range of feelings.

My behaviour may be ambiguous, in many different ways, but if my smile was always like the Mona Lisa's people would leave me out of the conversation.

It belongs to the very concept of emotion that it is *visible*. We do not observe certain facial contortions and, like a physician formulating a diagnosis, proceed to make inferences to the existence in the other person's consciousness of feelings such as pain, grief, joy and so on (*Z* 225). The very idea that we are all like patients with mysterious sicknesses, who are also all doctors having to diagnose one another's inner life from rather vague symptoms, is the rather uncanny picture conjured up by the metaphysical claim that I alone know what I really feel.

In discussion with a doctor who is questioning whether I have the pain that I have mentioned, it may become appropriate for me to say 'I know I am in pain'; but this would be insisting or protesting, it would not mean that I had observed my sensation again and was confirming my report. There may also be doubt about what I really feel, on this or that occasion. I may need the help of a psychiatrist to discover my true feelings. That only shows how untenable the belief is that I have privileged access of some interesting kind to the contents of my own mind. Other people may know what I am feeling before I realize it myself.

---

[11] James, *Radical Empiricism*, p. 42.

What needs to be punctured is the illusion that I always see my sensations before I release a description of them upon the unsuspecting company. That puts me once again in the position of the disengaged subject watching his own private stream of consciousness and occasionally reporting on it to the outside world.

To say that one's sensations are private is like saying that one plays patience on one's own (*PI* 248): it is perfectly obvious to everybody else what is going on. If we can never get away from the radical ambiguity of other people's outward demeanour we should have to agree that a baby's smile might be faked or forced (249); deceit simply cannot be built into our most fundamental relationships. A dog cannot deceive us (250); a whole cultural–linguistic network has to be in place before pretending becomes a possibility.

Wittgenstein comes back to the imaginary private language: if I identify my sensations with words that have developed from my natural sensation-expressions (screaming, weeping and so on), then my language is not essentially private. It might be a highly complicated code, extremely difficult for anyone else to break, but the regularity of the connections between my vocabulary and my almost animal ejaculations would make it, in principle, intelligible to other creatures of my physical kind. Thus the private language fantasy leads to the question of the place of the human body:

> But suppose I didn't have any natural expression for the sensation, but only had the sensation? And now I simply *associate* names with sensations and use these names in descriptions. (*PI* 256)

To get me into a position to make naming my sensations, and describing them, the metaphysically fundamental acts of which I am capable, however, I have to be detached from the natural expressiveness of my body. To save the idea that my sensations must be inwardly identifiable, independently of my having mastered expressions that other people understand, requires my being disembodied. The paradigm of designating objects applies to the recognition of the objects before my mind's eye only if I get out of my body:

> What would it be like if human beings never showed their pains (did not groan, grimace, etc.)? Then it would be impossible to teach a child the use of the word 'tooth-ache'. (*PI* 257)

If the little animal never held his jaw, gnashed his teeth etc., we should not be in a position to give him words for his feelings. He would be, but for his consciousness, under a general anaesthetic.

At this point Wittgenstein has the mentalist–individualist on the run. He now has to postulate that the infant is a genius, with the creative imagination to invent a name for the sensation, to provide his own description for the array of inner items, without any help from other people or the surrounding culture. When he used his special word, of course no one else could understand him. He could not explain to anyone else what the word meant to him – but then, if you cannot explain a thing to someone else, do you really understand it yourself? There is no way of escaping other people:

> When one says 'He gave a name to his sensation' one forgets that a great deal of stage-setting in the language is presupposed [*schon viel in der Sprache vorbereitet sein muss*] if the mere act of naming is to make sense. And when we speak of someone's having given a name to pain, what is presupposed [*das Vorbereitete*] is the existence of the grammar of the word 'pain'; it shows the post where the new word is stationed. (*PI* 257)

The metaphor of setting the stage is the translator's, but it faithfully reminds us of how much else must already be in place before the practice of naming *anything*, not to mention our sensations, even becomes a possibility.

We are left with a 'ceremony' in which 'I concentrate my attention on the sensation – and so, as it were, point to it inwardly' (*PI* 258). The disembodied consciousness is now curved introspectively upon itself. In any case, as Wittgenstein brings out with his final irony, the very word 'sensation' belongs to our common language (*PI* 261): to maintain the fantasy of a private language for one's experience gets one to the point of wishing to come out with a still unarticulated sound; a word so elemental that it brooks no explication. But then, as Wittgenstein cruelly observes, even such a pure sound would be an expression only in some conversation, which brings us back into the public world. It is as if one wanted to perform an act of meaning something without having to make use of anybody else's signs. It is, as it were, 'a contamination of the sense that we express it in a particular language which has accidental features, and not as it were bodiless and pure' (*PG*, p. 108). But it is only by cutting out the human behaviour which is the expression of sensation that we can generate the private language fantasy (*PI* 288).

The point of exploring the private language fantasy is, then, to retrieve the natural expressiveness of the human body, and to reaffirm the indispensability of belonging to a community: two obvious facts that the metaphysically dictated conception of the self trivializes and occludes.[12]

SEEING YOUR SOUL

Wittgenstein's exploration of the private language fantasy is a central part of his attempt to free us from thinking of the contents of our minds on the model of physical objects. Of course there is more detail to it, and it is surrounded with more considerations that I either can or need expound here: my purpose is only to persuade theologically minded readers that Wittgenstein's argument is of much deeper significance for their enterprise than might at first appear. The model of the inner life that seems intuitively appealing leaves us in the grip of mental pointing at private objects. Readers often feel, however, that Wittgenstein wants to eliminate the inner life altogether. He puts the objection to himself in the following little dialogue:

> 'But you surely cannot deny that, for example, in remembering, an inner process takes place'. – What gives the impression that we wanted to deny anything? When one says 'Still, an inner process does take place here' – one wants to go on: 'After all, you *see* it'. And it is nevertheless this inner process that one means by the word 'remembering'. (*PI* 305)

The voice that protests on behalf of the reality of the inner life is itself impelled to appeal to its *visibility*. When we think of someone as 'deep', or as having 'inner strength' or 'inner resources', we should automatically fill it out with stories about that person's style of life, or remarks about the character in his or her face, and the like.

> The impression that we wanted to deny something arises from our setting our faces against the picture of the 'inner process'. What we deny is that the picture of the inner process gives us the correct idea of the use of the word 'to remember'. We say that this picture with its ramifications stands in the way of our seeing the use of the word as it is. (*PI* 305)

This seems to me one of the most important methodological remarks in the *Investigations*.

[12] The bibliography on the private language argument spreads like bindweed: I recommend Rush Rhees, 'Can there be a private language?', and John W. Cook, 'Human beings'.

The idea that we can do no better than *believe* that someone else is in pain (*PI* 303) is tied up with the deeply attractive doctrine that the function of language is essentially to convey thoughts – 'which may be about houses, pains, good and evil, or anything else you please' (*PI* 304). I have to guess or infer from your face that you are in pain – because you have to stop to observe your feelings before you report them. My radical uncertainty about what you are thinking goes with your having your thoughts before your mind's eye long before putting them into words. The inner life is always being construed as a set of objects that I may choose to depict.

In trying to wean us away from that model Wittgenstein is passionately concerned to put us back in touch with the inner life which that model obscures; but the effect of his argument on the dedicated partisan of the radically inaccessible mystery of the self is to protest:

'Are you really a behaviourist in disguise? Aren't you at bottom really saying that everything except human behaviour is a fiction?' (*PI* 307)

To this Wittgenstein replies laconically:

If I do speak of a fiction, then it is of a *grammatical* fiction.

Talk of pains seems so like talk of houses, for example, that sensations are pushed into the role of describable objects. To conceive of feelings and thoughts as objects before the mind's eye is to fill our heads with fictitious entities that have been induced by certain analogies between describing pains and describing houses. Wittgenstein is only reminding us that these analogies are deeply misleading. The private language fantasy has been explored in order to bring out that there is nothing that I can find in myself, which I cannot show other people, at least in principle. When he says that there is not even a sensation that I can designate in a radically private language he is cutting the ground from beneath much grander claims to unique and incommunicable experiences.

This sounds as if he is trying to empty our heads of all that matters most. To deny that my sensations (at least!) are some kind of thing, of which I have a certain knowledge independently of my presence in a community, seems to deprive me of what is most surely my own. The anti-behaviourist protest is an essential part of Wittgenstein's argument. If we are not angered or bewildered by his destruction of the private language fantasy, it is surely only because we have not allowed our attachment to the paradigm of the inner life as constituted of quasi-objects really to be questioned.[13] To clear the mind of these objects, far from being the behaviourist move that the mentalist–individualist fears, is rather, for Wittgenstein, to free the mind from the alienating power of the metaphysical conception of the self. The model of the inner life which seems so inevitable only estranges us from ourselves, and, of course, from each other.

True enough, with adults at least and particularly in certain cultures, it will often be doubtful whether people are having certain sensations: I shall have to look for tell-tale signs, guess or infer their feelings, and so on. But could it be that, *in every case*, I should have nothing stronger than conjecture or hypothesis to go on? If we had only a belief or a theory, as a result of certain inferences, that someone else was in pain, would that not once again be cutting out the spontaneous, almost animal, expression of pity, say, and offering help? 'Pity, one may say, is a form that the conviction that someone else is in pain takes' (*PI* 287). There is no need, on every occasion, for a reflective pause to make inferences from certain signs. The arm goes out to comfort the injured man or the bereaved woman. The action of being sympathetic is already seeing the other person's pain or grief. This is Wittgenstein's argument.

To say that we go to the help of an injured person because we have the *belief*, drawn from analogy with our own case, that the other person is going through a pain-experience, puts the cart before the horse (*Z* 542). Being sure that someone else is in pain, doubting whether he is, and so on, are instinctive kinds of relationship (*Verhältnis*) to the other human being – and what we *say*, on such occasions, is an extension of this primitive behaviour (*Z* 545).

We want to say that our actions, not to mention our utterances, spring from *thought* – as if they would otherwise not be worthy of the rational creatures that we are. Wittgenstein combats this rationalism with expressions such as 'reaction', 'instinctive relationship', 'primitive behaviour', 'forms of life', and the like. Such phrases give rise to suspicions of behaviourism – but that makes his point. We are so dominated by the soul/body dichotomy that it becomes difficult to acknowledge a whole range of characteristically human activities which are neither the result of ratiocination nor the effect of mechanical conditioning.

Our attitudes towards each other often *are* based on calculation. The point is simply that our *theories* about people depend on our being related to one another in ways that come out all the time in *unreflective*

[13] Cavell, *Claim of Reason*, p. 91

reactions – which are no less intelligent, rational and human for being as natural and automatic as comforting an injured man or a bereaved woman, or shunning them in dread.[14]

Wittgenstein is reluctant to say that we have a theory that other people have minds:

> My attitude towards him is an attitude towards a soul [*eine Einstellung zur Seele*]. I am not of the *opinion* [*Meinung*] that he has a soul. (*PI*, p. 178)

Confronted with a creature like myself, however enigmatic its expression, I do not, even momentarily, entertain the hypothesis that it too may have a mind and a soul. True enough, on many occasions, you look at a certain person's face and say 'I wonder what's going on behind that face' (*LW* 978). The exceptional case, which may well be traumatic, in appropriate circumstances, need not become the norm. Once again, if we remember countless ordinary situations, there is no room for the fear (or the desire) that we are radically unintelligible to one another: 'The exterior does not have to be regarded as the facade behind which the mental powers are working away'. Rather, as Wittgenstein writes in a variant to that last remark: 'If someone is talking to me quite obviously holding nothing back then I'm not even tempted to think that way' (*LW* 978). I am simply engaged with the other person's mind as I listen to him, or respond in numerous other ways. My attitude towards *him* is already a reaction to his *mind*.[15]

> Do I *believe* in a soul in someone else, when I look into his eyes with astonishment and delight? (*RPP* I, 268)

Far from concealing the soul, the body reveals it. With many such reminders Wittgenstein mocks the inclination to 'postulate' minds in our neighbours.

The metaphysically conceived body gets between one mind and another. Bodiliness is then what isolates human beings from each other. The dream (or nightmare) of an incorporeal, wordless, unmediated presence of one bare soul to the next then becomes almost inevitable. In the private language fantasy Wittgenstein tries to voice the feeling of one's being *ultimately*, at least at the level of one's rawest sensations, accessible only to oneself, or to a being in a transcendent enough position

---

[14] Malcolm, 'Wittgenstein: the relation of language to instinctive behaviour'.
[15] Winch, '*Eine Einstellung zur Seele*'.

to see into one's soul. It is as if I were able to rise above, to escape beyond, the primitive forms of life which I might otherwise have to accept. Against such deeply seductive inclinations, supported as they apparently are by the facts of frequent difficulty in understanding people, Wittgenstein keeps reminding us of what is obvious: our language-bearing bodiliness opens the space where we meet each other in the first place.

GRAMMAR FOR A PRIVATE 'I'

It remains a deeply compelling thought that I am an object – to be sure an object of a very special kind, 'ethereal' and even 'gaseous' if you will – but an object of which I am the best guarantor because I am the only witness on the scene. My consciousness, understood as something essentially mental and spiritual, seems to be inherently self-identifying. My consciousness, after all, is nothing if it is not *self*-consciousness.

Philosophy, as practised by Wittgenstein, is a 'fight against the bewitchment of our understanding by the devices of our language' (*PI* 109). No linguistic instrument has bred such confusion as the first person singular pronoun – and Wittgenstein's remarks about this have given rise to a great deal of interesting debate:[16]

> We feel that in the cases in which 'I' is used as subject, we don't use it because we recognize a particular person by his bodily characteristics; and this creates the illusion that we use this word to refer to something bodiless, which, however, has its seat in our body. In fact *this* seems to be the real ego, the one of which it was said, 'Cogito, ergo sum'. (*BB*, p. 69)

Clearly, Wittgenstein is out to explode (what he thinks of as) the Cartesian picture of the self.

He has made an important distinction. The cases in which the word 'I' is used as object, as he says, are exemplified by my saying such things as 'I have grown six inches' and 'I have a bump on my forehead'. In such cases there is no difficulty: the pronoun 'I' is being used demonstratively, to indicate the object referred to. I might be wrong about how much I had grown: I need someone else's help, or at least a tape measure, to establish my height. It might only be by catching my reflection in a mirror

---

[16] See, e.g., Anscombe, 'The first person', in *Metaphysics and the Philosophy of Mind*, chapter 2, and, putting the opposite view, Madell, *The Identity of the Self*; but I owe most to the remarkable paper by J. R. Jones, 'How do I know who I am?'.

that I notice the bruise on my forehead. In such cases the word 'I' might be replaced by 'this body'.

The word 'I' is used as subject, according to Wittgenstein's distinction, in such cases as 'I see so-and-so', 'I think it will rain', and 'I have toothache'. I do not need anyone else to tell me that I have toothache. I may be wrong about the imminence of the rain but I cannot be mistaken about my *thinking* that it will rain. I may very well point to myself when I say 'I am in pain', but this is different from touching my forehead to indicate my bruise, which I may have been surprised to discover. 'I don't feel it', I may say of the bruise; but it makes no sense to say 'I don't feel it' of the toothache.

While it would sound odd enough to say, of myself, 'This body has grown six inches', it would make sense. To attempt the same substitution in the case of 'I am in pain' is much more problematical: 'This body is in pain'. I might ascribe growth to my body, but it is surely to *myself* that I ascribe pains, feelings and so forth. Thus the self appears, on cue, as the referent for the word 'I'. 'That which has pains or sees or thinks', as Wittgenstein says (*BB*, p. 74), is now almost inevitably conceived as the Cartesian 'thinking thing'. The body itself, although it reacts to a great variety of stimuli, even when one is asleep or unconscious, hardly seems the bearer of the sensations, moods, thoughts and so on, which characterize a human being. It seems, in short, that 'what has pain must be an entity of a different nature from that of a material object' (*BB*, p. 73). The ego must, in fact, be mental.

> Where our language suggests a body and there is none: there, we should like to say, is a *spirit* [*Geist*]. (*PI* 36)

Where the word 'I' is not used to identify a *material* object, we cannot help saying that it must refer to an *immaterial* one (*BB*, p. 47). Words, at least the important ones among them, such as 'I' surely is, name objects: the picture of the essence of language with which the *Investigations* opened once again reveals its power. The word 'I' has a meaning; it is the object for which the word stands (*PI* 1). That it is a very strange object is no objection: that is what everyone brought up on the metaphysically dictated conception of the self has thought all along. The word 'I' is the name for the essential thing about me: something bodiless, of course, which nevertheless has its seat in my body – the real ego (*BB*, p. 69).

It comes as a shock when, in the middle of a lengthy disquisition on 'consciousness', Wittgenstein asserts that the word 'I' is not a referring expression at all (*PI* 410). Where am I, one wants to ask, if I cannot refer to myself as 'I'? But the question is: what do I take myself to be when I protest that I can refer to myself as 'I'? We are so mesmerized by the paradigm of describing physical objects (cf. *Z* 40) that we naturally suppose that the self is an item that can be located. To be sure, the 'I' is systematically elusive,[17] but is that not simply because it is so hard to catch the real ego?

> 'When one thinks something, it is oneself thinking'; so one is oneself in motion. One is rushing ahead and so cannot also observe oneself rushing ahead. (*PI* 456)

The thing that one is, when it is doing its most characteristic thing, is so busy that it cannot get hold of itself. As William James said: 'The attempt at introspective analysis in these cases is in fact like seizing a spinning top to catch its motion, or trying to turn up the gas quickly enough to see how the darkness looks'.[18]

But it is extremely difficult to abandon the idea of the self as an admittedly very elusive and intangible 'something', presumably because the alternative seems to be that it must be a 'nothing' (*PI* 304). Wittgenstein, however, in notes that did not make their way into the *Investigations*, made a distinction that suggests a way out of this dilemma.[19]

He distinguishes between 'consciousness physiologically understood, or understood from the outside', and 'consciousness as the very essence of experience, the appearance of the world, the world' (*NL*, p. 254). In this second sense, which is equivalent to the use of the word 'I' as subject, consciousness is equated with the 'appearing' of the world – not with its 'look', but with its being there at all. This at once recalls some of Wittgenstein's earliest extant notes:

> All experience is world and does not need the subject . . .
> What kind of reason is there for the assumption of a willing subject?
> Is not *my world* adequate for individuation? (*NB*, p. 89)

Why cannot 'my world' individuate me just as plausibly as the putative 'real ego'? Being irresistibly inclined to speak of the self does not mean that we are forced to assume its existence as some kind of object. Rather, if the self is recognized as co-ordinated with the world (*TLP* 5.64), the

---

[17] Theologians are bound to remember the essay by Ian Ramsey, 'The systematic elusiveness of "I" '.

[18] *Principles of Psychology*, vol. I, p. 244.

[19] Here I am particularly dependent on J. R. Jones.

temptation no longer arises to picture it as an item in the world or detached from it. The self need not be regarded as an object in the world along with all the rest except for its being invisible, singularly elusive, and so on. Nor need it be the disengaged ego, surveying the world from a god's eye point of view. The soul need be neither an ethereal entity concealed in a fleshy envelope nor a transcendental spectator of the passing scene. For, just as there is nothing in the visual field that allows us to infer that it is seen by an eye, there is nothing in the world to fill the role of the self (*TLP* 5.633).

Wittgenstein's 'fundamental ideas', the ones that came to him 'very early in life' (*RW*, p. 158), as distinct from 'the most consequential ideas' in the *Investigations*, which he attributed to Piero Sraffa's stimulating criticism (*PI*, p. x), surely include the idea that solipsism, when it is unravelled, coincides with pure realism (*TLP*, 5.64): 'I am my world' (5.63). The self is not to be found anywhere *in* the world of experience because it is the *source* of that experience – but it is not *outside* the world either: 'rather, it is a limit of the world' (5.632). That the world is *my* world is something that discloses itself in the fact that the limits of language – the only language that I understand (*not* a 'private language'!) – mean the limits of my world. There is no world for me or anyone else other than the world that the language gives us. It is a world that we have in common: the predicament of private worlds is an illusion. And it is when I talk about the world that *I* appear on the scene, in the glory of my self if you like. But until I speak or act, *I* am not to be found; and then it is this human being that you encounter. The only satisfactory representation of the self is, after all, *der Mensch*: the human being (*RPP* I, 281).[20]

When I realize that there is no such object as I am strongly inclined to take myself to be, the world reappears as the place where I am at home. My consciousness, as Marx and Engels did not quite say,[21] is my relation to my surroundings.

But such sayings are too dark for the *Investigations*. Perhaps this is how Sraffa's criticism comes into the story, but the fact is that Wittgenstein gave up talking about the self and the world and spoke of 'consciousness' only to make fun of it (e.g. *PI* 412–20). He had come to think that the only liberating way to deal with the prejudices about the self that are generated by the use of the word 'I' is to bring the word back from its application in the metaphysical tradition, to the use to which it is

---

[20] See the splendid paper by Virgil C. Aldrich, 'On what it is like to be a man'.
[21] *Collected Works*, vol. 5, p. 44, but crossed out in manuscript.

put in the language where it is at home (*PI* 116).[22] We are tempted by metaphysical prejudices to try, when we use the word 'I', to grasp the essence of the thing which it supposedly names – and we are off in pursuit of chimeras (*PI* 94).

The dark sayings of the *Tractatus* give way to 'the synopsis of trivialities' (*WLDL*, p. 26). The idea that thought is a hidden process, or that the self is an invisible entity, must be Wittgenstein's favourite example of the metaphysical prejudices that pervade our culture. To equate the self with the world of experience is a radical way of bringing it out into the open, so to speak, without eliminating it. The 'I' is not hidden in the head; it is the world viewed.

From 1930 onwards, for Wittgenstein, the most satisfactory way of showing that thought lies open to us was by recalling an immense variety of obvious facts: 'But the proper synopsis of these trivialities is enormously difficult, and has immense importance'. Reading the *Investigations*, and the allied later writings, is much more demanding intellectually than reading the *Tractatus*.[23] What was so dramatically put in terms of the self's being individuated by its world requires to be teased out in immensely greater detail, so Wittgenstein came to think, if we really are to be released from the pictures that the devices of our language seem inexorably to impose (*PI* 115).

THE SELF AT HOME

The later writings are more demanding, largely because they are incomparably entertaining. Wittgenstein once said to Norman Malcolm that 'a serious and good philosophical work could be written that would consist entirely of *jokes*'.[24] Perhaps he was thinking of the *Investigations*. The butt of some of the later writing's best satire is, at any rate, the would-be hidden 'I'.

Of course you can sometimes discover a wish or a fear by self-observation – 'by observing your own reactions' (*RPP* II, 3). Introspection, as a method of finding yourself, depends on remembering situations that you have been in, imagining how you might have behaved

[22] In the official translation – 'in the language-*game* which is its *original* home' – neither of the italicised words is justified by the German text.
[23] Bertrand Russell: 'The later Wittgenstein, on the contrary, seems to have grown tired of serious thinking and to have invented a doctrine which would make such an activity unnecessary', *My Philosophical Development*, p. 161.
[24] *Memoir*, 1984, p. 28.

differently, and the like: it does not isolate you from your surroundings. All the time, Wittgenstein reminds us, or strives to persuade us, that it is the surroundings that are essential to our conversation, not the mental accompaniment of speech that one is so inclined to consider essential (*RPP* II, 204). What is going on in people's minds when they are talking to me, he says, is normally not an issue:

> it would make no sense if somebody who had a pleasant conversation with me were thereafter to assure me that he had spoken entirely without thinking. But this is not because it contradicts all experience that a person who can speak in this way should do so without thought processes accompanying his speech. Rather, it is because it comes out here that the accompanying processes are of no interest whatsoever to us, and do not constitute thinking. We don't give a damn about his accompanying processes when he engages in a normal conversation with us. (*RPP* II, 238)

It is only when I distrust someone, for example, that I begin to wonder what lies behind his words:

> If I don't distrust him, I don't pay any mind to what is going on inside him. (Words and their meaning. The meaning of words, what stands behind them, doesn't concern me in normal conversation. Words flow along and transitions are made from words to actions and from actions to words. When someone's performing mathematical calculations he doesn't stop to think whether he is doing it 'thoughtfully' or 'parrot-like'.) (*RPP* II, 603)

It is when something goes wrong (I make a slip), that I stop and do it more thoughtfully, or carefully, or slowly or imaginatively or in a hundred other ways in which I show that I am not a parrot. It is when I suspect that you are deceiving me, or yourself, that I begin to see a gap between your words and your mind. But I should be mad, literally, to see that gap between *everybody's* words and mind *all the time* – and just as mad if I supposed that the gap is usually a perfect fit.

When a man groans he may be joking or feigning; but that does not mean that, on all other occasions, his groaning is the perfect outward match for some inner awareness of pain. Sometimes when I hear someone speak I suspect that he is pretending or lying: there *is* something 'behind' his words. But again that does not mean that, under normal circumstances, when I listen to what he is saying I suppose that his words are like windows on his inner states of mind.

Wittgenstein piles up the trivialities. 'I don't know what is going on inside him' means that I could not reconstruct or imagine situations to account for his behaviour (*LW* 197): it is not the mystery inside him but my lack of knowledge of his past and present circumstances that makes him incomprehensible. 'He is incomprehensible to me means that I cannot relate to him as to others' (*LW* 198), but it is a question of our relationship. I can hide my thoughts from someone by hiding my secret diaries – and that might be hiding something that would interest him (*LW* 974). But I can hide my thoughts from you just as effectively by telling you them in a language that you have never learned (*RPP* II, 564). The cases in which the other person, or his thoughts and feelings, are concealed from me have to be the exception: it is tempting then to wonder whether the inner life of others is really always hidden (*RPP* II, 558–9). It is then that we find ourselves insisting that the *meaning* that gives sense to what we say is something in the mental domain:

> But it is also something private! It is the intangible *something*; comparable only with consciousness itself.
> How ludicrous this could seem! In fact it's, as it were, a dream of our language. (*PI* 358)

It would be funny, but the idea that consciousness is an intangible quasi-object in my own case, as in that of anyone else, simply blinds us from ourselves.

   In hundreds of such remarks Wittgenstein brings out the power of the picture of the hidden thoughts behind the facade of my face, and of the invisible soul inside the carapace of my body. The very idea of the self that is supposed to capture my uniqueness as a spiritual being, and preserve my subjectivity against the encroachments of modern science, simply gets in the way of my seeing what I am. Picturing meaning or thought as a private object in the mind's eye keeps me from recognizing the countless ways in which my mind is at work in my ordinary everyday encounters with other people in our common environment. The model of the self as an intangible and private object alienates us from ourselves:

> The confusing picture is this: that we observe a substance – its changes, states, motions: like someone observing the changes and motions in a blast furnace. Whereas we observe and compare the attitudes [*Verhalten*] and behaviour [*Benehmen*] of human beings. (*RPP* I, 312)

Again and again, that is to say, we return to the paradigm of the material object, deny its materiality, visibility and so on, and think that we have found our true selves. The relationships and demeanour of human beings towards one another disappear from sight. The problems with which this chapter has been concerned, and many others like them, then become inevitable.

CHAPTER 5

Suspicions of Idealism

Why do I not satisfy myself that I still have two feet when I want to get up from a chair? There is no why. I simply don't. This is how I act.

(OC 148)

MISINTERPRETING WITTGENSTEIN

It is at first disconcerting to see how determinedly many philosophers insist that Wittgenstein's later work represents an ingenious revival of metaphysical idealism, or a perverse kind of solipsism,[1] or a new form of epistemological scepticism.[2] Further reflection suggests that these readings only bear out Wittgenstein's suspicions about the power of metaphysical idealism. Indeed, as I go on to show, it occasionally confuses his faithful translators as well as his interpreters.

Consider first the currently most influential interpretation of the later writings.[3] The exegesis is clinched with the following putative quotation from *Zettel*:

We have a colour system as we have a number system. Do the systems reside in *our* nature or in the nature of things? How are we to put it? – *Not* in the nature of things. (Z 357)

Bernard Williams naturally takes this remark to mean that, if the colour and number systems that we have do not originate in the nature of things in the world around us, they must originate in our minds. The remark leaves no third possibility open. In rejecting some vulgar realist philosophy according to which we have names for the colours of flowers, animals, cars etc., simply because these items pop up before us and flaunt themselves so importunately that they all but name themselves, Wittgenstein had to go to the other extreme and conclude that the colour system is our invention and thus mutable by decree, arbitrary, 'pure convention'

[1] J. N. Findlay, *Wittgenstein: a Critique*.
[2] Saul A. Kripke, *Wittgenstein on Rules*, subjected to (I think) devastating critique by Colin McGinn, *Wittgenstein on Meaning*.
[3] Bernard Williams, 'Wittgenstein and idealism'.

and such like. The notion can be filled out to become somewhat more plausible: colour systems differ from one culture to another, whole communities might be colour blind, it is apparently easy to imagine some radically alternative colour scheme to the one we chance to have inherited.

In his zeal to draft Wittgenstein into the idealist camp, and then to refute him, Williams has rewritten the clinching text, which actually runs as follows:

> We have a colour system as we have a number system. Do the systems reside in *our* nature or in the nature of things? How are we to put it? – *Not* in the nature of numbers or colours. (*Z* 357)

Far from residing in our minds, the colour system lies in a certain collaboration between our nature and the nature of things. The remark which Williams hails as the last word in showing Wittgenstein's idealism turns out to be one of his most explicit repudiations of the realist/idealist dilemma. There would be no colour system but for our being on the scene: but that does not mean that we are in a position to revise it at will. In fact, Wittgenstein goes on at once to discuss how revisable the colour system is and remarks:

> It is obvious at a glance that we aren't willing to acknowledge anything as a colour intermediate between red and green. (Nor does it matter whether this is always obvious, or whether it takes experience and education to make it so.) (*Z* 359)

But for our presence on the scene the difference between primary and secondary colours would not be noticed, and noticing it no doubt requires a certain education of our perceptions; but it is a difference that we cannot revise or eliminate.

The revealing misquotation comes from quite a lengthy discussion in which Wittgenstein plays with our knowledge of colours precisely to release us from the sense of having to choose between realism and idealism. However much we bent our will to it, we could not make room in the conversation for the claim that red is not a primary colour: there are language-games we *cannot* learn (*Z* 339). Wittgenstein's energy is mostly devoted here to extracting and exploding pro-idealist inclinations:

> 'If people were not in general agreed about the colours of things, if undetermined cases were not exceptional, then our concept of colour could not exist'. No: – our concept of colour *would* not exist. (*Z* 351)

To say more, to yield to the temptation to say '*could* not exist', is to let in the possibility that we might after all be in a position to identify the colours of things independently of our having the words, as if the concept of colour resulted from our agreeing in our sense-impressions first. The fact that we generally agree in colour judgements *is* our having the language:

> How do I know that this colour is red?
> – It would be an answer to say: 'I have learnt English'. (*PI* 381)

The mentalist–individualist inclination is to say that I know that the colour is red before I have learnt to speak at all, or that I learn the public words merely to label the experiences I have already privately and inwardly identified. Wittgenstein reminds us that, whatever we are inclined to say, identifying a thing's colour is a skill that is interwoven with language.

But even authorized translators have, without noticing, read idealist inclinations into Wittgenstein's text:

> One can say: Whoever has a word explained by reference to a patch of colour only knows *what* is meant to the extent that he knows *how* the word is to be used. That is to say: there is no grasping or understanding of an object, only the grasping of a technique. (*RPP* II, 296)

That these two sentences contradict one another suggests that something has gone wrong. The proposal that we have no grasp of *objects*, but 'only' of *techniques of using words*, feeds grist generously to those who want to read Wittgenstein as an arch-idealist. But a correct translation of this remark would read as follows:

> One can put it this way: If you are going to explain a word to someone by pointing to a patch of colour he will know *what* you mean only to the extent that he knows *how* the word is being applied. That is to say: there is no way of grasping the object here, of understanding it, except by grasping a technique [*Es gibt hier kein Erfassen, Auffassen des Gegenstandes, ausser durch ein Erfassen einer Technik*].

You cannot explain the word 'red' simply by pointing to an object unless your interlocutor is already able to discriminate between size and colour, one colour and another, and so on, not to mention being able to *refer* in the first place. It is a familiar point from the first 60 or so remarks in the *Investigations*: I can understand what you mean, in a case like this, because I have acquired a certain technique. Wittgenstein is not suggesting that we do not grasp the object but only a certain linguistic skill. That certainly would be an exotic form of idealism! He is denying that one is able to get hold of anything independently of one's being initiated into certain common practices.

One of the least cryptic remarks in which Wittgenstein voices a position that is neither realist nor idealist is thus inadvertently slanted in a radically idealist direction. A momentary lapse over a German conjunction has left us with a translation that places him firmly in the idealist camp. He is made to endorse the myth that the self is cut off from grasping things in the world, being confined to grasping nothing but words.

The text goes on:

> On the other hand, one could certainly say that a certain grasping, apprehending, of the object is possible *before* any grasping of a technique, for we can simply give someone the order 'Copy *this*' and he can then copy, for example, the colour, or the shape and size, or only the colour but not the exact shade, etc. And here copying achieves what, in the case of a physical object, taking it in one's hand achieves.
> – It is as if we could apprehend what is meant, the colour for example, with a particularly fine pair of mental tweezers, without taking anything else along with it. (*RPP* II, 296)

Thus Wittgenstein returns to satire. His interlocutor, dazzled by the paradigm of designating material objects, has once again betrayed his susceptibility to the appeal of the mythical private ostensive definition.

The interest of Bernard Williams's misquotation, and of the slip in the authorized translation, lies in the way that readers who are themselves no doubt anti-idealist may be momentarily blinded, either by Wittgenstein's strategy of voicing all the sides in the debate or simply by the cunning of their subterranean metaphysical confusions. Whatever the explanation, they project an idealist intention on manifestly anti-idealist remarks.

The two remarks just discussed are interesting because they are so clearly and illuminatingly anti-idealist. Indeed, they would suffice to establish Wittgenstein's anti-idealist credentials. Things do not reveal their properties to us as if we were totally passive recipients, with no contribution of our own to make. Nor are we absolutely free to impose whatever grid we like upon the raw data of sensation. The colour and number systems belong in the realm of that interplay of nature and culture which is 'the natural history of human beings' (*PI* 415). There is no getting hold of anything in the world except by a move in the network of practices which is the community to which we belong. This reaffirms the only *a priori* in Wittgenstein's philosophical vision of human life: our *Lebensformen*.

ALTERNATIVE CONCEPTUAL FRAMEWORKS

For a long time now, since the expansion of ethnography and social anthropology in the wake of European colonization of the rest of the world, people have been troubled (or charmed) by the thought that human beings may now be, or may always unwittingly have been, totally unintelligible out of their native culture. With the nearing possibility of intergalactic travel, the prospect of communication with radically alien beings is perhaps no longer entirely in the realm of science fiction.

Theologians have always had problems about communicating with a radically alien being. More recently, some have insisted on an irreducible pluralism in theological work, even within such an apparently homogeneous tradition as the Roman Catholic one.[4] Different cultures, across history and geography, transact their cognitive business with the world so differently that intellectual understanding between them comes to seem difficult if not impossible: so the story goes.

But just how radically incommensurable may conceptual frameworks intelligibly be? If we have extremely difficult problems when we move from one theological environment to another, for example, that is one thing. If the differences are insuperable, so that translation of concepts becomes impossible, then we are no longer in one world.

In a much discussed paper Donald Davidson has argued, initially on Wittgensteinian grounds, that the notion of radically different conceptual frameworks is incoherent.[5] He begins by arguing that we cannot split our concepts from our language in any fundamental way, to make it appear that 'it is only wordlessly if at all that the mind comes to grips with things as they really are'. Under pressure from the metaphysical tradition we are no doubt easily taken in by the thought that language is merely a medium or an apparatus that remains outside the minds that (deign to) employ it. As Davidson notes, the mentalist–individualist mythology remains powerful: 'There are, for example, theories that make freedom consist in decisions taken apart from all desires, habits and dispositions of the agent; and theories of knowledge that suggest that the mind can observe

[4] Karl Rahner, *Theological Investigations*, vol. XI, pp. 3–23, esp. p. 7.
[5] 'On the very idea of a conceptual scheme', in *Inquiries*, chapter 13.

the totality of its own perceptions and ideas'.[6] Voluntaristic and introspectionist doctrines continue to dog people, but, pretending for the moment that his readers are all over *that* hump, Davidson invites us to equate conceptual systems with languages. He can then rephrase the question: might there be languages that defy being translated into each other?

To keep the exciting prospect of radically alternative conceptual schemes in play, then, we have to show that there could be an untranslatable language. Much of what people say *is* untranslatable, of course, or would prove so troublesome that we do not bother. We may just have to learn Arabic if we want to understand camels. It is hard to do physics in Gaelic. Speakers of many non-European languages had best learn some English if they need to repair lorries. But for a radically different conceptual scheme we have to envisage a language which no stranger could ever learn.

An unlearnable language is another version of the private language fantasy, which we discussed in chapter 4. An untranslatable language, so Davidson now argues, would not be a language. Surrounded by naked creatures displaying the same physical constitution as ourselves we might be bewildered by the sounds that they directed at one another; but sooner or later, once we had got the hang of how certain snatches of speech matched or meshed with phenomena in the environment, such as rain, darkness etc., and activities like cooking, eating and so on, we could begin to translate. We could not but understand beings of our own kind, at a level which rules out radically untranslatable languages.

We may want to play up the difficulties of translation. We may think that such difficulties, across history and cultures, are all too obvious. There is room for differing emphases on continuity and discontinuity, but the heady doctrine that there might be several mutually unintelligible and incompatible representations of the world, all of which were equally viable and workable and even 'true', seems to have nothing in it.[7] And the reason it collapses takes us back to the natural expressiveness of the human body in a variety of public situations.

Davidson, who does not regard himself as a follower of Wittgenstein (rightly so, as we shall see), thus disposes of the notion of incommensurable conceptual frameworks. But Wittgenstein himself gave a good deal of attention to the matter, although, characteristically, not in those terms.

---

[6] Ibid., p. 185.
[7] But see Nelson Goodman, *Ways of Worldmaking*.

On one occasion, when he approached this issue, he asked us to imagine a community in which everyone was raised from infancy to give no expression whatsoever to feelings. Showing emotion is regarded as infantile, the training in the poker face and the stiff upper lip is very severe, people are ridiculed or punished for betraying feeling, and so on. They are a people with totally expressionless faces, so much so that shamming pain is impossible for them:

> 'Shamming', these people might say, 'What a ridiculous concept!' (As if one were to distinguish between a murder with one shot and one with three.) (Z 384)

It is this stony-faced community of zombies, or something equally outlandish, that we have to imagine in order to see how radically different conceptual schemes might be possible:

> I want to say: an education quite different from ours might also be the foundation for quite different concepts.
> For here life would run on differently. – What interests us would not interest *them*. Here different concepts would no longer be unimaginable. In fact, this is the only way in which *essentially* different concepts are imaginable. (Z 387–8)

If the connection between sensations of pain and expressions of pain, to take Wittgenstein's favourite example, had been educated out of people – 'if there were for instance no characteristic expression of pain, of fear, of joy' (PI 142) – then we should find them impossible to talk to:

> 'These people would have nothing human about them'. Why? – We could not possibly make ourselves understood to them. Not even as we can to a dog. We could not find our feet with them [*Wir könnten uns nicht in sie finden*]. (Z 390)

Literally the meaning is: we could not find ourselves in them, we could not put ourselves in their place. Since they never expressed emotion we could not react to them – unless with horror: 'These people have nothing human about them'. We could not speak to them.

On another occasion Wittgenstein put it like this:

> If you came to a foreign tribe, whose language you didn't know at all and you wished to know what words corresponded to 'good', 'fine', etc., what would you look for? You would look for smiles, gestures, food, toys. . . . If

you went to Mars and men were spheres with sticks coming out, you wouldn't know what to look for. Or if you went to a tribe where noises made with the mouth were just breathing or making music, and language was made with the ears. (*LC*, p. 2)

It seems to me that, in appropriate settings, a tribe who communicated with their ears (elaborate wigglings) would not be beyond the reach of a tribe who have traditionally preferred their tongues: but Wittgenstein's appeal is, in any case, to the human way of *acting*.

For Davidson, to think of a conceptual framework is to think of a *language*; but for Wittgenstein, to think of a language is to think of some *activity* such as warning, pleading, reporting and innumerable others (*PI* 19). We should be well along the way to understanding an alien people when we saw pain, fear, joy, etc., in their faces and actions. They might have practices which we should wish them to abandon; they might have things to teach us. Mutual understanding would often be difficult, and on particular issues quite unattainable. But there would always be an immense range of activities, such as slaking thirst, erecting shelters, helping the sick, and so on, where we collaborated, understanding one another's reactions immediately. In the process we should no doubt weep and joke with one another, and so 'find our feet' with one another: 'What is essential for us is, after all, spontaneous agreement, spontaneous sympathy' (*RPP* II, 699).

As long as our inherently physical reactions of welcoming and shunning, threatening and comforting, and so on, in a host of situations, are mutually intelligible, we must already be deep enough into conversation to learn each other's language. It follows, then, that we could not be divided by *insuperable* differences of conceptual framework.

Both Davidson and Wittgenstein argue against the very idea of essentially different conceptual frameworks, but the difference between them is important. Davidson writes as follows:

Why must our language – any language – incorporate or depend upon a largely correct, shared, view of how things are? First consider why those who can understand one another's speech must share a view of the world, whether or not that view is correct. The reason is that we damage the intelligibility of our readings of the utterances of others when our method of reading puts others into what we take to be broad error. We can make sense of differences all right, but only against a background of shared belief.[8]

[8] 'The method of truth in metaphysics', esp. pp. 199–200, in *Inquiries*, chapter 14.

But note his terms: 'a *view* of the world . . . our *readings* . . . our *method* . . . a background of shared *belief* . . .'. For Wittgenstein, however, what we share lies at the level, not of views, readings, method, and belief, but of *reactions* and *forms of life*.[9]

For Wittgenstein, it is our bodiliness that founds our being able, in principle, to learn any natural language on earth. In contrast to the metaphysical conception of the self, where our bodies supposedly get between us and prevent a meeting of minds, Wittgenstein reminds us of the obvious fact that the foundation of mutual understanding is the human body, with its manifold responsiveness and expressiveness. Paradoxically, it is not our bodies but our minds that get in the way of our understanding each other.

THE COMMON HUMAN WAY OF REACTING

But what if we reacted differently from one another? Wittgenstein puts it like this:

> Suppose you came as an explorer into an unknown country with a language quite strange to you. In what circumstances would you say that the people there gave orders, understood them, obeyed them, rebelled against them, and so on?
> The common human way of acting (*die gemeinsame menschliche Handlungsweise*] is the system of reference by means of which we interpret an unknown language. (*PI* 206)

The system of reference is the way that human beings generally react to one another – but the protest that naturally arises against this remark soon voices itself in the following little exchange:

> 'So you are saying that human agreement [*die Übereinstimmung der Menschen*] decides what is true and what is false?' – It is what human beings *say* that is true and false; and they agree in the *language* they use. That is not agreement in opinions [*Meinungen*] but in form of life [*Lebensform*]. (*PI* 241)

The protest to the effect that it must be something more fundamental than consensus among human beings that settles what is correct seems to

[9] Davidson is compared with Wittgenstein by Anthony Manser, 'Language, language-games and the theory of meaning'.

assume that the agreement is at the level of views and beliefs. The fear is that Wittgenstein is offering a form of idealism – as if what we come back to is *ideas*. Does he mean that it is a consensus of opinions?

> Is this what I am saying? No. There is no *opinion* at all; it is not a question of *opinion*. They [the truths of logic] are determined by a consensus of *action*: a consensus of doing the same thing, reacting in the same way. There is a consensus but it is not a consensus of opinion. We all act the same way, walk the same way, count the same way. (*WLFM*, pp.183–4)

As he said at the outset of the *Investigations*, in the tale of the purchase of five red apples, setting himself against Augustine's portrait of the mental ego in the infant body: 'Well, I assume that he *acts* as I have described. Explanations come to an end somewhere' (*PI* 1). His later writing, his later philosophy if you will, treats as fundamental, not ideas or truths of logic or the many other candidates that the tradition has proposed, but *human action*.

It is certainly what people *say* that is true or false; but what makes it possible for them to affirm or deny anything in the first place is not views or beliefs but, more fundamentally, their being engaged in patterns of activity which already contain the concept of being right and wrong. The 'agreement' between human beings that makes possible our living together in one world and, among much else, our acting and thinking logically, lies in our already being 'attuned'[10] to one another in a whole range of unhesitating reactions. Indeed, as Wittgenstein says with unusual emphasis even for him, 'Following according to the rule is FUNDAMENTAL to our language-game' (*RFM* VI, 28).

FOLLOWING THE RULE BLINDLY

It is hard to accept that following the rule is so fundamental to our use of language:

> I feel that I have given the rule an interpretation before I have followed it; and that this interpretation is enough to *determine* what I have to do in order to follow it in the particular case. (*RFM* VI, 30)

At least, if I am subjected to enough mentalist–individualist pressure, that is my feeling. Once again, of course, occasions often arise when I

[10] Cavell, *Claim of Reason*, p. 32.

take thought before carrying out normal procedure in the given situation. But it misrepresents the phenomenon of following the rule to suppose that some act of reflection has to be present, however tacitly and fleetingly, on every occasion.

Wittgenstein devotes many pages to describing the 'physiognomy' of all that belongs to what we call 'following a rule' in everyday life (*PI* 235). The metaphysically inspired inclination is to say that understanding a sign is always a fresh insight or interpretation: it is how I take the rule, not how I am trained to react, that finally counts. How I am trained to use a sign seems quite unimportant in comparison with the construction that I am apparently always free, and indeed obliged, to put on it. In effect, how could a being such as I am, with my self-consciousness, have to knuckle under to the dictates of a material sign! And once again, in starting to uncover and neutralize the attractions of the doctrine that understanding is always interpretation, Wittgenstein invites the criticism that he is a behaviourist:

> Let me ask this: what has the expression of a rule – say a sign-post – got to do with my actions? What sort of connection is there here? (*PI* 198)

This is hardly an objective inquiry. Whether it is heard as bluster or cunning or in a dozen other possible tones, the question demands a reply that is respectful of our metaphysical dignity. With mock timidity Wittgenstein replies:

> Well, perhaps this one: I have been trained to react to this sign in a particular way, and now I do so react to it.

That is easily put down – Wittgenstein talks as if 'I' am a Pavlovian dog, trained to slaver at the bell:

> But that is only to give a causal connection; to tell how it has come about that we now go by the sign-post; not what this going-by-the-sign [*dieses Dem-Zeichen-Folgen*] really consists in.

What we want is a proper philosophical account of sign-following, and what we expect to hear is that it is because we breathe life into these dead signs that they have any meaning (*PI* 432). Once again the dilemma appears: if we cannot countenance a behaviourism that reduces us to animals that react automatically to stimuli, then we are left with a mentalism that frees (or condemns) the individual to make a decision at every step. To this, Wittgenstein replies, somewhat enigmatically:

> On the contrary; I have further indicated that a person goes by a sign-post only in so far as there exists a regular use of sign-posts, a custom.

The gap that there seems to be between the embodiment of a rule (e.g. a sign-post) and my behaviour (following it) calls out to be filled with something more exciting than a mere *reaction*. But, in a characteristic move, Wittgenstein fills the gap that his anti-behaviourist interlocutor would bridge with a special mental act of *meaning* the rule, with the longstanding custom of the community. Reaction to the sign, although unattended by deliberation or reflection, is a perfectly respectable way of behaving which in no way diminishes my status as a self-conscious rational being. The sign-post on occasion leaves room for doubt about the way I am to go (*PI* 85); but, under normal circumstances, it is rational to follow it – blindly.

Otherwise the door stands open to radical scepticism:

> It may easily look as if every doubt merely *revealed* an existing gap in the foundations; so that secure understanding is only possible if we first doubt everything that *can* be doubted, and then removed all these doubts. (*PI* 87)

(That Descartes is somewhere in the background need not be doubted.) The signs will often be damaged or obsolete; the rule may permit so many exceptions that it has to be reinterpreted; but to deny that a man 'really understands' the system when he simply reacts appropriately to the signs, whilst it may boost the claims of rational self-consciousness, also surrenders us to madness:

> I can easily imagine someone always doubting before he opened his front door whether an abyss did not yawn behind it; and making sure about it before he went through the door (and he might on some occasion prove to be right) – but that does not make me doubt in the same case. (*PI* 84)

DOING WITHOUT PRESUPPOSITIONS

It is amazingly easy to believe that the alternative to behaving 'thoughtlessly' is behaving with the full panoply of reasoning, reflecting and conscious deciding. It can even seem irresponsible and irrational not to keep, at least at the back of one's mind, a monitoring watch on the possibility that one is always being deceived (cf. *RPP* II, 591). Wittgenstein tries to draw out this obsessive thought in such examples as those that follow.

> A doctor asks: 'How is he feeling?' The nurse says: 'He is groaning'. A report on his behaviour. But need there be any question for them whether the groaning is really genuine, is really the expression of anything? Might they not, for example, draw the conclusion 'If he groans, we must give him more analgesic' – without suppressing a middle term? Isn't the point the service to which they put the description of behaviour? (*PI*, p. 179)

The nurse's report on the patient's behaviour immediately leads to their giving him more painkillers. They do not first assure themselves that his groaning is in fact an expression of pain – although it is possible, in many imaginable circumstances, that he might be feigning, or groaning with sorrow for his sinful life. The temptation is to say that the medical team are working on the hypothesis that the patient is in pain – as if they had entertained the other possibilities and excluded them. Their reaction would be rational only because it rests on the presupposition that the patient's groaning is an expression of his sensation – as if we always had to consider the possibility that the outward demeanour and the inner experience had some bizarre connection. There seems to be room, and even need, for a middle term: 'If he groans, and assuming that he is not feigning, then we must give him more analgesic'. They are at least making a *tacit* assumption, it seems necessary to say; but 'Then the transaction of our language-game *always* rests on a tacit presupposition' (*PI*, p. 179).

On another occasion Wittgenstein resorts more openly to satire:

> 'We're always making presuppositions; if they aren't correct then, of course, everything is different'.
> – Do we say this, for example, when we ask someone to go shopping? Are we presupposing that he is human, and that the store is not a Fata Morgana? Presuppositions come to an end. (*LW* 354)

No doubt, in a metaphysical mood, people might be inclined to say that, even in this case, we are presupposing that he is human (he might have been an angel or an android), and that the village shop is not a mirage or a film set. No doubt, we might hasten to add, these presuppositions become automatic; but all the same – our life rests on a web of belief, our everyday transactions rest on a foundation of all but certain hypotheses of an extremely general kind.

These examples, and many more like them, are designed to trap us into realizing just how seductive and compelling the idea is that language rests on rationality, and human action upon self-consciousness. Behaviour, if it is to be significant, seems to have to rely on injections of meaning from one's inner mental store; language seems to be the invention of a being with a highly developed intelligence; and so on.

Against all such thoughts Wittgenstein summons us back to the obvious:

> Did we *invent* human speech? No more than we invented walking on two legs. (*RPP* II, 435)

In all such matters we return to a level where nature and culture cannot be disentangled. Language neither grew on human beings like hair nor did they sit down and invent it. Language is not the product of thought or will:

> I want to regard man here as an animal; as a primitive being to which one certainly grants instinct but not ratiocination. As a creature in a primitive state. For any logic good enough for a primitive means of communication needs no apology from us. Language did not emerge from some kind of ratiocination [*Raisonnement*]. (*OC* 475)

Indeed, even the famous Cartesian doubt, the paradigm of modern intelligence, is rooted in animal instinct:

> I really want to say that hesitations in thinking begin with (have their roots in) instinct. Or again: the language-game does not have its origin in *reflection*. Reflection is part of the language-game. And that is why concepts are at home in the language-game. (Z 391)

Methodical scepticism, far from being the mark of disembodied intellect, has its roots in human animality:

> Doubt . . . is an instinctive way of behaving. A way of relating to someone else [*ein Verhalten gegen den Andern*]. (*RPP* II, 644)

It is a way of relating to someone else which is *primitive*:

> But what is the word 'primitive' meant to say here? Presumably that the way of behaving is *pre-linguistic*: that a language-game is based *on it*, that it is the prototype of a way of thinking and not the result of thinking. (Z 541)

Human beings have primitive reactions (Z 540), ways of behaving and relating to one another which give rise to various uses of signs and eventually, among much else, and quite rarely, to ratiocination, reflection and doubt. The metaphysically dictated doctrine that everything that people do and say, if it is to be worthy of their dignity as self-conscious and autonomous intellectual entities, must issue from thought and will (supposed, to be sure, to be interior, invisible and private), is an illusion that has to be deflated once and for all.

The more he wrote, the more deeply opposed Wittgenstein became to that doctrine. Again and again, by a synopsis of trivialities, he drives us back, against all our metaphysical inclinations, to discover ourselves in 'the whole, consisting of the language and the activities with which it is interwoven' (*PI* 7): in Hölderlin's phrase, 'the conversation which we are'.[11]

The tacit presupposition or, more generally, the suppressed middle term, needs to be exposed as another piece of nonsense of the kind it is wounding for the intellect to discover (*PI* 119). With the age-long emphasis on rational and autonomous consciousness, the metaphysical tradition entrenches the myth that there has to be an element of reflection or deliberation in every respectable human action. Otherwise actions fail to be intelligent or free – and the people in whose daily lives reflection and deliberation seldom occur drop into the margins of history. Wittgenstein, with his radical anti-idealism, keeps reminding us that our action, on the whole, is an unreflective and instinctive reaction to the manifold pressures and appeals of the common order to which one belongs. And the point of reminding us of this really rather obvious fact, is to persuade us not to be ashamed of it. The interesting question is why we are so prone to insert this element of conscious reflection into any action that is to count as intelligent and voluntary; and why we are so reluctant to let go of this inclination.

The opening story, one comes to suspect, is a joke at the expense of the self-conscious individual (*PI* 1). There is something uncanny, surrealistic, even mechanical and inhuman about the shopkeeper who takes apples one by one from the box, checking the colour of each against a chart on the wall, and reciting the numbers as he counts them out. A young child might do this, but an adult who acted so reflectively and deliberately would strike us as a bit queer. Shopping, trade at any level, occasions much more reflection and deliberation than many human activities. The

---

[11] 'Seit ein Gespräch wir sind': a line in the unfinished poem 'Versöhnender der du nimmer geglaubt', *Poems and Fragments*, p. 428.

apples may not be ripe, the shopkeeper may be trying to cheat us, and so on. But what would a world be like in which every human activity was carried out with intense concentration and self-conscious deliberation? Would that make the activity any more human?

The inclination to want our doing to be one with our consciousness, at least as an ideal, for failing to reach which we need to apologize, finally requires *theological* treatment. For the truth of the matter, at least according to the classical theological tradition, is that doing and knowing, activity and consciousness, are one and the same only in God.

By doggedly recalling obvious facts, and by satirizing the metaphysically induced myth that so frequently conceals them, Wittgenstein tries to release his readers from the inclination to say that human beings and their activities are to be understood in terms of 'consciousness'.

> But doesn't one say that human beings have consciousness and that trees, or stones, do not? (*PI* 418)

The protesting voice of 'common sense' is raised at once, to which Wittgenstein slyly replies:

> What would it be like if it were otherwise?
> Would human beings all be unconscious?

The 'common sense' notion of 'consciousness' is fraught with metaphysical prejudice: Wittgenstein tries to bring the word back into a setting in which it has a place – people pass out of consciousness when rocks drop on them or they are given a general anaesthetic. But this does not satisfy the metaphysical voice:

> No; not in the ordinary sense of the word. But I, for instance, should not have consciousness – as I now in fact have it.

Back to the infallible evidence of my own case: I am conscious that I am conscious – if you will: '*cogito ergo sum*'. And of course I am not bound by the *ordinary* sense of the word.

> In what circumstances should I say that a tribe had a *chief*? And the chief must surely have *consciousness*. Surely we can't have a chief without consciousness! (*PI* 419)

Sarcasm indeed! To say whether a community has a leader I should look for certain patterns of relationship within the group, watch for who speaks first, or perhaps last, or who never speaks at all but (like the lord whose oracle is in Delphi) merely gives a sign, and so on. My evidence would all be in the open, even if my theory of group processes kept me from understanding it for years. The chief's having consciousness would not interest me, unless the priests of the tribe drugged him on certain occasions or he gave his orders in a trance-like state.

> But can't I imagine that the people around me are automata, lack consciousness, even though they behave in the same way as usual? (*PI* 420)

People might *behave* in apparently intelligible ways, but how do you know what is going on *inside*? The difference between us and androids is that we have consciousness and they do not!

With Descartes' Second Meditation in mind, presumably, Wittgenstein tries the experiment:

> If I imagine it now – alone in my room – I see people with fixed looks (as in a trance) going about their business – the idea is perhaps a little uncanny. But just try to keep hold of this idea in the midst of your ordinary intercourse with others, in the street, say! Say to yourself, for example: 'The children over there are mere automata; all their liveliness is mere automatism'. And you will either find these words becoming quite meaningless; or you will produce in yourself some kind of uncanny feeling, or something of the sort

The doctrine that our behaviour depends on 'consciousness' is redundant.

That does not mean that our behaviour is any the less rational or accountable. To be ashamed of having to found our mental and spiritual activities on our primitive reactions to one another in our common world would amount to being ashamed of our bodiliness – and that, once again, takes us back to religion. ('And the eyes of them both were opened, and they knew that they were naked; and they sewed fig leaves together, and made themselves aprons'.)

'For it isn't as though everything we say has a conscious purpose; our tongues just keep going [*unser Mund geht eben*]', as Wittgenstein once remarked (*CV*, p. 64); and that is perfectly all right, in the conversation that we are. It does not mean that we are mindless, thoughtless. Indeed not: what would it be like if we never uttered a word except after reflecting?

RADICAL ANTI-IDEALISM

If Descartes' famous *'Cogito ergo sum'* – 'I think, therefore I am' – were turned inside out we should hear something like Wittgenstein's retrieval of the true state of affairs: granted our manifold community in standard reactions, it is occasionally possible for a man or a woman to reflect and deliberate. But if idealism, in the philosophical sense, means that ideas are more fundamental than action, or that meanings are all in the head, then it is hard to imagine a more radically non-idealist way of thinking than Wittgenstein's. The meanings that establish the house of reason are not inside our individual minds. They are out in the open, constituting the space, wherever two or three gather to exchange gifts or threats or stories and songs.

Wittgenstein's suspicions of rationalism come out very clearly in the following text:

> Reason [*Vernunft*] – I feel like saying – presents itself to us as the gauge *par excellence* against which everything that we do, all our language games, measure and judge themselves. – We may say: we are so exclusively preoccupied by contemplating a yardstick that we can't allow our gaze to *rest* on certain phenomena or patterns. We are used, as it were, to 'dismissing' these as irrational, as corresponding to a low state of intelligence, etc. The yardstick rivets our attention and keeps distracting us from these phenomena, as it were making us look beyond [*nach oben hin*].[12]

The claim of reason is so exorbitant in our metaphysically inflated self-understanding that it is hard for us to acknowledge what is obvious: the phenomena, including the language games that give rise to the possibility of rational thought in the first place. It is as if one particular style of architecture had captivated us so deeply that we looked askance at all other buildings. We cannot let our eyes *rest* on certain phenomena, we are compelled to try to see through them to something more important. But Wittgenstein urges us to remain with the phenomena:

> The aspects of things that are most important for us are hidden because of their simplicity and familiarity. (One is unable to notice something – because it is always before one's eyes.) The real foundations of his enquiry do not strike a man at all. Unless *that* fact has at some time struck him. –

[12] In 'Ursache und Wirkung: Intuitives Erfassen', p. 400.

And this means: we fail to be struck by what, once seen, is most striking and most powerful. (*PI* 129)

The 'real foundations', for a student of Marx,[13] are forms of material production, in food, tools, shelter and so on. A clue to what Wittgenstein meant is perhaps to be found in notes that he made in 1931 on Frazer's *Golden Bough*. In another part of the notebook in which he first made the remark about the 'real foundations' he wrote as follows:

> That a man's shadow, which looks like a man, or that his mirror image, or that rain, thunderstorms, the phases of the moon, the change of seasons, the likenesses and differences of animals to one another and to human beings, the phenomena of death, of birth and of sexual life, in short everything a man perceives year in, year out around him, connected together in any variety of ways – that all this should play a part in his thinking (his philosophy) and his practices, is obvious, or in other words, this is what we really know and find interesting. (*RFGB*, p. 6)

If that text indicates even only part of what might be meant by the 'real foundations' of our practices, including our inquiring, thinking and philosophy, then the conversation that we are is very firmly rooted in the *natural* order that pervades and sustains our culture. 'The complex nature and the variety of human contingencies' is a 'natural foundation' for the formation of a certain concept (*Z* 439). If several of Wittgenstein's friends in the early 1930s were exponents of historical materialism, perhaps his emphasis was rather on a biological or physical materialism.[14]

The idealist (I come to the realist in chapter 6) is, for Wittgenstein, the man who has to have a *reason* for accepting the existence even of his own hands (*OC* 24). All that we do and say has to rest upon some assumption or hypothesis, some view or belief, or, more generally, some web of beliefs. Our relation to the world, on this account, is essentially cognitive. What is primary and foundational, according to Wittgenstein, is, however, neither ideas nor beliefs nor any other class of mental events, but human beings in a multiplicity of transactions with one another. His remarks, as he said (*PI* 415), are contributions to the natural history of human beings – but the words need to be weighed: the *history* of the *nature* of *human beings*. There is plenty of room for the study of history, just as for human biology; but with his remarks on the natural history of human beings, drawing attention to phenomena which are ignored only

---

[13] e.g. Marx, *A Contribution to the Critique of Political Economy*, p. 20.
[14] Sebastiano Timpanaro's term, in *On Materialism*.

because they are so obvious, Wittgenstein returns us to ourselves as we are, prior to any science (*PI* 126), not to mention metaphysical inflation of the signs that we use (*PI* 116). With his emphasis on action and life, practice and primitive reactions, Wittgenstein's way of thinking is as non-idealist as any philosophical reflection could be. His metaphysics-free vision of human life is radically non-idealist.

> Language – I want to say – is a refinement, 'in the beginning was the deed'.
> . . .
> I want to say: it is characteristic for our language that it springs up on the foundation of stable forms of life, regular ways of acting.[15]

Goethe's famous remark – '*Im Anfang war die Tat*' – cited, incidentally, in Bukharin's lecture in London in 1931,[16] rules out even a suspicion of idealism in Wittgenstein's project.

---

[15] 'Ursache und Wirkung', pp. 403–4, my translation.
[16] 'Theory and practice', *Science at the Cross Roads*, p. 12.

CHAPTER 6

Assurances of Realism

One man is a convinced realist, another a convinced idealist and teaches his children accordingly. In such an important matter as the existence or non-existence of the external world they don't want to teach their children anything wrong.

(Z 413)

WITTGENSTEIN'S VIEW OF A CLASSICAL CONTROVERSY

The alternative to idealism, in philosophical discourse, is, of course, realism. Since Plato's 'ideas', in the theory of Forms, are 'real', it has been argued, with brilliance and plausibility, that ancient philosophy should be described as 'realism'.[1] The term 'idealism' is then available for the spread of mentalist–subjectivist themes in post-Cartesian philosophy, where ideas have taken up residence in the head. That accords well enough with Wittgenstein's few references to idealism, because he always links it to solipsism: his idealists are tempted to say that we never know what is in each other's mind. But this epistemological scepticism, which breeds a certain fideism about the contents of other people's minds, whilst it is typically Cartesian, nevertheless derives from the rediscovery, in the sixteenth century, of the works of Sextus Empiricus (floruit c. 200 AD), which in turn made available the thought of Pyrrho of Elis (floruit c. 300 BC). It is thus a plausible story that the Cartesian turn to the self-certainty of the individual consciousness, which inaugurated modern philosophy, should be understood as a reaction to Pyrrhonian scepticism. It has been argued also that Descartes was trying to do better than certain fideistic defences of Roman Catholic traditionalism against Calvinist individualism.[2]

However all that may be, and the theological resonances alone would be well worth exploring, I want here only to show that Wittgenstein, although certainly not an idealist (as I hope chapter 5 made clear), is not an ordinary realist either.

[1] Bernard Williams, 'Philosophy', in *The Legacy of Greece*, esp. pp. 204–5; M. F. Burnyeat, 'Idealism and Greek philosophy: what Descartes saw and Berkeley missed'.
[2] Popkin, *History of Scepticism*, chapter 1.

The only remark in the *Investigations* in which the controversy between idealists (solipsists) and realists is mentioned in these precise terms runs as follows:

> For *this* is what disputes between Idealists, Solipsists and Realists look like. The one party attack the normal form of expression as if they were attacking a statement [*Behauptung*]; the others defend it, as if they were stating [*konstatierten*] facts recognized by every rational man. (*PI* 402)

That is to say: idealists attack a normal expression such as 'I am in pain' as if it were typically a report on one's inner life, while realists bluffly reply that they can see no difficulty here: I suppose, on analogy with my own case, that you are in pain when you say 'I am in pain'.

The controversy between idealism and realism lies at the heart of the *Investigations*. It is no great exaggeration to say that Wittgenstein's later work centres upon dissolving this dilemma. But, as he remarked (*RFM* VI, 23), it is an immensely hard task, having escaped from the toils of idealism, to avoid succumbing to a facile and uncritical realism. In notes made early in 1950 he spoke of refusing both 'the scepticism of the idealist' and 'the assurances [*Versicherungen*] of the realist' – the only 'answer' to the two parties, when the idealists say that we do not know that the external world exists, and the realists reassure them, is to say:

> this assertion [*Behauptung*], or its opposite [e.g. 'There are physical objects'], is a misfiring attempt to express what can't be expressed like that. And that it does misfire can be shown; but that isn't the end of the matter. One must come to see that what presents itself as the first expression of a difficulty, or of its solution, may in addition be a completely misguided expression. (*OC* 37)

Apart from anything else, this remark gives an illuminating insight into Wittgenstein's method:

> one who has a just censure of a picture to make will often at first offer the censure where it does not belong, and an *investigation* is needed in order to find the right point of attack for the critic. (*OC* 37)

His 'investigations', perhaps one may say, are devoted to finding the right point of attack upon the picture – and the picture, in this case as so often elsewhere, is 'a picture of the essence of human language' (*PI* 1).

It is a picture, an *idol*, of the nature of the conversation that we are which surrounds the working of language with a haze that makes clear vision impossible (*PI 5*). The idealist's sceptical inclinations, but also the realist's bluff assurances, are equally dependent upon the myth that speaking, and *a fortiori* thinking and meaning, are, fundamentally, ostensive definition of physical objects.

To return to the discussion in the *Investigations* (*PI* 402), and without rehearsing the preparation for it from the very beginning, it will suffice to place it in the following context:

> Is a sum in the head less real than a sum on paper? – Perhaps one is inclined to say some such thing; but one can get oneself to think the opposite as well by telling oneself: paper, ink, etc. are only logical constructions out of our sense-data. (*PI* 366)

That mental arithmetic is *more* real than working it out with pencil and paper should have some appeal for people who are inclined to make mental and spiritual activity autonomous – who see it as in effect creating its own objects, to cite one definition of idealism.[3] The variety to which Wittgenstein alludes here, with its reference to 'logical constructions' and 'sense-data', is usually called 'phenomenalism'. It may be traced at least from John Stuart Mill[4] to A. J. Ayer,[5] but Wittgenstein was more likely to have been alarmed by Eddington's popular science books, which start from the premise that we are directly aware of nothing but the contents of our consciousness.[6] The effect of phenomenalist doctrines is that statements about material objects, trees, stars, smells, rainbows etc., can be translated into statements about sense-data, which are, then, as given to our consciousness, necessarily mind-dependent. There are physical objects: the realist is permitted to go on talking about trees, stars and so on, but he has to understand that – *really* – these things are all reducible to sense-data. As Mill said: 'Matter is the permanent possibility of sensation'.

Thus, if it was put to them in these terms, some might incline to say that counting in the head is *less* 'real': doing it on paper is visible, observable, material, empirically more real. Others, arguing that, as sense-data, everything in our experience is mind-dependent, including paper and pencil, would be inclined to say the opposite.

---

[3] MacKinnon, *Explorations*, p. 24.
[4] *Examination of Sir William Hamilton's Philosophy*, chapter 11, appendix to chapter 12.
[5] *Foundations of Empirical Knowledge*.
[6] Hallett, *Companion*, p. 763.

Criss-crossed by several other themes, the phenomenalist line of thought is voiced again in the following protest:

> But when I imagine something, or even actually *see* objects, I have *got* something which my neighbour has not. (*PI* 398)

It is not just when I mentally picture something but also when I am looking at some item of middle-sized dry goods in the world:

> I understand you. You want to look about you and say: 'At any rate only *I* have got THIS'.

The deeper motivation of sense-data theory is, Wittgenstein suggests, the desire to be in a position to say that *my* experience of the world is absolutely unique: I have, in a sense, my own private version of the world. On the wilder shores of subjectivist idealism *the* world is real only for me; in the milder climate of phenomenalism I only have, more plausibly, my own private world within the world.

Wittgenstein goes on to pummel his phenomenalist interlocutor:

> Might I not ask: In what sense have you *got* what you are talking about and saying that only you have got it? Do you possess it? You do not even *see* it. Must you not really say that no one has got it? And this too is clear: if as a matter of logic you exclude other people's having something, it loses its sense to say that you have it.

I could not know what it would be for me to have something which no one else could have; I am back in the divine illusion that I generate my own inner life. But Wittgenstein now turns more sympathetically towards his adversary:

> But what then is the thing you are speaking of? It is true I said that I knew within myself what you meant. But that meant that I knew how one thinks to conceive this object, to see it, to make one's looking and pointing mean it. I know how one stares ahead and looks about one in this case – and the rest.

The inward concentration on the sensation turns out to be a staring at the world around – as in the case of the man who looks at the sky and says to himself 'How blue the sky is!':

When you do it spontaneously – without philosophical intentions – the idea never crosses your mind that this impression of colour belongs only to *you*. And you have no hesitation in exclaiming that to someone else. And if you point at anything as you say the words you point at the sky. I am saying: you have not the feeling of pointing-into-yourself, which often accompanies 'naming the sensation' when one is thinking about 'private language'. Nor do you think that really you ought not to point to the colour with your hand, but with your attention. (*PI* 275)

Sense-data theories steer inexorably towards the myth of the private ostensive definition (*PI* 380); phenomenalism feeds off a particular picture of the essence of human language (*PI* 1).

Consider now the following remark:

It's true I say 'Now I am having such-and-such an image', but the words 'I am having' are merely a sign to someone *else*; the description of the image is a *complete* account of the imagined world. (*PI* 402)

The world as mentally pictured is *completely* represented in the description of what I am imagining. 'The mental picture is the picture which is described when someone describes what he imagines' (*PI* 367). But the tempting confusion is now to say that I don't describe the world, or the blue sky, as I find it, but that I describe the mental picture. Instead of saying 'I am in pain', to go back to the favourite example, I might just as well make a sign with my hand and then describe my sensation:

You mean: the words 'I am having' are like 'I say! . . .'. You are inclined to say it should really have been expressed differently. Perhaps simply by making a sign with one's hand and then giving a description.

It is as if every statement that I make should really be regarded as a description of my inner life (*PI* 24). Everything that I say should be understood as a report of how the world seems to *me*. If we do not keep the multiplicity of language-games in view, that is to say, we fall under the sway of the paradigm of designating material objects. We then naturally incline to model the inner life on a parade of immaterial objects that are subject to private interior ostensive definition.

This brings us to the controversy between idealism and realism, as it looked to Wittgenstein:

When as in this case ['I have such-and-such a sensation' should really be interpreted as a description of my inner life], one is not happy with the

expressions of our customary language . . . there is an *idée fixe* in our heads
which conflicts with the model of our customary way of expressing
ourselves. We are then tempted to say that our way of expressing ourselves
does not describe the facts as they really are. As if, for example, the
proposition 'He has pains' could be false in some other way than by that
man's *not* having pains. As if the form of expression were saying something
false even when the proposition *faute de mieux* asserted something true.
(*PI* 402)

And *this* is what the ancient controversy looks like to Wittgenstein. The
phenomenalists allow the realist to go on talking about material objects –
we have no better way of talking; but *really*, of course, our experience is
always of sense-data. And since my sense-data are items in my inner life,
of which you cannot have a first-hand description, we are back in the
predicament of private worlds.

When I say 'He is in pain' the idealist wants to add: 'So it seems to
you': the relation between physical objects and sense-data he takes to be
contingent. He is warning me that matching my sense-data with the
squirming and shrieking object on the floor is a tricky and precarious
business. The realist laughs the problem off. He sees no difficulty in the
idea of my supposing, thinking, or imagining, that someone else has what
I have – 'But the trouble with the realist is always that he does not solve
but skip the difficulties which his adversaries see, though they don't
succeed in solving them' (*BB*, p. 48). Content to make suppositions on
analogy with his own case, the realist simply misses the problem that the
idealist strives to articulate.

THE CONTROVERSY RENEWED

In effect, then, although not denying that the world is full of physical
objects, the idealist is inclined to say that our knowledge is of these things
as they appear to us. We can have knowledge of how things look to us,
but not of how they are in themselves. Human experience, however rich
and strange, however austere and bare, is never knowledge of mind-
independent realities. The best we can do is to build upon our sense-data,
or the appearances, or our ideas, but always on something which is
already in the realm of the mind. 'The temper of Realism', on the other
hand, to quote Samuel Alexander, 'is to de–anthropomorphize; to order
man and mind to their proper place among the world of finite things; on
the one hand, to divest physical things of the colouring which they have
received from the vanity or arrogance of mind; on the other, to assign

them along with minds their due measure of self-existence'.[7] The difficulty for the realist, if he is to take these words seriously, is that he has to work for his position, instead of just assuming, as he is traditionally inclined to do, that it is simply 'common sense'.

Starting in 1959 with a famous lecture on 'Truth',[8] Michael Dummett has continued to argue that, in many domains, realism has had far too easy a victory. Although frequently described, in the relevant literature, as an anti-realist *tout court*, he seems to me to be probing the obtusities of realism rather than recommending neo-idealism. All that I need to note here, however, is his transformation of the terms of the debate.

Hitherto, realists have characteristically held that experience is knowledge of that which is independent of our minds. Under Dummett's tutelage, philosophers now regard the controversy as bearing upon certain classes of *statements*: for example, mathematical statements, statements about other minds and about the past, and so on. The question at issue, he then says, is whether statements in these classes possess an objective truth-value, independently of our means of knowing whether they are in fact true or false. The realist sees no difficulty in saying this. Dummett, thereby opening the anti-realist case, argues that statements of these classes cannot be true or false unless it is in principle possible for us to know whether they are. The point that he is making he puts as follows:

> The realist holds that we give sense to those sentences of our language which are not effectively decidable by appealing tacitly to means of determining their truth-values which we do not ourselves possess, but which we can conceive of by an analogy with those which we do. The anti-realist holds that such a conception is quite spurious, an illusion of meaning, and that the only meaning we can confer on our sentences must relate to those means of determining their truth-values which we actually possess. Hence, unless we have a means which would in principle decide the truth-value of a given statement, we do not have for it a notion of truth and falsity which would entitle us to say that it must be either true or false.[9]

The terms of the controversy have thus been greatly, and no doubt irreversibly, sharpened. The theological implications of this way of putting it are also very considerable. For a realist, as Dummett says, 'the truth of a statement [of an appropriate class] involves the possibility in

---

[7] 'The basis of realism', p. 279.
[8] *Truth and Other Enigmas*, pp. 1–24.
[9] Ibid., p. 24.

principle that it should be, or should have been, recognized as true by a being – not necessarily a human being – appropriately situated and with sufficient perceptual and intellectual powers'.[10] The realist treats statements of the disputed class as if they must be either true or false, even if God alone knows. The most dramatic example of this realist move that Dummett cites is the Molinist[11] theory of *scientia media*: a knowledge ascribed to God of things that do not, but would, exist, if certain conditions were realized, and which are thus 'intermediate' between mere possibilities and actual future events. (The purpose of the theory is to reconcile God's foreknowledge with human free will.) The realist has no difficulty in imagining how the world and history might be described from a standpoint outside space and time: 'The anti-realist takes more seriously the fact that we are immersed in time: being so immersed, we cannot frame any description of the world as it would appear to one who was not in time, but we can only describe it as it is, i.e., as it is now'.[12]

It may be noted in passing that, in an unpublished paper which is apparently in effect a reconstruction of Bishop Berkeley's argument for the existence of God, Dummett has suggested that 'anti-realism is ultimately incoherent but that realism is tenable only on a theistic basis'.[13] The theological ramifications of Dummett's reformulation of the controversy between realism and anti-realism may thus turn out to be of immense importance.

As things stand, however, the anti-realist project is engaged in laying bare this quasi-theistic assumption which the realist makes, no doubt unwittingly and naively. The realist is challenged to explain how an assertion is capable of being true or false when the evidence for or against it is, in principle, unavailable – at least, by tacit implication, to *us*. That is to say, for the realist view to prevail, the existence of a supratemporal perspective on the world is covertly admitted. A realist approach to the truth-value of assertions in certain specifiable classes apparently trades on the presence of a higher being. From a theological point of view, then, the anti-realist project amounts to an attempt to bring out the theistic element in realist philosophy. In particular, may those who have no truck with any form of theism go on, philosophically, as realists?

The renewal of the controversy has profound theological (as well as

---

[10] Ibid., p. 314.
[11] Ibid., p. 362. Luis de Molina (1535–1600), the Jesuit theologian, has given his name to this attempt to defend free will.
[12] Ibid., p. 369.
[13] Ibid., xxxix.

many other) implications.[14] To follow them out would take me far beyond my purposes here. But, in returning to Wittgenstein's version of the controversy between realism and idealism, I want briefly to reconsider the dilemma in the light of Dummett's reformulation.

Again in 1959, in a fateful review of Wittgenstein's *Remarks on the Foundations of Mathematics*,[15] Michael Dummett found him to be such an extreme anti-realist, as regards mathematical statements, that he speaks of his 'constructivism' and 'full-blooded conventionalism'. In old-fashioned terms, Wittgenstein's philosophy of mathematics is interpreted as a form of subjectivist idealism. Reacting against the realist picture, that the truths of mathematics are objectively *there*, waiting for the human mind to discover them, Wittgenstein would have been saying that we simply compose them. This interpretation of Wittgenstein's philosophy of mathematics has been challenged, and to my mind radically undermined, by D. S. Shwayder, in a much less celebrated paper which is nevertheless a great deal more scathing in its criticism of some of the detail of Wittgenstein's understanding of mathematics.[16] But, since there are fashionable writers in philosophy as in many other disciplines, Dummett's review lends authority to a now widespread belief that Wittgenstein's later work licenses anti-realist inclinations in every disputable domain. It has certainly spread to theology: 'Everywhere [Wittgenstein] is a thoroughgoing constructivist and voluntarist: logical necessity is created by the rules governing language. If he is a non-realist about religion, he is also a non-realist about everything else'.[17] A non-theistic form of subjectivist idealism, deriving from the anti-realist interpretation of Wittgenstein's writings on mathematics, is thus drafted into the service of a version of Christianity according to which it is, like mathematics and art and everything else, entirely subject to the will of its human creators.

Taking the case of assertions about other people's mental states, we may say that Wittgenstein sought to expel psychologism from realism without giving in to the other extreme of behaviourism. The realist, being content to make guesses or inferences from people's behaviour on something like the argument from analogy with his own case, subscribes without qualms to the central myth of psychologism,[18] which is that

---

[14] MacKinnon, *Explorations*, chapters 10 and 11.
[15] *Truth and Other Enigmas*, pp. 166–85.
[16] 'Wittgenstein on mathematics'.
[17] Cupitt, *The Sea of Faith*, p. 222
[18] Psychologism was identified by Gottlob Frege (1848–1925), whose work Wittgenstein held in the highest regard.

meanings are hidden away in the privacy of the head. We have no means of knowing what is going on in other people's minds, even when they tell us, but that is not a problem. Many assertions that we make must be true or false, though we are not in a position to judge.

We laugh at people who make assertions that they are in no position to support with appropriate evidence. Most people's views about the late novels of Henry James, or the price of herring at Stornoway, have little call on anyone's attention. We also often make assertions in one domain which we venture to support with parallel instances or analogues from some other domain where we are (more) at home. Difficulties already suggest themselves at this point, at least for theologians who need arguments from analogy. But the anti-realist asks, more generally, what it means for us to be able to say that an assertion (in an appropriately disputable domain) is true or false, when there is in principle no way in which we can verify it.

The anti-realist suspects, then, that we cannot find meaning in assertions (of one of the disputable classes) unless it is related to the means of verifying them that we (human beings) actually possess. We are, as Michael Dummett says, 'immersed in time'. The anti-realist's inclinations are therefore towards 'pervasive anthropocentrism'[19] and 'the temporalization of rationality'.[20] It is a position easy to reduce to the logical positivism of the 1930s: we know the meaning of an assertion (of the appropriate class) only when we have the apparatus to verify it – and we should do best to stay well within the realms of the empirically observable and testable.

As regards understanding other people, we should dispense with talk about invisible and uncheckable mental states, and so on, and stay with the behaviour that we can see: behaviourism is the natural alternative to mentalist–individualist mystifications.

In its new formulation, the controversy is even more obviously about the place of the self in the world. If we cannot mean what we say unless we have a way of verifying it, the constraints upon what we assert as true or false may drive us to remain within the limits of empiricism and, in religion, silence us altogether. (We may also go on talking religiously, but recognizing that we say nothing that could be true or false.) An anti-realist temper might, however, deepen our sense of the finitude and historical character of human consciousness so that participation in discussion of the hermeneutical problem would prove an easy transition

---

[19] MacKinnon, *Explorations*, p. 154.
[20] Rorty, *Consequences of Pragmatism*, p. xli.

to the Hegelian tradition.[21] The realist temper might, on the other hand, as Samuel Alexander said, be 'to de-anthropomorphize': to return us to a world, that is to say, about which we need not cease to speak, even though it far exceeds our capacity to understand.

'Not empiricism and yet realism in philosophy, that is the hardest thing' (*RFM* VI 23): with this remark, written in 1943/44, Wittgenstein surely makes it clear that he at least was not satisfied with anti-realism.

NOT EMPIRICISM

The empiricist cast of mind feeds on thoughts of the following kind. One is directly affected by *things*, people and the sounds they make included. Our knowledge of the world, eventually embodied in our talk about it, is built up from the impact that 'visuo-tactile continuants' (in Ayer's happy phrase) have upon individuals of our kind. In R. F. Holland's words:

> To set up in business an individual only has to be exposed to the elements with his senses unshuttered . . . Every mind is a complete and independent factory, where raw materials enter, are processed and emerge cut and dried. And when at the end each mind's eye surveys the products of its owner's efforts, perceiving an agreement here and a disagreement there, and so having knowledge, the results will be found to coincide with those of the rest, as though by pre-established harmony.[22]

This epistemology, if it makes sense at all, takes as foundational something that is in fact a rare and immensely sophisticated activity. To feel rain on the skin, or to get down to some level of bare sensory stimulation, is already to abstract oneself from the hurly-burly which is one's native element. Epistemology cannot *begin* with the individual's awareness of objects in the environment. We are always immersed in things, desiring or fearing them, actually coping with them in innumerable ways. It is when things break down, or when we learn to see them with the hard-won 'innocent eye' of certain painters, that we become aware of them as *objects*, temporarily out of the pragmatically encountered and emotionally construed environment in which they are normally experienced.

The idea is nevertheless almost irresistible that knowledge is founded

[21] See Richard J. Bernstein, *Beyond Objectivism and Relativism*.
[22] *Against Empiricism*, p. 12.

on one's individual sense-impressions, which, as it turns out, are amazingly like everybody else's. To say that seeing the colour of some apples is quite a sophisticated skill that requires training and practice, and which thus manifests one's membership of an epistemological community, sounds odd to many people. To be sure, they might concede that one is not able to tell people about the sensation or perception until one has acquired some of their language; but this only brings us back to Wittgenstein's exploration of the private language fantasy. Whatever the desire to get to some stratum of rockbottom experience on the individual's part, we have to return to the level of the unreflective reactions, patterned responses and so on, that constitute the world into which the individual is born. The given, we have to say, is the common forms of life in which one participates from the outset – not one's sense-data.

The inclination to isolate the effects that the world has on me prior to my having the public words, and prior to the world's being worded, is once again the dream that tradition and community are dispensable. It is as if I alone, untutored, self-reliant, lacking history and kin, could possess the world, untrodden, uninterpreted, yielding itself to me alone. If the realities of social life are so alienating that people feel themselves to be floating individuals with passively receptive bodies, it is not surprising that being subjected to the impact of a multi-media spectacular becomes a plausible image of the epistemological situation. The idea that, *ultimately*, I depend on nothing but my own sensations for my vision of the world no doubt appeals to the entrepreneurial spirit. Empiricism is perhaps the appropriate epistemology for a private enterprise economy.[23]

THE HARDEST THING

Whether it is psychologism or empiricism, the question of the place of the self in the world is always treated as if it were settled already in a way that gives priority to the individual. But consider these remarks from the important text that Wittgenstein completed in 1930:

> What I wanted to say is that it is remarkable that those who ascribe reality only to things and not to our ideas move about so unquestioningly in the world as idea and never look outside it.

[23] For some interesting suggestions see Sabina Lovibond, *Realism and Imagination in Ethics*, pp. 9–24.

That is: how unquestioned the given still is. It would be the very devil if it were a tiny picture taken from an oblique, distorting angle. The unquestioned – *life* – is supposed to be something accidental, marginal; while something over which I never normally puzzle at all is regarded as the real thing! (*PR* V, 47)

We have been tempted into the habit of thinking that either *die Dinge* or *unsere Vorstellungen* must be the primary thing, but the choice betwen realism and idealism overlooks *das Leben*: that is Wittgenstein's suggestion.

Even those who insist most strongly on the priority of *things*, rather than that of our *ideas*, and who thus may be regarded as anti-idealist, go on unquestioningly within 'the world as idea', *die Vorstellungswelt*. Realists, for all their passionate insistence on our having knowledge of things outside our minds, never look outside[24] the world as *representable*. They too, that is to say, take it for granted that the debate is about matching ideas in our heads with items in the world.

The simple but crucial point that Wittgenstein is making here comes out in the immediately preceding passage:

> That it doesn't strike us at all when we look around us, move about in space, feel our own bodies, etc., etc., shows how natural these things are to us. We do not notice that we see space perspectively or that our visual field is in some sense blurred towards the edges. It doesn't strike us and never can strike us because it is *the* way we perceive. We never give it a thought and it's impossible we should, since there is nothing that contrasts with the form of our world. (*PR* V, 47)

We cannot get outside our skins to compare our relationship to the world with some alternative. But the model of meaningful activity as essentially based upon designating objects blinds both sides in the realist/idealist debate to our embodied condition.

Realists, just as much as idealists, fail to acknowledge that *das Leben* is 'the given': these *Lebensformen* that, in a later and more celebrated formula, are what has to be accepted (*PI*, p. 226). In effect, Wittgenstein implies here, realists are as oblivious as idealists to 'the real thing', *das Eigentliche*, which, again in a much later phrase, he refers to as 'the bustle of life', *das Getriebe des Lebens* (*RPP* II, 625). Obsession with representing reality makes the unrepresentable bustle of life seem

---

[24] According to the official translation they 'never long to escape from it'; but that seems to go beyond the original.

contingent and marginal. The 'stenographer', in Bukharin's phrase, takes the place of 'the real subject, i.e. social and historical man'[25]

In this perspective, realists remain as wedded as anyone else to the idea that the primary act of meaning is representing. Any importance that designating objects may have, as Wittgenstein has argued from the beginning of the *Investigations*, depends on a matrix of activity within which connections between words and their referents arise in the first place. But the hard thing is to break free of the obsession with representation, and of the accompanying picture of the self as observer of the passing scene.

In responding to Michael Dummett's questioning of the assumptions of realism, philosophers continue to take it for granted that meaning should be seen in terms of representation.[26] Of course they recognize that we ask questions, give orders and so on; but, amazing as this may seem by now, theorists of meaning in the realist interest show a great inclination to focus on indicative sentences and to regard others as reducible to that type.[27] Understanding language is characteristically taken as understanding how we represent objects by words. This inevitably encourages a view of the self as a detached spectator in the world.

To understand language as a form, or rather as a multiplicity of forms, of expressive activity, as Wittgenstein encourages us to do, is to rehabilitate the self as a responsive agent in vital connection with others of the same kind (*mostly*: I would not exclude certain domesticated animals). The rapport, or the friction, that exists between human beings, depends very little on use of techniques of representing. 'Words have meaning only in the stream of life', as Wittgenstein says (*RPP* II, 687), with that emphasis on the primacy of 'life' which characterizes his later philosophy.[28]

Regarding ourselves as detached observers of the passing scene encourages us to treat language as representation of reality, and thought as mirror-image of the world (*PI* 96). However natural and venerable it may be to think along such lines, it is yielding to metaphysical antipathy to *life*. Wittgenstein challenges this entire tradition in a sentence:

Would it be correct to say our concepts reflect our life?
They stand in the middle of it. (*RC* III, 302)

[25] Bukharin, 'Theory and practice', in *Science at the Cross Roads*, p. 7.
[26] Charles Taylor, 'Theories of meaning', *Philosophical Papers*, vol. 1, pp. 248–92.
[27] Ibid., p. 279.
[28] Characterized by Derek Bolton as 'life-philosophy', in 'Life-form and idealism', p. 271.

Our *life* has traditionally been regarded as accidental and marginal to the great metaphysical debates about words and things, thought and reality, self and world, and so on. Once 'the unquestioned – *life*' is opened up to philosophical consideration, the halo departs from certain traditional cruces. The detached self and the passing scene are recalled to the community in life which has always been the only 'given'. To ask, then, whether our life is mirrored in our concepts only shows the absurdity of the metaphysical impulse to get our minds out of our world. Concepts are among the tools which express and direct our vital interests (*PI* 569– 70); they permeate our life – as the system of our language permeates our life (*RC* III, 303).

Copying is only one way of coping. We are, when we think, often trying to represent the facts as exactly as possible. Objective depiction without subjective expression remains an inalienable ideal of our civilization. The world allows itself to be pictured. The ability to make pictures of reality easily comes to seem the defining characteristic of the mind, and human nature itself begins to seem definable in terms of rationality as representation.[29] We are led to wonder at the amazing fact that *thought* is the unique correlate of *reality* (*PI* 96). We feel as if we had caught reality in our net (*PI* 428). We then feel the want of a theory to explain how mere sentences manage to represent reality (*PI* 435). Thus we return to the opening pages of the *Investigations*: the controversy between realists and their opponents leaves unquestioned the assumption that dispassionate representation of items in the world is the paradigm of meaningful activity. Our very existence as rational beings, never mind our mastery of techniques of depiction, depends upon our being bound together as participants in innumerable vital activities, in that *Sprachspiel* which is 'the whole, consisting of the language and the activities with which it is interwoven' (*PI* 7).

We cannot catch reality in our net because it is the bustle of life of which we are part. The idea that thought, or language, represents the reality 'out there', however natural and intuitively appealing, draws us easily into supposing that the whole hurly-burly may be treated as just one more object to be represented, as if we could get outside it to view it from somewhere else. This is one more way in which the individual is tempted to imagine himself detached from the world, disengaged from the common forms of life, with the language interwoven with them, which are the real *a priori* of any intelligent behaviour at all, never mind representing and depicting.

[29] Apart from Taylor, see also James C. Edwards, *Ethics Without Philosophy: Wittgenstein and the Moral Life.*

Characteristically, Wittgenstein never says it in so many words, but the central thrust of his later writing is to remind us that our techniques of designating objects (themselves more varied than we tend to think) fit into a whole set of shared practices without which there would be no possibility of our ever being in a position to make those movements of disengagement from the hurly-burly to picture this or that element or aspect of it. He just gets on, quietly and patiently, with the task of loosening the hold of the idea that knowledge is principally representation of reality, and that the rational animal is primarily the master of objective depiction.

We have to renounce the idea that meaning is primarily a matter of representing, and that the self is a monological observer, in order to retrieve a holistic respect for the innumerable significant moves that we make in the conversation that we human beings are.[30] There is something more to understanding language than just successfully matching words with things: the anti-realist doubts about the complacencies of realist epistemologies certainly have that much *prima facie* justification. In the perspective of Wittgenstein's *Lebensphilosophie*,[31] however, the ancient controversy between realists and idealists, even in its most modern form, remains entirely within the boundaries of the metaphysical tradition.

THE END OF METAPHYSICS

The hardest thing, philosophically, is to free reflection from the bewitching power of the devices of our language (*PI* 209). The very signs that enable us to act rationally, and, among much else, to reason and reflect, in the first place, raise fantasies that alienate us from ourselves. Our signs are so natural that we come to imagine that we could communicate without them: meaning becomes a purely mental activity (*PI* 693). Our reliance on language is so complete that we become oblivious of it. Our dependence for our status as rational agents upon the materiality of signs, once overlooked, soon tends to be played down and even denied. Thus the metaphysical paradigm of the self is generated. (The metaphysical tradition might even be defined as the age-long refusal to acknowledge the bodiliness of meaning and mind.)

For Wittgenstein, we may say, a philosopher in the realist tradition who endorses arguments from analogy with his own case to other

[30] Taylor, *Philosophical Papers*, vol. 1, p. 282.
[31] In German histories of philosophy *Lebensphilosophie* means Nietzsche, Bergson, and others, from 1870 to 1920, who sought to undermine the metaphysical tradition.

people's thoughts and feelings, remains captivated by metaphysical antipathy to the body.[32] The other person's face ceases to show anger or grief and becomes a diagram that he has to decipher. The idealist is so troubled by this radical delay between feelings and mien that epistemological solitude appears to be our fate. The realist, with his reassuring arguments, does not dissolve the hiatus between the face and the soul but complacently endorses it. He has an argument (from analogy with his own case) to show that it is 'No problem'. Under imaginative enough anti-realist pressure, however, a non-dualistic realism may become available.[33]

The retrieval of the notion of intrinsically expressive behaviour is, philosophically, enormously hard work. It goes against the grain of our metaphysical prejudices: If what I do is significant it is apparently because my action is the outwardly visible effect of hidden events in my secret consciousness. Against this overpoweringly plausible line of argument Wittgenstein quoted this remark by Goethe: 'Don't look for anything behind the phenomena; they themselves are the theory' (*RPP* I, 889). Normally, the meaning is on the surface. Appearances do not always deceive, or require deliberate interpretation. But it is easy to suppose otherwise:

> I observe his face closely. Why? What does it tell me? Whether he is sad or cheerful, e.g. But why am I interested in that? Well, if I get to know his mood, it is like when I have got to know the condition of a body (its temperature, for example); I can draw various kinds of conclusion from this. (*RPP* I, 890)

The message that I read off his face, when I scrutinize it, is the mood that lies behind, and now I can make various inferences. But this cannot be the normal case:

> 'We *see* emotion'. – As opposed to what? – We do not see facial contortions and make inferences from them (like a doctor framing a diagnosis) to joy, grief, boredom. We describe a face immediately as sad, radiant, bored, even when we are unable to give any other description of the features. – Grief, one would like to say, is personified in the face. This belongs to the concept of emotion. (*Z* 225)

Again and again, Wittgenstein reminds us, a person's grief or joy is perceptible in his or her bearing, under normal circumstances.

---

[32] Lovibond, *Realism and Imagination*, p. 206.
[33] See John McDowell's work.

The idealist has identified a profound and terrifying problem: my thoughts and feelings may be radically incommunicable, my inner life may be totally unsharable. But the assurances of the realist, while they take the drama out of the predicament of epistemological solitude, leave the metaphysical picture of the self undisturbed. The difficulty is to show that our understanding of meanings is normally a *perception* of meanings, and thus not a matter of inferrings to radically private inner states of consciousness of which the words or gestures would only be effects.[34]

The difficulty comes out in the following sequence of remarks:

> If I give someone an order it is *quite enough* for me to give him signs. And I should never say: These are of course only words, and I have to penetrate behind the words. Equally, when I have asked someone something and he gives me an answer (i.e. a sign) I am content – that was what I expected – and I don't object: That's a mere answer. (*PI* 503)

Under normal circumstances we operate unhesitatingly with signs; it never occurs to us to try to 'transcend' them. Wittgenstein reminds himself of this obvious fact, before getting to the nerve of the problem:

> But if you say: 'How am I to know what he means when I see nothing but the signs that he makes?', then I say: 'How is *he* to know what he means when he has nothing but the signs either?' (*PI* 504)

Seeing the gestures, or hearing the sounds, that the other person makes, seems to require supplementation: perceiving the signs seems only to be a preliminary to understanding what he means by them. To this line of thought, which plays on the impulse to dualism, Wittgenstein once again replies that it is just as mysterious that *I* know what I mean if I have nothing better than words to express my meaning. That is to say: the desire to have meanings that are independent of signs leaves me in a state of inarticulacy as much as it blocks my immediate perception of what other people mean.

> Must I understand an order before I can act on it? – Certainly, otherwise you wouldn't know what you had to do! – But once again there is a jump from *knowing* to doing! (*PI* 505)

Reacting to an order – leaving your room when the fire alarm rings, for

[34] Gareth Evans and John McDowell (eds.), *Truth and Meaning*, p. xxii.

example – might often be automatic, but it seems correct to say that there is always *some* delay between understanding it and behaving appropriately. There has to be a mental act of understanding to bridge the gulf between the words of the command and its fulfilment (cf. *PI* 431). Everything that we human beings do must be preceded by a moment of *knowing* – supposedly to protect our dignity as rational beings. Wittgenstein imagines his metaphysical alter ego on the parade ground, taking part in some complicated drill:

> The absent-minded man who at the order 'Right turn!' turns left, and then, clutching his forehead says 'Oh! Right turn' and does a right turn. – What has struck him? An interpretation? (*PI* 506)

In such a case, as Russell noted, 'there need not be anything mental, but merely a habit of the body'[35] – but that 'merely' betrays his metaphysical prejudices. For Wittgenstein, in contrast, there need be nothing defective in a habit of the body. The more automatic a driver's reaction on the motorway, the more spontaneous a gesture of compassion or affection, the more practised a posture at prayer, and so on, in innumerable different situations, the less need there is for the mental intermediary.

But this little sequence ends as follows:

> 'I am not merely saying this, I mean something by it'. – When we consider what is going on in us when we *mean* (and don't merely say) words, it seems to us as if there were something coupled to these words, which otherwise would run idle. – As if they, so to speak, connected with something in us. (*PI* 507)

Sometimes – in some people's lives perhaps often – a gap opens up between what is said and what is meant. People in police states have to practise deception, people in religious countries may have to resort to hypocrisy. The fact that our minds and our signs can so easily drift apart need not generate the belief that our mere words are always meaningless unless we deliberately inject meaning into them – but to feel something of the plausibility of that belief is to understand the power of the metaphysical devaluation of the habitual expressiveness of the human being.

It is not enough to say that the epistemological scepticism that Cartesian idealism propagates, and the reassuring arguments of unreconstructed realism, are equally grounded on a piece of nonsense: 'For

[35] *The Analysis of Mind*, pp. 80–1.

them after all it is not nonsense' (OC 37). Wittgenstein's exposure of a piece of nonsense has no purchase on anyone's attention unless the speculative mind is wounded by running against the boundary of the language (PI 119). The critic had first to conduct an investigation to find the right point of attack of the whole idealist/realist controversy (OC 37). The debate, Wittgenstein clearly implies, is sustained by a picture of our cognitive situation in which, because of our bodiliness, we are compelled to delay all attributions of intellectual and emotional properties to other people.[36] Again and again he reminds us of the facts of ordinary conversation. That picture gets its captivating power only by super-imposing a metaphysically, and ultimately theologically, dictated defa-mation of the human body upon 'our *life*'.

This antipathy to the body is, of course, a Christian heresy. It is labelled, theologically, as 'Manichean', 'Gnostic', 'docetic', and the like. The plethora of pejoratives is a measure of its recurrence. Few people in our culture today would admit to thinking their bodies to be evil, or their minds to be sparks of the eternal temporarily imprisoned in these habitations of fleshly corruption. Few readers of the New Testament nowadays would say that the central figure must have been a god in human guise. However, our mental hospitals are full of people damaged by such ideas, or, at any rate, using them to voice their distressing self-contempt. From pornography to torture, many everyday phenomena in our society trade on something very like hatred of the fleshly. For that matter, the 'Adoptionist' trends in some modern Christology may often best be understood as vigorous protests against the crypto-Monophysitism in the practice of a great deal of Christian worship.[37]

Wittgenstein's critique is directed at much less blatant varieties of the Gnosticism that is disseminated throughout our culture. His *Lebens-philosophie*, if we may call it that, sounded to him, a month or so before his death, rather like 'pragmatism' (OC 422). His emphasis on 'our life', on 'action' and on the human being as the best model of the mind, certainly puts an end to the picture of the solitary disembodied consciousness that the metaphysical tradition favours. The metaphysical tradition just *is* the disavowal of the mundane world of conversation and collaboration in which human life consists. In countless, often almost invisible, ways, the metaphysically generated fantasy of the human estranges us from ourselves. The aim of Wittgenstein's 'spiritual exercises' is to liberate us from that disseminated antipathy to bodiliness

---

[36] McDowell, 'Criteria, defeasibility, and knowledge', p. 469.
[37] T. F. Torrance, 'The mind of Christ in worship'.

which is the last remnant of heretical theology in what we are naturally inclined, in moments of reflection, to say about ourselves and our relationships with one another.

Philosophy, traditionally, begins in wonder.[38] There is a sense in which Wittgenstein's work puts an end to metaphysics by inviting us to renew and expand our sense of wonder:

> I should like to say: you regard it much too much as a matter of course that one can tell anything to anyone. That is to say: We are so much accustomed to communication through speaking, in conversation, that it looks to us as if the whole point of communication lay in this: someone else grasps the sense of my words – which is something mental: he as it were takes it into his own mind. If he then does something further with it as well, that is no part of the immediate purpose of language. (*PI* 363)

[38] Plato, *Theaetetus*, 155 d.

PART THREE

Theology without the Mental Ego

CHAPTER 7

Wittgenstein's Theological Investigations

'Wisdom is grey'. Life on the other hand and religion are full of colour.
(CV, p. 62)

THEOLOGY AS GRAMMAR

In the course of the *Investigations* Wittgenstein makes only one reference to theology as such. It comes in the following context:

> One ought to ask, not what images are or what happens when one imagines anything, but how the word 'imagination [*Vorstellung*]' is used. But that does not mean that I want to talk only about words. For the question as to the nature [*Wesen*] of the imagination is as much about the word 'imagination' as my question is. And I am only saying that this question is not to be decided — neither for the person who does the imagining, nor for anyone else — by pointing; nor yet by a description of any process. The first question also asks for a word to be explained but it makes us expect a wrong kind of answer.
> Essence [*Wesen*] is expressed by grammar. (*PI* 370–1)

The next remark sends us parenthetically back to reconsider some much earlier reflections on grammar, language, ostensive definition, and so on (cf. *PG*, p. 184). It is followed by the reference to theology:

> Grammar tells us what kind of object anything is. (Theology as grammar.) (*PI* 373)

To ask what ideas, mental pictures and so on *are*, is to invite the thought that it should be possible to locate them, by introspection or description. 'We are up against one of the great sources of philosophical bewilderment: a substantive makes us look for a thing that corresponds to it' (*BB*, p. 1). The recommendation that we should consider how words for the inner life are used in conversation if we want to understand what they mean provokes the protest that we are being asked to talk 'only' of words, whereas we want to get, by some supposedly more direct, non-linguistic way, straight to the thing itself. The paradigm of meaning as designating material, or quasi-material, objects, once again reveals its sway.

The question of what the inner life is, Wittgenstein insists, is not to be settled by ostensive definition, or by description of any interior goings-on, neither for the subject nor for the observer. The answer lies in attending to the kind of things that we are permitted to say about these matters, by the rules of the conversation. The kind of object that a thing is comes out in the kind of things that it is appropriate to say about it. This evidently goes for 'God' as much as for 'imagination'. To explain what the word 'God' means we have to listen to what it is permissible to say about the subject.

In an earlier version of these thoughts, Wittgenstein said what happens with the words 'God' and 'soul' is that 'Even though we give up explaining these words ostensively, by pointing, we don't give up explaining them in substantival terms', and he went on:

> Luther said that theology is the grammar of the word 'God'. I interpret this to mean that an investigation of the word would be a grammatical one. For example, people might dispute about how many arms God had, and someone might enter the dispute by denying that one could talk about arms of God. This would throw light on the use of the word. What is ridiculous or blasphemous also shows the grammar of the word. (*WLAA*, p. 32)

This account seems absolutely right.[1] Theology, in practice, has always included a great deal of critical reflection on what people are inclined to say about the divine. It is very much a question of learning to trace what may rightly be said, and what has to be excluded as inappropriate or obsolete. Ridiculous and blasphemous claims may well cast far more light than innocuous assertions of what it is permissible to say. (Of course, if people never spoke of the divine, such theological discussion would not arise; but they are not so dumb.)

Wittgenstein's remarks on explaining words like 'imagination' and 'God' conclude as follows:

> The great difficulty here is not to represent the matter as if there were something one *couldn't* do. As if there really were an object, from which I

[1] J. G. Hamann said that he, 'like Luther, turned the whole of philosophy into a grammar', a remark quoted by Fritz Mauthner as a motto in his *Beiträge zu einer Kritik der Sprache*, 1901–2, which Wittgenstein had certainly looked at: see Gershon Weiler, 'On Fritz Mauthner's critique of language', esp. p. 85.

derive its description, but I were unable to show it to anyone. – And the best that I can propose is that we should yield to the temptation to use this picture, but then investigate how the *application* of the picture goes. (*PI* 374)

It is easy enough to *say* that we no longer explain these words in the substantival terms that turn the referents into mysterious objects. It is more instructive, Wittgenstein implies, to give in to the paradigm of designating material objects and see what confusion it creates for us. It still seems that, if I have a conception of God, for example, I have to have something facing me from which I derive a description: the fact that I cannot show others my picture of God only confirms what epistemically impotent creatures we mortals are. But there is nothing here that we are incapable of doing. It is an illusion to think that we either could or could not get a picture of the object: there is no such object.

That little aside – 'Theology as grammar' – thus has considerable importance, methodologically. Moreover, the importance is not that this is what theologians have often been doing all along; the important thing is to understand why they have had to do this – because they will have to go on doing it so long as people are adjusted only to consider the designating of physical objects (Z 40).

Theology as grammar is, then, the patient and painstaking description of how, when we have to, we speak of God. But why is it that we doubt it can be in mere words or signs or bodily activities that we discover anything interesting about our inner selves or about the divine? Why is it that we are so strongly tempted to turn away from what we say and do, as if these were not 'significant' enough? Again and again Wittgenstein reminds us that we have no alternative to attending to the signs, the repertoire of gestures and so on that interweave our existence. We have no access to our own minds, non-linguistically. We have no access to the divine, independently of our life and language. It goes against the grain, so captivated are we by the metaphysical tradition, but Wittgenstein keeps reminding us of the obvious fact: we have nothing else to turn to but the whole complex system of signs which is our human world.

The great question remains: why do we retreat from our world; why do we withdraw from the body in the hope that more direct illumination about our minds and about the gods is to be found by gaining access to something other than what we say and do? This is the hidden theological agenda of Wittgenstein's later writings. In effect, by remarking that theology is grammar, he is reminding us that it is only by listening to what we say about God (what has been said for many generations), and to how what is said about God ties in with what we say and do in innumerable other connections, that we have any chance of understanding what we mean when we speak of God.

FAITH UNDER THE LEFT NIPPLE

The only other overt theological reference in the *Investigations* is offered as a quotation from Luther.[2] It is introduced in the following way:

> Does it make sense to ask 'How do you know that you believe?' – and is the answer: 'I know it by introspection'?
> In *some* cases it will be possible to say some such thing, in most not.
> It makes sense to ask: 'Do I really love her, or am I only pretending to myself?' and the process of introspection is the calling up of memories; of imagined possible situations, and of the feelings that one would have if . . .
> (*PI* 587)

There is no reason to say that the believing in question here includes religious believing, nor to exclude that. It might happen, Wittgenstein is saying, that, if challenged over some doctrine of faith, I should have to examine my conscience to decide if I believed it: 'Do I really *believe* that, or am I only pretending to myself?' In such cases, introspection, far from being private inspection of some object-like datum, would be remembering past situations, imagining possible ones, assessing the depth of one's feelings and the like. In most cases, if asked whether you believe a thing or love someone, you do not have to go through any of this – you would say yes or no, unhesitatingly. In *some* cases, however, for instance if asked whether you (still) believed the gospel, you would reflect on what you (still) find it possible to do, you might imagine what life would be like if you gave up these practices, you might eventually discover, even with some surprise, that, given the things that you say and do without undue strain and embarrassment, you count as a believer – or not: but you need not struggle to locate some burning faith-sensation in your head or heart.

Against this background Wittgenstein writes:

> 'In my heart I have determined on it'. And one is even inclined to point to one's breast as one says it. Psychologically this way of speaking should be

[2] Where Wittgenstein found the phrase has baffled Luther scholars: see Hallett, *Companion*, p. 563.

taken seriously. Why should it be taken less seriously than the assertion that belief [*der Glaube*] is a state of mind? (Luther: 'Faith [*der Glaube*] is under the left nipple.') (*PI 589*)

A man lays a hand on his chest when he takes an oath, as he may clutch his brow when he is solving a problem. Why should such instinctive gestures be taken less seriously than theories that faith is an inner state, thought is in the head, love is in the will and so on? Faith, like thought, is often *visible*.

Compare this remark:

If the picture of thought in the head can force itself upon us, then why not much more that of thought in the soul?
The human body is the best picture [*Bild*] of the human soul. And how about such an expression as: 'In my heart I understood when you said that', pointing to one's heart? Does one, perhaps, not *mean* this gesture? Of course one means it. Or is one conscious of using a *mere* figure [*Bild*]? Indeed not. – It is not a figure [*Bild*] that we choose, not a simile [*Gleichnis*], yet it is a figurative expression [*ein bildlicher Ausdruck*]. (PI, p. 178)

Besides gestures which reveal my thoughts or feelings to others because, for both them and me, certain meanings have been deliberately attached to these signs, a whole repertoire of primitive enactments of significance has to be acknowledged, in which the thought or feeling does not exist prior to, or apart from, the physical expression. Beating one's breast, touching the sternum, clutching the brow, shedding tears and innumerable other physical expressions, are no more subject to our choice than being a living human being is only one possible realization of the human soul. To regard such significant gestures as 'merely' arbitrary and conventional would be to let in the idea that the soul, or the mind, could exist in some better shape than the living human being. These gestures are no more 'adopted' simply to display one's meaning or feeling than the body is a puppet jerked by a little man inside. Such gestures *are* one's meaning or feeling this or that. There is no need to insist that belief, regret, delight etc., are 'really' states of mind, or that faith is better described as a state of mind. In saying, if he ever did, that faith is under the left nipple, Luther would have been satirizing the mentalism that keeps overcoming Christian discourse and piety in the metaphysical tradition.
    A certain flexibility is allowed:

Suppose one tribe says love is in the right side of the chest, and another tribe says it is in the left side of the chest; would you worry very much about which was right? But you would *worry about* 'love is in the nose'.[3]

The repertoire of expressive gestures varies, even quite considerably, across cultures and eras. But for all that, Wittgenstein insists, there is a primitive expressiveness about the human body, in appropriate circumstances, which needs no backing in states of mind, or theories, that supposedly authorize it:

> A man says 'O God' and looks up to heaven. Now, it is this which can teach us the sense of the proposition that 'God lives on high'. We might say, very roughly, of people whose nature it is to kneel down on certain occasions and fold their hands, that in their language they have a personal God.[4]

Of course, after centuries of the metaphysical way of thinking about ourselves, we now want to say that people do not, or at least should not, kneel on any occasion unless they have certain theories in their heads to justify doing so. Some gestures, like some language-games (*PI* 23), become obsolete and get forgotten. It would be eccentric or degrading or ridiculous to revive them.[5] But our reactions, in many situations, are already as significant as they could be, without any mental or spiritual injection supposedly from within. The gestures of commitment, regret, delight, compassion and so on, are as likely to be at the origin of the inner mental states (if any) as they are to be the effect. Indeed, but for the natural expressiveness of certain primitive reactions we should not have any interesting mental or emotional states in the first place.

Faith, like hope and much else, is embedded in human life, 'in all of the situations and reactions which constitute human life' (*RPP* II, 16). But instead of simply saying what anyone knows and must admit, we find ourselves overcome by a myth of mental processes (*Z* 211): faith becomes something so inward and spiritual that it can never be exhibited to anyone else, and the believer soon finds that he too does not know whether he has it.

---

[3] Notes taken by A. C. Jackson of Wittgenstein's lectures 1946–7, quoted by Hallett, p. 623.

[4] Unpublished TS 219 in the *Nachlass*, dated 1932–3, quoted by Hallett, p. 427.

[5] Not that Wittgenstein liked kneeling: 'I cannot kneel to pray because it's as though my knees were stiff. I am afraid of dissolution (of my own dissolution), should I become soft', (*CV*, p. 56).

WHETHER GOD EXISTS

Thus, those two asides (*PI* 373 and 589), in the otherwise apparently quite non-theological surface of the *Investigations*, open lines of reflection which are both profoundly Wittgensteinian and of considerable theological interest. In fact, from the early *Notebooks* to the final pages of *Culture and Value*, theological questions lie between the lines of all Wittgenstein's writings. It is hard to think of a great philosopher, at least since Nietzsche, whose work is equally pervaded by theological considerations (unless Heidegger counts).

Consider this remark, which dates from 1950:

> When someone who believes in God looks around him and asks 'Where did everything that I see come from?' 'Where did everything come from?', he is *not* asking for a (causal) explanation; and the point of his question is that it is the expression of such a request. Thus, he is expressing an attitude towards all explanations. – But how is this shown in his life? It is the attitude that takes a particular matter seriously, but then at a particular point doesn't take it seriously after all, and declares that something else is even more serious. (*RC* III, 317)[6]

Coming from people who are already believers, such questions express a dissatisfaction with all possible scientific answers to them (cf. *TLP* 6.52). Their attitude, the way they are engaged with things, will appear in other areas of life – anger at people's dying unfulfilled and the like. But the believer's longing is, at any rate, for no causal explanation. He wants to contemplate what he sees around him from a non-scientific point of view. It is as if he wants to do something that is possible *before* all scientific discoveries and inventions (*PI* 126). Explanations come to an end, and where they end, where they find their limit, is in a certain reaction. The question is in effect an exclamation: 'How extraordinary that the world should exist'.[7]

The passage continues:

> Someone may for instance say it's a very grave matter that such and such a man should have died before he could complete a certain piece of work; and yet, in another sense, this is not what matters. At this point one uses the words 'in a deeper sense'.

[6] Much better than the translation in *CV*, p. 85.
[7] Wittgenstein takes this line in 'A lecture on ethics', dated 1929–30.

> Actually I should like to say that in this case too the *words* you utter or what you think as you utter them are not what matters, so much as the difference they make at various points in your life. How do I know that two people mean the same when each says he believes in God? And just the same goes for belief in the Trinity. A theology which insists on the use of *certain particular* words and phrases, and outlaws others, does not make anything clearer (Karl Barth). It gesticulates [*fuchtelt*] with words, as one might say, because it wants to say something and does not know how to express it. *Practice* [*Praxis*] gives the words their sense. (*CV*, p. 85)

That passage contains much more than I want to disentangle here, but the drift is obvious enough.

As with the Luther references, it is hard to locate a text which Wittgenstein might have had in mind. Drury reports that he tried out some Barth on Wittgenstein in 1930 and was stopped after a few minutes: 'I don't want to hear any more. The only impression I get is one of great arrogance' (*RW*, p. 119). In 1940 he received a letter from Wittgenstein in which he said that he was reading Barth: 'This writing must have come from a remarkable religious experience' (*RW*, p. 146). Drury reminded him of the earlier episode; Wittgenstein never mentioned Barth to him again. He no doubt had access in Cambridge libraries to the original works; but a likely text for him to have been leafing through (it is not clear that he read many books from beginning to end, except novels) is the first half-volume of *Church Dogmatics*, in which Barth writes:

> In the raw material of dogmatics, the first object is a series of expressions which, more or less constantly and emphatically, usually make up the spoken matter of proclamation in the whole Church ... But here, as everywhere, these expressions acquire their meaning from the associations and contexts in which they are used.[8]

Such a remark would surely have caught the eye of the philosopher who is reported as saying, in 1938:

> If I had to say what is the main mistake made by philosophers of the present generation, including Moore, I would say that it is that when language is looked at, what is looked at is a form of words and not the use made of the form of words. (*LC*, p. 2)

Anyway, the point is clear: it is in what we *do* when we use them that our words have their sense. Fixation upon certain words and phrases,

[8] *Church Dogmatics*, vol. 1, part 1, p. 86.

abstracted from their place in the conversation of the community, obviously generates a great deal of theological confusion – even if it is true to say, as Wittgenstein did in 1929: 'There is no religious denomination in which the misuse of metaphysical expressions has been responsible for so much sin as it has in mathematics' (*CV*, p. 1). Words and phrases have to be reclaimed from metaphysical application and attended to in the language in which they are at home (*PI* 116). In theological reflection on Christian discourse, it is the practices into which words and phrases are interwoven that we need to remember. Whether I mean the same by saying 'I believe in God' as other people do when they say the same thing will come out at various places in our lives: our practices, aspirations, hopes, virtues, and so on. It will show in the rest of what we do whether we have faith in God. It will not be settled by our finding that we make the same correlation between our words and some item of metaphysical reality.

Thus, my attitude to all explanations of the world's existence comes out in such questions as 'Why is there anything rather than nothing?', and such exclamations as 'How extraordinary that the world should exist!' – *if I am already a believer*; and what these cries of wonder (or protest) amount to in practice will come out in many of the things that I do, or refrain from doing.

This no doubt suggests how the doctrine of the creation of the world fits into the context of an already existing religious faith. But people, who are not yet, or no longer, believers in God, often want to know how to establish the existence of a deity in the first place. About this Wittgenstein also had some thoughts.

It must be said that, like many another, his faith in God seems to have been strained, if not undermined, by the rationalistic apologetics then common in Roman Catholic circles. In 1930, for example, he made this remark to Drury:

> It is a dogma of the Roman Church that the existence of God can be proved by natural reason. Now this dogma would make it impossible for me to be a Roman Catholic. If I thought of God as another being like myself, outside myself, only infinitely more powerful, then I would regard it as my duty to defy him. (*RW*, pp. 107–8)

Leaving aside whether this dogma (of the First Vatican Council, 1869–70) ever meant that the deity's existence could be proved by simply anyone, irrespective of circumstances, moral considerations etc., it is also contestable that it is 'another being like myself' whose existence is at issue – though that is how people generally view the matter, whether or not they think they can do the trick.[9]

By 1949, however, Wittgenstein had a more interesting view:

> God's essence is supposed to guarantee his existence – what this really means is that what is here at issue is not the existence of something. (CV, p. 82)

The allusion must be to the celebrated thesis of Thomas Aquinas, in a text he had to hand:[10] that, while in every created thing essence and existence are distinct, in God they are identical. Whatever its difficulties, and whether or not it secures the radical difference between everything and God that Aquinas thought it did, to Wittgenstein it seemed to have nothing to do with existence:

> Couldn't one actually say equally well that the essence of colour guarantees its existence? As opposed, say, to white elephants. Because all that really means is: I cannot explain what 'colour' is, what the word 'colour' means, except with the help of a colour sample. So in this case there is no such thing as explaining 'what it *would* be like if colours *were* to exist'.

What we mean by the word 'colour' depends on the pervasiveness of the colour system throughout what we say and do. There is no position from which the existence of the colour system might have been a discussable hypothesis. We could not answer the question 'What difference does the existence of colour make?' by pointing to an item in the environment. We have to recall how our conversation is shot through with colour language. There is no 'essence' of colour that might be abstracted from the existence of the colour system in our perception of the world.[11] The grammar of God-talk, Wittgenstein thus suggests, is more like talking about the colour system than about any particular colour.

He goes on as follows:

> And now we might say: There can be a description of what it would be like if there were gods on Olympus – but not: 'what it would be like if there

[9] See Lubor Velecky, 'Flew on Aquinas'.

[10] Wittgenstein had the first two volumes of the Latin-German Pustet edition, containing *Summa Theologiae*, I, qq. 1–26: like the 'Five Ways' the thesis that essence and existence are identical in God is in q. 3. Wittgenstein is quoted as saying that he found Aquinas 'extremely good in his formulation of questions but less satisfactory in his discussion of them' (Hallett, p. 761).

[11] I am following Rowan Williams, 'Religious realism', pp. 15–16.

were such a thing as God'. And to say this is to determine the concept 'God' more precisely.

The Greek gods are like white elephants – items in a system; but the inclination to speak of *God* as an item (that may or may not exist) has to give way to the analogy of the colour *system*. The important question is how we learn to speak of God in the first place:

How are we taught [*beigebracht*] the word 'God' (its use, that is)? I cannot give a full grammatical description of it. But I can, as it were, make some contributions to such a description; I can say a good deal about it and perhaps in time assemble a sort of collection of examples.

A few examples suffice to remind us of how we are initiated into the use of the word 'God'. They will have to do with such multifarious activities as blessing and cursing, celebrating and lamenting, repenting and forgiving, the cultivation of certain virtues and so on. There will be little place for the inferring of some invisible entity's presence.

The question of the existence of God as commonly conceived comes either too late or too early to have a place in the conversation:

A proof of God's existence ought really to be something by means of which one could convince oneself that God exists. But I think that what *believers* who have furnished such proofs have wanted to do is to give their 'belief' an intellectual analysis and foundation, although they themselves would never have come to believe as a result of such proofs. Perhaps one could 'convince someone that God exists' by means of a certain kind of upbringing, by shaping his life in such and such a way. (*CV*, p. 85)

It is hard to imagine how people would awaken to the possibility of religious faith, in the Judeo-Christian or any other tradition, by having it proved to them that there is something more powerful (etc.) than anything in the world. On the other hand, it is easy to think of people who have wanted to analyse and justify their faith by securing rational grounds for it but who then find themselves no longer able to believe in God.

Wittgenstein continues as follows:

Life can educate one to a belief in God. And *experiences* too are what bring this about; but I don't mean visions and other forms of sense experience which show us the 'existence of this being', but, e.g., sufferings of various sorts. These neither show us God in the way a sense impression shows us

an object, nor do they give rise to *conjectures* about him. Experiences, thoughts — life can force this concept on us.
So perhaps it is similar to the concept of 'object'. (*CV*, p. 86)

It is not that God is perceived or surmised as an object — the *concept* 'object' fits into the conversation quite differently from all talk about any particular object. It is easy to imagine people who do most of what we do, but without having the *concept* of an object at all. That is to say: talking of God *is* like talking of an object, provided that we remember how different the concept of an object is from the concept of a table or a star or a theorem. If the similarity between tables, refrigerators and motor cars never struck us we could live happily without the notion of middle-sized dry goods. But, for various reasons, connected with the metaphysical impulse and scientific curiosity, the concept of an object has forced itself irreversibly upon our culture. Analogously, Wittgenstein suggests, given certain experiences, sufferings, reflections and so on, the concept of God has forced its way into our lives.

It is difficult to bring out the profundity of Wittgenstein's suggestion because it is also so obvious. He might be reminding us of how the concept of the divine has been developed in, for example, the Judeo-Christian tradition. He is certainly reminding us, once again, that words are not always correlatable with the objects for which they supposedly stand.

A CEREMONIOUS ANIMAL

In 1929, when Drury was still contemplating ordination in the Church of Ireland, Wittgenstein lamented the 'infinite harm' done by 'Russell and the parsons between them' — evidently because they had colluded in immuring people ever more deeply in rationalistic apologetics. He went on as follows:

> I would be afraid that you would try and give some sort of philosophical justification for Christian beliefs, as if some sort of proof was needed.
> . . .
> The symbolisms of Catholicism are wonderful beyond words. But any attempt to make it into a philosophical system is offensive. All religions are wonderful, even those of the most primitive tribes. The ways in which people express their religious feelings differ enormously. (*RW*, p. 102)

'*All* religions are wonderful' seems something of an exaggeration, but these remarks are reported from conversation and obviously must not be taken too seriously. Much of what Drury reports was provoked by things that he himself said. In 1943, for example, he visited Wittgenstein in Newcastle and, while they walked by the river in Durham, he told him of his visit to the temples of Luxor, saying how shocked he had been at finding a bas-relief of the god Horus with an erect phallus, in the act of ejaculation and collecting the semen in a bowl – to which Wittgenstein responded:

> Why in the world shouldn't they have regarded with awe and reverence that act by which the human race is perpetuated! Not every religion has to have St Augustine's attitude to sex. Why, even in our culture marriages are celebrated in church; everyone present knows what is going to happen that night, but that doesn't prevent it being a religious ceremony. (*RW*, p. 148)

It is as if Drury had allowed certain rationalistic questions about the justification for certain religious symbols and ceremonies to get in the way of seeing how expressive of awe and reverence at certain *non*-religious activities (such as procreation) these symbols and ceremonies are, or have been.

Soon after it appeared, Wittgenstein and Drury discussed F. R. Tennant's *Philosophical Theology* (*RW*, p. 90). This massive two-volume work is an immensely impressive intellectual feat of exactly the kind of philosophical justification for the Christian religion that Wittgenstein regarded as totally irrelevant.[12] In effect, Tennant treats theism as a hypothesis which is arguable in the sort of way that, for example, Darwinist theory is.

On the other hand, Wittgenstein was fascinated by William James's *The Varieties of Religious Experience*.[13] In a letter to Russell, in 1912, Wittgenstein wrote:

> Whenever I have time I now read James's Varieties of religious experience. This book does me a *lot* of good. I don't mean to say that I will be a saint soon, but I am not sure that it does not improve me a little in a way in which I would like to improve *very much*: namely I think that it helps me to

[12] Fellow of Trinity College, Cambridge, F. R. Tennant (1866–1957), a clergyman with a background in the natural sciences, published the first volume, *The Soul and its Faculties*, 1928, and the second, *The World, the Soul and God*, 1930.

[13] Gifford Lectures at Edinburgh, William James's *Varieties* appeared in 1902 and had been reprinted 20 times by 1912.

get rid of the *Sorge* (in the sense in which Goethe used the word in the 2nd part of Faust).[14]

In 1930 Wittgenstein advised Drury to read the book: he had already done so, and commented that he enjoyed reading James – 'He is such a human person' – to which Wittgenstein made the interesting reply: 'That is what makes him a good philosopher; he was a real human being' (*RW*, p. 106). Drury, opposing von Wright's alignment of Wittgenstein's intense seriousness with Pascal's narrow religiosity and fideism, insists that his delight in the pleasures of reading William James indicates a quite different orientation (*RW*, p. 93).

It is easy enough to see that Wittgenstein would have sympathized with James's mockery of theologians as 'the closet-naturalists of the deity':

> What is their deduction of metaphysical attributes but a shuffling and matching of pedantic dictionary-adjectives, aloof from morals, aloof from human needs, something that might be worked out from the mere word 'God' by one of those logical machines of wood and brass which recent ingenuity has contrived as well as by a man of flesh and blood.[15]

James insists on the secondary character of intellectual constructions, and on the primacy of feeling and instinct in founding religious beliefs: 'Ratiocination is a relatively superficial and unreal path to the deity'.[16]

In opposition to (what he takes to be) standard theological procedure, James makes feeling, rather than reason, foundational in religion. But Wittgenstein's later work strives to show that neither feeling nor reason but *action* is the foundational thing. It is consistent with this that he should lay emphasis on ceremony, on symbolism, in religion, because it is not 'thought up', or to be regarded (normally) as glimpses of interior spiritual states. Just as unsurprisingly, James's psychologistic inclinations remain one of the great quarries in the *Investigations*. In the end, although seeking to defend feeling at the expense of reason, and thus to rehabilitate the primitive and unreflective, James concludes that 'The genuineness of religion is . . . bound up with the question whether the prayerful consciousness be or be not deceitful'.[17] In fact 'the fountainhead of much that feeds our religion' turns out to be the transmarginal or subliminal region of the self. For all his pragmatism – 'The truth of the

[14] *Letters to Russell, Keynes and Moore*, p. 10. (*Sorge*: care, anxiety, grief.)
[15] *Varieties*, p. 446.
[16] Ibid, p. 448.
[17] Ibid, p. 466.

matter can be put in this way: *God is not known, he is not understood: he is used* – sometimes as meat-purveyor, sometimes as moral support, sometimes as friend, sometimes as an object of love'[18] – William James has as private and individualistic a conception of the self as one will meet anywhere in the copious literature of modern philosophy.

Varieties, for all the rich and strange things with which it is packed, shows very little interest in rites, ceremonies etc. In 1931 Wittgenstein asked Drury to get hold of a copy of Frazer's *The Golden Bough*, saying that he had long wanted to read it, and they spent some weeks reading the first volume together (*RW*, p. 119).[19] This led to one set of remarks (*RFGB*, pp. 1–12). Towards the end of his life he was reading the one-volume edition of *The Golden Bough* and some pencil notes, probably made after 1948, have survived (*RFGB*, pp. 13–18). They are of great theological interest.[20]

Frazer tries to explain the custom of sacrificing the priest-king in the sacred grove at Nemi. It goes far beyond my purposes here to show whether Wittgenstein reads Frazer fairly: his objection is that Frazer tries to make the custom intelligible to people who think in his own rationalist categories. The custom thus becomes the result of *Dummheit*: 'But it never does become plausible that people do all this out of sheer stupidity' (*RFGB*, p. 1). People can be persuaded to abandon practices if they are convinced that they are based on mistaken *views*, but, so Wittgenstein insists, many religious practices are not generated by views of any kind. Frazer thinks that it is sometimes hard to get at the view, but that is what Wittgenstein contests; very often, at the bottom of the practice, there is nothing that might be called a view or a belief or a theory, which would then be open to correction. Frazer's account of religious practices, in other words, is permeated by the idealistic metaphysical prejudices that Wittgenstein strove to expose.

The explanation of the practice which Frazer needs to satisfy his rationalistic inquiry is redundant, Wittgenstein argues. The satisfaction that is supposed to be provided by the explanation is already available if only we listen to the story of the ceremony. Indeed, Frazer himself, with

[18] Ibid, p. 506.
[19] Fellow of Trinity College, Cambridge, J. G. Frazer (1854–1941) published *The Golden Bough* in 1890, in two volumes which he twice revised and expanded. It had great influence on writers such as D. H. Lawrence and T. S. Eliot, and classical scholars, especially at Cambridge.
[20] See the interesting papers by Richard H. Bell, 'Understanding the fire-festivals'; Frank Cioffi, 'Wittgenstein and the fire-festivals'; and Christopher Cherry, 'Meaning and the idol of origins'.

all his best explanatory intention, tells it 'in a tone which shows that something strange and terrible is happening here': the question 'Why *this*?' is already answered: 'Because it is terrible':

> In other words, the very thing that strikes us in this episode as terrible, impressive, horrible, tragic, etc., anything but trivial and insignificant, is what brought about the ceremony in the first place. (*RFGB*, p. 3)

Compared with the story of what happened, the explanation is banal. The rationalistic attempt to find the deeper psychological or evolutionary significance of the ceremony only distracts us from the deep significance that a description of the event already communicates: 'One would like to say: This is what took place here; laugh, if you can'.

The sacrifice of the priest-king is no different in kind from religious actions that we might ourselves perform, Wittgenstein says, and he lists some examples: confessing one's sins, kissing a loved one's picture, baptism, adoption ceremonies, Schubert's brother's cutting up scores to give fragments to favourite pupils after the composer's death and so on. Frazer's trouble is lack of imagination: 'What narrowness of spiritual life we find in Frazer! And as a result: how impossible for him to understand a different way of life from the English one of his time!' (*RFGB*, p. 5).

The principle according to which such practices are related to one another is much more common than Frazer allows: 'we find it in ourselves [*in unserer Seele vorhanden*]' (*RFGB*, p. 5). The phenomena of the natural world, of death, of birth and of sexual life, and much else, none of which is specially mysterious but any of which may become so to us, prompt certain human reactions: 'We could almost say, man is a ceremonious animal' (*RFGB*, p. 7). In other words: 'When we watch the life and behaviour of people all over the earth we see that apart from what we might call animal activities, taking food etc., etc., people also carry out actions that bear a peculiar character and might be called ritualistic'. But these customs are not adopted because of views that people have; they are too primitive and unreflective for that, they are *reactions*, in certain situations. And the sense of these observances is much clearer than Frazer's explanations, finally because 'there is something in us too that speaks in support of those observances by the savages' (*RFGB*, p. 8).

SOMETHING DEEP AND SINISTER

The later set of notes takes this a little further:

Yes, but that which I see in those stories is something they acquire, after all, from the evidence, including such evidence as does not seem directly connected with them – from the thought of man and his past, from the strangeness [*das Seltsame*] of what I see in myself and in others, what I have seen and have heard. (*RFGB*, p. 18)

Frazer, like many educated people in our rationalistic culture, fails to acknowledge the tenacity of certain ancient practices, their continuity with present ones, their resonances and surrogates in our own experience. A theory about the origins of a religious custom does not explain its significance:

> What I want to say is: What is sinister, deep, does not lie in the fact that that is how the history of this practice went, for perhaps it did not go that way . . .
> What makes human sacrifice something deep and sinister anyway? Is it only the suffering of the victim that impresses us in this way? All manner of diseases bring just as much suffering and do *not* make this impression. No, this deep and sinister aspect [*dies Tiefe und Finstere*] is not obvious just from learning the history of the external action, but *we* insert it from an experience in ourselves. (*RFGB*, p.16)

These perhaps dreadful practices already make sense to us before we look for explanations in terms of causes or purposes. To deny this is, once again, to deny what human beings are like: *das Seltsame* is in us all.

Wittgenstein's deeper point thus becomes clear. To deal with religious practices by taking them to rest on mistaken hypotheses about the world is to evade the truth about ourselves. It is to say: all this is alien, it has nothing to do with us now. Moreover, when it is something as sinister as sacrificing a human being, the temptation to go in for Frazer's kind of explanation becomes overwhelming. But Wittgenstein wants to remind us of the deep continuities between the sensibility of our primitive ancestors and our own. He insists on this continuity – and on our desire to deny it – because to deny it is to deny something about our own nature.

In effect, Frazer's theorizings conceal our kinship with his savages by assuming that their customs can be made intelligible to modern civilized men round Cambridge college dinner tables only by dispassionate observation – as if these tables were not occupied by beings at least as sinister as any dancing savage. By resorting to scientific objectivity we have a method of disowning biological and historical continuity with our ancestors. Frazer's approach to the sacrifice of the priest-king enables him to avoid facing what it is in human beings that makes the custom so disturbing in the first place. Confronted with horrors, Dr Johnson said, we take refuge in incredulity. We can also go for explanation – but, sometimes at least, it is ourselves that we need to understand, and, understandably, we prefer not to.

The point has been well made by Bernard Williams.[21] Reviewing J. L. Mackie's demonstration of the incoherence of the arguments for the probability of God's existence that certain modern philosophers of religion favour, Williams, himself an atheist, notes that Mackie's refutations leave the real question intact. The intellectual case for accepting the God hypothesis is so full of holes that no rational person could accept it; but it is a mistake, in demonstrating this, to leave it as if religion must therefore be something alien to humanity and its needs, 'now simply abandoned by advanced thought'. What is required, from the atheist, is an account of religion that understands it as expressing needs that will have to be expressed in some form when the belief in God has disappeared. As Williams writes elsewhere: 'Humanism – in the contemporary sense of a secularist and antireligious movement – seems seldom to have faced fully a very immediate consequence of its own views: that this terrible thing, religion, is a *human* creation.'[22]

Religion, in other words, has to do with something deep and sinister in *us*. Its power is not ended by refutations of arguments for the existence of the deity. Religions are an expression of human nature long before they give rise to reflections about the divine. Certain modern reflective procedures tempt us to forget that. Objective study of primitive religion gets in the way of our seeing how savage our own religion is. We prefer a certain interpretation of other people's behaviour to understanding what is deep and sinister in ourselves – and thus we do not have much understanding of the savages either.

That considering the execution of an innocent man is a more promising starting point for sustaining Christian theology than proving that God exists might be one unsurprising conclusion.

THE AROMA OF COFFEE

There is much else in Wittgenstein's writings, particularly in *Culture and Value*, that bears explicitly on theological matters. I have noted only four

[21] *The Times Literary Supplement*, 11 March 1983, p. 231.
[22] *Morality*, p. 94.

topics here, without exhausting what might be said about any of them. Talking about God has to be reflection on how the word 'God' is used in our conversation. Faith, in appropriate circumstances, is visible in one's behaviour; it is not some undetectable inner object. Arguments for the existence of the deity come either too late or too early to be of much use to anyone. Finally, to understand the power of religion we have to rediscover the strangeness in our own nature that makes stories of religious customs intelligible. In all of these matters Wittgenstein's suggestions are entirely consonant with that change in the position of the self which the strategies of the later writing are meant to accomplish. Language, the living human being, our life, human nature: Wittgenstein's watchwords in the philosophy of psychology are also contributions of central importance to a theology that starts where we are; a theology for ceremonious animals, so to speak, rather than for cerebrating solipsists; a theology that starts from the deep and sinister thing in human nature, rather than from a hypothesis about a deity; theology *naturalized*, so to speak.

Wittgenstein's writings also contain a great deal that has less explicit bearing on theological matters. Consider only one example:

> Describe the aroma of coffee. – Why can't it be done? Do we lack the words? And *for what* are words lacking? – But whence comes the idea that such a description must after all be possible? Have you ever felt the lack of such a description? Have you tried to describe the aroma and not succeeded?
>
> ((I should like to say: 'These notes say something glorious, but I do not know what'. These notes are a powerful gesture, but I cannot put anything side by side with it that will serve as an explanation. A grave nod. James: 'Our vocabulary is inadequate'. Then why don't we introduce a new one? What would have to be the case for us to be able to?)) (*PI* 610)

This text is a labyrinth of paths but the thread is a question to which Wittgenstein often returns: what gives rise to the very idea of a description that we are powerless to achieve? The curiously double-bracketed paragraph brings out the point.

Listening to a piece of music I say: 'These sounds say something glorious', and I feel defeated that I cannot say it. I want a paraphrase, when there is no other way of expressing the meaning. The powerful gesture which is the music seems to call for some rationale. There is an incipient sense of frustration that something indescribable is eluding our powers of description.

Our own inner life is the paradigm of the indescribable, as William James was suggesting in the phrases to which Wittgenstein alludes: 'This absence of a special vocabulary for subjective facts hinders the study of all but the very coarsest of them. . . . Our psychological vocabulary is wholly inadequate'.[23] Bertrand Russell made the same complaint: 'We have no vocabulary for describing what actually takes place in us when we think or desire, except the somewhat elementary device of putting words in inverted commas . . . We need a new vocabulary if we are to describe these occurrences otherwise than by reference to objects'.[24] Wittgenstein puts this desire for an unattainably better vocabulary in these terms:

> But one would like to say: 'The interior life of a human being simply cannot be described; it is so extraordinarily complicated and full of scarcely tangible experiences. Like a brew of coloured mist in which every shape is only a transition to other shapes – to other transitions. – Why, take just visual experience! Your gaze wanders almost incessantly, how could you describe it?'
> – And yet I do describe it!
> – 'But that is only a pretty crude description, it gives only the coarsest features of your experience'.
> – But isn't this just what I *call* description of my experience? How then do I arrive at the concept of a kind of description that I cannot possibly give? (*RPP* I, 1079)

If the words are lacking, we introduce new ones. William James, in *The Principles of Psychology*, revolutionized our psychological vocabulary, so profoundly that his achievement has been forgotten. His younger brother, shortly to enter his third manner, opened up fiction to new ways of describing extremely subtle psychological states. A great deal of ordinary conversation consists in exchanging stories of our experiences. What gives rise to the idea that our stories are inherently inadequate?

The aroma of coffee is no more intrinsically indescribable than the bouquet of a fine claret or a barrowload of dung. Granted that we have a great deal else in common, with which comparisons may be made, and that the description is for some purpose ('And *for what* are words lacking?'), there is no reason to doubt that we shall succeed. Indeed, when we have tried to describe the aroma of coffee, have we ever failed? What kind of description are we hankering for when we feel inclined to lament the inadequacy of our descriptive skills?

[23] *Principles of Psychology*, vol. I, pp. 195, 251.
[24] *Outline of Philosophy*, p. 12.

The voice of common sense assures us that we describe things as well as we need to; but the idea of a description that is infinitely finer than our clumsy powers can ever achieve is not as easily expelled.

According to students' lecture notes, Wittgenstein once made the following suggestion:

> One often has the experience of trying to give an account of what one actually sees in looking about one, say, the changing sky, and of feeling that there aren't enough words to describe it. One then tends to become fundamentally dissatisfied with language. We are comparing the case with something it cannot be compared with. It is like saying of falling raindrops, 'Our vision is so inadequate that we cannot say how many raindrops we saw, though surely we did see a specific number'. (*WLAA*, p. 63)

The fact is that, since it makes no sense to talk of the number of drops we see during a shower of rain (people would smile patiently if we did), we need not reproach ourselves for being powerless to say precisely how many we saw. The example is deliberately crude, but it startles us into realizing that we do have an ideal of exactitude or completeness at the back of our minds which very easily imposes itself inappropriately. (After all, I *must have* seen a specific number of raindrops.)[25]

Much more deeply, however, Wittgenstein sought to bring out the power of 'the strange illusion' which possesses us 'when we seem to seek the something which a face expresses whereas, in reality, we are giving ourselves up to the features before us' (*BB*, p. 166). It is as if, when we look at a man's face, we had to check the outward expression against 'a mould ready for it in our mind'. We are back with the argument from analogy with our own case to the existence and nature of other people's psychological properties. When we respond to someone's expression it seems that we have made a lightning comparison of his exterior with the supposedly inaccessible interior. We cannot take anyone at face value; the meaning is concealed behind the phenomena.

Wittgenstein goes on as follows:

> that same illusion possesses us even more strongly if repeating a tune to ourselves and letting it make its full impression on us, we say 'This tune says *something*', and it is as though I had to find *what* it says. And yet I know that it doesn't say anything such that I might express in words or pictures what it says. And if, recognizing this, I resign myself to saying 'It

[25] Like Funes the Memorious, in Borges's *Labyrinths*.

just expresses a musical thought', this would mean no more than saying 'It expresses itself'. (*BB*, p.166)

But why should I have to 'resign myself' to the music? What impels anyone to think that what the music expresses might be expressed otherwise, and better?

In effect: why do the sounds and shapes of our world have to be constantly compared, of course unfavourably, with celestial sounds and ethereal shapes? The aroma of coffee is indescribable only if no objects of comparison are available. We simply give ourselves up to the features before us: people's faces do not normally mask their thoughts and feelings. Our language is not just a tolerable *façon de parler*, as if *faute de mieux*. It is not a failure on our part that we cannot say what the music expresses. We do better to awaken to the possibility that our way of life is the incomparable thing that it is, without compulsively contrasting it all the time with alien alternatives. The metaphysical picture of what we are, far from securing our uniqueness, only obscures it.

It might even be that, in this rare allusion to music, double-bracketed into the ironic remark on describing the aroma of coffee, Wittgenstein is hinting at the most important thing that he could not say in the course of the *Investigations* (cf. *RW*, p. 160). In a letter from the Russian front, dated 9 April 1917, to his friend Paul Engelmann, who had sent him a poem by the early nineteenth century poet Johann Ludwig Uhland, Wittgenstein wrote:

> The poem by Uhland is really magnificent. And this is how it is: if only you do not try to utter what is unutterable then *nothing* gets lost. But the unutterable will be – unutterably – *contained* in what has been uttered![26]

Nobody could be very confident about what that remark means. But since (if I am right) Wittgenstein's philosophical reflections are in large part, however indirectly, readings between the lines of the story of the soul in the Western metaphysical tradition, a quotation from St Augustine may be the most appropriate comment:

> At the harvest, in the vineyard, wherever men must labour hard, they begin with songs whose words express their joy. But when their joy brims over and words are not enough, they abandon even this coherence and give themselves up to the sheer sound of singing. What is this jubilation, this exultant song? It is the melody that means our hearts are bursting with

[26] Engelmann, *Letters*, pp. 6–7; Uhland's ballad, with translation, pp. 83–4.

feelings words cannot express. And to whom does this jubilation most belong? Surely to God, who is unutterable. And does not unutterable mean what cannot be uttered? If words will not come and you may not remain silent, what else can you do but let the melody soar?[27]

---

[27] On Psalm 32, Sermon 1, 7–8 (office reading on 22 November, feast of St Cecilia).

CHAPTER 8

Questions in the Philosophy of Theology

There are problems I never get anywhere near, which do not lie in my path or are not part of my world. Problems of the intellectual world of the West that Beethoven (and perhaps Goethe to a certain extent) tackled and wrestled with, but no philosopher has ever confronted (perhaps Nietzsche passed by them). (*CV*, p. 9)

THE PHILOSOPHY OF THEOLOGY

I have been suggesting that theologians are in a good position to understand Wittgenstein. They will not only benefit from the discipline that he imposes on what is said about the notion of a person, they have the knowledge of history to identify his quarry. Much theological reflection, not to mention everyday Christian piety and discourse, is permeated by the conception of the knowledge-seeking self which his later work is out to deconstruct. (I am not suggesting that this is the only thing he is doing, or the only concern in his later work which is of considerable theological interest; but one thing at a time). On the other hand, this picture of the cognitive subject has roots, far beyond modern philosophy, in religious ideas about the soul. The mentalist–individualist conception of the self owes much of its imaginative power and psychological appeal to the vitality of the myth of the soul as a ghost inside the body. In more specifically Christian terms, it is the Origenist theology which secretes a philosophy of psychology that tends to represent human beings as angels fallen into flesh.

Whether any such doctrine should be ascribed to Origen himself need not concern us here.[1] The Second Council of Constantinople (AD 553) endorsed the repudiation of a string of allegedly Origenist errors that a provincial council, ten years earlier, had made. The heresies of some monks in Palestine were the principal objects of censure. These monks

[1] See Lampe, 'Christian theology in the Patristic period', esp. p. 81.

were understood to hold the view that the human soul is inserted into a body as a punishment, and that the human body is therefore a degrading place of exile. (Interestingly enough, their other heresy was to conceive the origin of the world as necessary, and thus to deny the freedom of the divine creativity.)

Thus crystallized at a certain epoch in the history of Christianity, the myth of the soul as imprisoned in the body was roundly condemned and officially disowned. One of the consequences of such public disavowal of a doctrine as heresy is, however, that people no longer feel able to own up to their private fears, or desires, that it might be the truth. The louder the official denunciation of a doctrine, the longer it takes for people to work themselves properly free of its subterranean effects. In any case, the history of Christian spirituality shows that antipathy to the body reappears, in more or less disguised and virulent forms, with such predictability that the religion of the Incarnation has clearly not altogether extirpated it.

The only real problem for theologians in reading Wittgenstein lies in reluctance to acknowledge that the myth of the soul, even after all these centuries of official ecclesiastical rejection, has as strong a grip on our imagination as it ever had on Origen or his monkish followers.

We are then free to enjoy doing Wittgenstein's exercises. Since his games are designed precisely to overcome that antipathy to the body which marks the metaphysical way of thinking, it is obvious that, once over the preliminary shock, reading Wittgenstein is a pleasure.

Antipathy to the human body, in our world of pornography and torture, is a phenomenon that must frighten many other people besides those with theological commitments. The fetish of dispassionate objectivity in real knowledge, and the correlative retreat into subjectivism in morals and aesthetics, dominate many people's lives in our culture. Wittgenstein certainly did not suppose that what he was doing, even if it were understood, would achieve very much. Consider a remark he wrote in 1937:

The sickness of a time is cured by a change in people's way of life and the sickness of philosophical problems could be cured only through a changed way of thinking and of living, not through a medicine invented by an individual.

Suppose that using the motor-car produced or encouraged certain sicknesses, and that humanity was plagued by this sickness until, from some cause or other, as the result of some development or other, it abandoned the habit of driving. (*RFM* II, 23)

Even if he is thinking of his own work there, as the invention of a therapy for metaphysical illusions, he is surely saying that those illusions are nourished by a certain social order that needs to be changed:

> I am by no means sure that I should prefer a continuation of my work by others to a change in the way people live which would make all these questions superfluous. (*CV*, p. 61)

At this point, in 1947, when his deepening concentration on questions in the philosophy of psychology, both in writing and in classes, suggests that he had found the way of working that he could teach to others, he doubted whether a future of good philosophy was preferable to a social revolution that would make metaphysical illusions impossible.

On the other hand, whatever his doubts about the value of his work, he also felt that he had instituted a way of doing philosophy which got down to the roots of metaphysics:

> Getting hold of the difficulty *deep down* is what is hard. Because if it is grasped near the surface it simply remains the difficulty it was. It has to be pulled out by the roots; and that involves our beginning to think about these things in a new way. The change is as decisive as, for example, that from the alchemical to the chemical way of thinking. The new way of thinking is what is so hard to establish.
>
> Once the new way of thinking has been established, the old problems vanish; indeed they become hard to recapture. For they go with our way of expressing ourselves and, if we clothe ourselves in a new form of expression, the old problems are discarded along with the old garment. (*CV*, p. 48)

The point is surely confirmed by the difficulty one feels by this stage of returning to the galaxy of modern theologians with which we started this quest for signs of the myth of the individual; it no longer seems necessary to correct or supplement or refute the kind of thing that we found them saying. After working through Wittgenstein's writings we simply have a different way of expressing ourselves.

This does not mean that all the philosophical problems in theology are solved. It becomes too awkward and embarrassing to enter into debate with Rahner about the transcendental subject, or with Küng about the gamble on theism, and so on: we have simply changed the subject. It therefore seems more useful, in the rest of this chapter, to outline, albeit very sketchily, some of the questions that might be, and already are being, treated differently, in the light of the Wittgensteinian considerations which it has been the purpose of this book to bring forward.[2]

Philosophers who are interested in theology, and theologians who go in for philosophy, almost equally rare breeds, tend to devote their energies to arguing for or against the hypothesis that there is a deity. Once that issue is settled, they are free either to give up theology or to get on with it. In the latter case, interestingly, they often show no sign of having any further theological problems. Philosophy, that is to say, concerns theologians only at the threshold. Once the foundations of the theological enterprise have been secured, it is often thought that no further philosophical assistance is required.

But theology cannot do without philosophy as easily as that. The work that customarily goes under the heading of the philosophy of religion, at least in the Anglo-American analytical tradition, usually concentrates on discussing reasons for Christian faith in terms of something like proofs of the deity's existence. These are obviously such difficult questions that it is not surprising if resolving them seems a worthwhile terminus. The question on which I have placed the emphasis in this book, on the other hand, reappears in one form or another over a range of issues that are internal to theological discussion. The picture of the self, along the mentalist—individualist lines that I have tried to indicate, dominates a great deal of modern theological theorizing, simply because it belongs to modern thought in general. I make no claim that this is the only, or even the most important, philosophical option that queers the modern theologian's pitch. The half dozen or so issues that I am going on to mention are not even the only ones that involve this particular option. Much more could and needs to be said. Philosophical investigation inside theology, in the English-speaking world at least, has hardly found its feet. Perhaps, lifting Donald MacKinnon's phrase, we should say that, since the philosophy of religion is currently so identified with one set of problems (what used to be called natural theology or Christian apologetics), we need many more practitioners of *the philosophy of theology*.[3]

SECRET THOUGHTS

We have come a long way, in our spirituality, from the case of the barren Hannah, in the temple of Shiloh, who prayed with her lips moving but

---

[2] Among the few attempts to do theology after Wittgenstein I would mention Ian Davie, *A Theology of Speech.*

[3] MacKinnon's phrase, *Explorations in Theology*, p. 147.

without making a sound, so that the guardian priest of the shrine thought that she was drunk, so unaccustomed was he, presumably, to anything but highly audible prayer (I Samuel:1). The parish clergy probably still prefer congregations that sing with gusto, but spiritual writers in the last three centuries or so have driven many devout people into believing that the only real prayer is silent, wordless, 'private'. They often have such a sense of failure in attaining this ideal that it is as if they were haunted by the thought that – *ideally* – one could learn to do sums in the head without ever doing oral ones (*PI* 385). The presence of other people then comes to seem an irrelevance or even a nuisance.

It becomes clear, as soon as we recall a few simple facts, that, in this case also, the inner life depends for its depth and character on connections with past and present situations, with tradition and community. But it is amazing how often devout people think that liturgical worship is not really prayer unless they have been injecting special 'meaning' to make the words work. The inclination is to say that participation consists in private goings-on inside the head, while, following Wittgenstein, we should want rather to see it primarily in the connections, the tie-ups, that one is making (*RRP* II, 261). It is not what is going on in the radical privacy of people's minds that makes the difference between a committee meeting and a bout of glossolalia. It is the surroundings, not the mental accompaniment of the people's talking, that make all the difference (cf. *RRP* II, 204).

It remains a temptation, however, to say that liturgical worship is normally 'lip-service', merely mouthing the words: occasionally saved from this by specially energetic injections of 'meaning'.

Consider this remark:

> We say 'The expression in his voice was *genuine*'. If it was spurious we think as it were of another one behind it. – *This* is the face he shows the world, inwardly he has another one. – But this does not mean that when his expression is *genuine* he has two the same. (*PI* 606)

It is very tempting, however, to say that the difference between genuine and spurious utterance is that in the former case my inward face and my outward face for once match. We are back under the spell of the idea that, normally, we are masked, as if hypocrisy in worship were the standard case.

No doubt the worshipper's participation is enhanced by peace of mind, a clear conscience, intelligent grasp of theological principles and the like; but, as a little reflection shows, none of these advantages is, in principle, different from following carefully in a missal or having left the little ones at home. Once again, the difficulty is to understand that we do not have to be either intensely concentrated or merely mechanical. Here, as in so many other situations, as Quine would say, 'banal messages are the breath of life'.

There is nevertheless a central strain in modern Christian piety which puts all the emphasis on people's secret thoughts and hidden sins. It gets to the point, in some traditions, that the worst sins of all become those that the individual performs entirely by himself. Wittgenstein recalls us, somewhat astringently, to the historical contingency of this belief:

> Only God sees the most secret thoughts. But why should these be all that important? And need all human beings count them as important? (Z 560)

Why should our secret thoughts be more important than the thoughts that come out only too effectively in what we say and do? Are our most secret thoughts always so deep that only God could understand them? Are our most secret thoughts so much more interesting than the thoughts that we communicate? Are our hidden sins so much worse than the sins that we commit against, and with, other people, out in the open, for everybody to see? (Is injustice not worse than solitary vice?)

Moreover, are there not many people who, for one reason or another, have little skill in keeping secrets or practising mental reserve? Have there not been people, indeed whole communities, who, although just as aware of living under judgement as we are, never imagined that secret thoughts were so special? There need be nothing at all going on in your mind, and still you may not pray like a parrot.

CARTESIAN PSYCHOLOGY IN MORAL THEOLOGY

The idea that secret thoughts and hidden sins are uniquely important trades on the myth that mind and will are essentially private and incorporeal. Mentalist individualism in epistemology breeds what has been called radical volitionism as regards human action.[4] When I raise my arm, to stop the traffic, to strike the other cheek, or whatever, it is as if I first make the inward decision to do so and then translate it into my arm's going up. It is very tempting to say that my will caused the arm to go up by triggering a chain of mental events which eventually issue in the observable action.

[4] O'Shaughnessy, *The Will*, vol. 1, passim.

This view of how the will comes into what I do is beautifully captured by Wittgenstein's favourite author, William James, who was, however, doubtful about it: 'Is the bare idea of a movement's sensible effects its sufficient mental cue, or must there be an additional mental antecedent, in the shape of a fiat, decision, consent, volitional mandate, or other synonymous phenomenon of consciousness before the movement can follow'.[5] For an action to be *willed*, and so possibly culpable, seems to require some preceding or accompanying private mental consent to it. Since people's actions are to be judged, not by what they *did*, but by what they *intended*, moral judgement is immediately confronted, in the mentalist–individualist tradition, with supposed difficulties about ever knowing what other people's intentions really are. I alone can say what I intended when I carried out a morally dubious action, because I alone have access to knowledge of how much internal consent I gave to it.

G. E. M. Anscombe argued, in 1958, that 'it is not profitable for us at present to do moral philosophy; that should be laid aside at any rate until we have an adequate philosophy of psychology, in which we are conspicuously lacking'.[6] Since then, many philosophers, among whom she has played an important part,[7] have followed Wittgenstein's advice: 'Sometimes an expression has to be withdrawn from language and sent for cleaning – then it can be put back into circulation' (*CV*, p. 39). The concept of a person, and so of mind and will, intention, responsibility, action etc., badly needed to be cleaned of mentalist–individualist presuppositions before moral argument could be worth while.

It may well be wondered whether moral theology has escaped from the spell of an illusory picture of the self. To see the lack of progress, consider only Anscombe's own example, in an essay written in 1961. She has sketched the so-called principle of double effect: the intended and the merely foreseeable effects of a voluntary action are often distinguishable, which means that we are not always answerable for a predictable consequence of some action that we perform. For example: a pregnant woman is diagnosed as having cancer of the uterus; it would be justified, according to this distinction, to go ahead with the hysterectomy despite the certainty of killing the unborn infant. But the problems surrounding the proper use of this principle need not detain us here: Anscombe, in this paper, is interested in the *im*proper application of the principle, and I am interested in how she links this with the mentalist–individualist picture of the self:

[5] *Principles of Psychology*, vol. II, p. xxvi.
[6] *Ethics, Religion and Politics*, p. 26.
[7] Her *Intention* is a classic.

From the seventeenth century till now what may be called Cartesian psychology has dominated the thought of philosophers and theologians. According to this psychology, an intention was an interior act of mind which could be produced at will. Now if intention is all-important – as it is – in determining the goodness or badness of an action, then, on this theory of what intention is, a marvellous way offered itself of making any action lawful. You only had to 'direct your attention' in a suitable way. In practice, this means making a little speech to yourself: 'What I mean to be doing is . . .'[8]

She refers to the papal censure of certain theories of the Laxist casuists (in 1679); but an interesting book might be written on the philosophical implications of the bedevilment of Catholic moral theology by Cartesian pictures of the inner life.[9] No matter what a man does, he is always able to direct his interior intention in some private way: the connection between action and intention is made to seem purely contingent.

Thus the way is cleared, Anscombe goes on to say, for suppressing doubts about obliteration bombing of cities:

The devout Catholic bomber secures by a 'direction of intention' that any shedding of innocent blood that occurs is 'accidental'. I know a Catholic boy who was puzzled at being told by his schoolmaster that it was an *accident* that the people of Hiroshima and Nagasaki were there to be killed; in fact, however absurd it seems, such thoughts are common among priests who know that they are forbidden by the divine law to justify the direct killing of the innocent.

It is as if we were in a position to keep our inward intentions above the mire of this unhappy world even when the actions that we perform seem downright wicked to those who only see the outside. A doctrine like this obviously helps to generate the idea that we could have weapons of mass destruction trained on innocent people while having the private intention never to fire them.

I am not saying that nuclear deterrence theory can only be morally justified by relying on Cartesian psychology, nor that Wittgensteinian considerations about action easily settle that question. I am only noting

---

[8] *Ethics, Religion and Politics*, pp. 58–9.
[9] Caricatured in Pascal's *Lettres provinciales* (1657), Laxism is expounded as a system in every moral theology textbook, but the underlying conception of the self has not been properly studied. Nor is there a modern study of the '*princeps laxistarum*', Juan Caramuel von Lobkowitz (1606–82), monk, bishop, military engineer and prolific author.

one important area of deep moral conflict where we first need to be sure that our philosophy of the self has been to the cleaners.

THE STATUS OF EMBRYOS

In the modern philosophical tradition the concept of *person* is tied up with notions of self-consciousness, rationality, autonomy etc. Important though these are, we have to remember the obvious fact that we are first of all animals of a certain kind. Long before we are knowing and willing selves, capable of reasoning and self-reflexiveness, and liable for moral reproach or admiration, we are living creatures in multiple response to our natural habitat. Even pre-Cartesian theologians, who spoke of the rational animal rather than the *res cogitans*, moved pretty briskly from our animality to the supposedly more theologically rewarding topic of our rationality. In more recent times, great emphasis on our freedom to make our own history has tended to deepen theological indifference to the fact that our rationality, however historically developed and culturally specific, is vitally and physically sustained by our natural surroundings: 'Epistemology takes second place to vitality'.[10]

It has recently been argued, however, explicitly in Wittgenstein's wake, that the concept of a person in terms of self-reflexiveness, autonomy etc. may prejudice discussion in another important area of moral conflict today: namely, the ethics of abortion and embryo experimentation.[11] The high theology according to which we are made to God's image by being endowed with understanding and self-direction, leaves us, when it has passed through the modern philosophy of the mental ego, somewhat at a loss to explain what is wrong with killing mere embryos. Whether a human embryo, or a dolphin, has the status of being a person comes to seem a question that we decide on the evidence.

Peter Singer, for example, who believes that many animals have a better right to life than human embryos, relies on inference from his own case to the existence of other people's minds or feelings: 'Neither in embryos nor in adults do we observe consciousness – we infer it from behaviour, or from the degree of the development of the nervous system'.[12] In effect, he endorses Mill's argument from analogy that other organisms are not automata: 'We can never directly experience the pain

[10] O'Shaughnessy, *The Will*, vol. 1, Introduction.
[11] Aidan O'Neill, 'After Warnock: the ethics of embryo experimentation'.
[12] Peter Singer and Deane Wells, *The Reproduction Revolution*, p. 97.

of another being, whether that being is human or not. When I see my daughter fall and scrape her knees . . . I accept that my daughter feels something like what I feel when I scrape my knee'.[13] Thus, *some* arguments in favour of experiments on human embryos are interwoven with notions of what a person is that, after Wittgenstein, are surely extremely implausible.

But it will not do, either, to reply, in the same terms, that human embryos *are*, potentially, these rational and autonomous creatures whose life we are obliged to respect. That very easily remains at the level of measuring capacities and abilities that the embryo now has (an empirical question), in terms of a future as a person (defined as an entity endowed with intellect and will).

If, on the other hand, Wittgensteinian considerations about the primitive reactions which are the *Lebensformen* that constitute the natural *a priori* for the existence of a human being are given due weight, then a very different context for the debate seems to appear. The embryo already exists in the closest relationship of physical dependence on an adult member of our species. Our being human has to be redescribed as our being animals of a certain kind, sharing from the beginning certain possibilities of interaction and response at the very physical level of vital functions. Paradoxically enough, the more animal we remember our-selves to be, the weightier the theological objections to abortion and embryo experimentation might become.

I should emphasize that Aidan O'Neill's argument needs much more explanation than it has been given here; I am concerned only to identify a question in moral theology where abandoning the metaphysical concep-tion of the self, far from weakening traditional abhorrence of abortion, might actually deepen it.[14]

THE SURVIVING EGO

People often wonder what happens to us when we die. Indeed, the appeal of religion for many people seems to lie mainly in its offering the hope of personal survival. True, the mainstream churches have difficulty in explaining how life after death is to be envisaged. In 1979, for example, members of the Roman Catholic communion were officially reminded of

---

[13] Singer, *Practical Ethics*, p. 60.
[14] Moral theology after Wittgenstein may be found also in Rodger Beehler, *Moral Life*, and Carol McMillan, *Women, Reason and Nature*.

178 *Questions in the philosophy of theology*

its commitment to 'the continuation and subsistence, after death, of the spiritual element, endowed with consciousness and will, in such a way that, although lacking the complement of its own body for a time, the "human I" itself subsists'.[15]

What is 'the human I' – this *'humanum ego'* which the text itself places in inverted commas? Talk of the 'I' is quite common in modern Roman Catholic theology: for example, the 'I' is said to be 'the centre of human (self) consciousness'; 'as the subject of intentional willing and thinking it can be distinguished conceptually from the soul, in the sense that the soul also includes states of feeling'.[16] (When the soul loses its feeling you are left with your 'I'.)

Interestingly, the same author goes on to celebrate our Cartesian inheritance: 'With Descartes, the "I" conceived itself independently of the divine "Thou" as autonomous act-centre of consciousness, excluding the external world together with its own body'. (After Wittgenstein, one is inclined to say: 'See how high the seas of language run here!') Indeed, Vetter continues, 'with the Cartesian principle *cogito ergo sum* we have a dichotomy between inside and outside that is decisive for the whole of modern times'. Here, as recently as 1960, and in the principal encyclopedia of theology in the German-speaking world, we have the Cartesian self regarded as one of the boons of modern times.

The 'human I' of the Roman pronouncement looks very like the mirror image of the 'I' in the German encyclopedia, not to say his alter ego, and both would be hard to distinguish from the hero of the Cartesian *Meditations*.

What Christians mean when they recite the ancient creeds, proclaiming that they 'look for the resurrection of the dead, and the life of the world to come' is a large and important question: I am saying merely that, after Wittgenstein, it is even more repugnant to think of a world peopled with mental egos.

It is not a new problem. Thomas Aquinas, after all, conceded that, prescinding from faith in the biblical promise that the dead shall be raised, the thesis of the immortality of the soul is very hard to make intelligible. 'The soul, being part of a man's body, is not the whole man': the soul's being the *form* of the man's body, as he would say, the living human being is more than a soul. Indeed, he says: 'My soul is not I' (*'anima mea non est ego'*). Thus, he is led to say: 'Even if my soul were to find salvation in some other world, neither I nor any man would so so'.[17]

---

[15] Congregation for the Doctrine of the Faith, 'De quibusdam quaestionibus'.
[16] A. Vetter, *Ich*, *Lexikon für Theologie und Kirche*.
[17] *I ad Corinthios*, 924.

On the face of it, then, Aquinas' *ego*, which is the human being whole and alive, is something other than the Roman pronouncement's *humanum ego*, or the German encyclopedia's *Ich*.

Aquinas could not bring himself to say that bodiless souls should be regarded as human beings. He was clear that we are animals, of a particular kind. He often says that, when human thought or choice occurs, it is the man thinking or willing, not his intellect or will. He nevertheless feels bound by the traditional Catholic doctrine that there is a space of time (aeons perhaps) between the individual man's death and the general resurrection of the dead. Against the grain of his philosophy, and surely aware that it is so, he hypothesizes non-human mental goings-on to occupy the minds of the dead while they wait for resurrection.[18] In the end, he finds himself defending the thesis that bodiless souls, brainless minds as we might say, manage to think in ways that, when alive, they never thought possible. Our minds finally become angelic when we are dead. No wonder that the epistemological predicament of the dead seemed to him to be *contra naturam*.[19]

It seems to impose itself on the Christian imagination that the soul of a dead man has to be pictured as a quasi-angelic being, even when, as in Aquinas, the philosophical intention is to maintain the uniqueness and integrity of the whole human being.

In a discussion of the concept of thinking Wittgenstein made the following remark:

> The soul is said to *leave* the body. Then, in order to exclude any similarity to the body, any sort of idea that some gaseous thing is meant, the soul is said to be incorporeal, non-spatial; but with that word 'leave' one has already said it all. Show me how you use the word 'spiritual [*seelisch*]' and I shall see whether the soul is 'incorporeal', and what you understand by 'spirit [*Geist*]'. (Z 127)

That is to say: listen to the kind of thing that people say, and have said for many generations, in a variety of contexts; and if it turns out that the immateriality of the soul is sometimes pictured as a gaslike substance, rather like ectoplasm, that survives the death of the body, it should not be very hard to find a dozen other uses of the word 'soul' that include no such picture.[20]

The meaning of a picture is, after all, in its *use*:

[18] *Summa Theologiae*, 1, 89.
[19] *Summa contra Gentiles*, 4, 79.
[20] Dilman, *Studies in Language and Reason*, passim.

Religion teaches that the soul can exist when the body has disintegrated. Now do I understand this teaching? – Of course I understand it – I can imagine plenty of things in connection with it. And haven't pictures of these things been painted? And why should such a picture be only an imperfect rendering of the spoken doctrine [*des ausgesprochenen Gedankens*]? Why should it not do the *same* service as the words [*die gesprochene Lehre*]? And it is the service which is the point. (*PI*, p. 178)

The *best* picture of the human soul, he goes on to say almost at once, is the human body, or, as a variant runs: 'The human being [*der Mensch*] is the best picture of the human soul' (*RRP* I, 281). In biblical stories as well as in many works of art we have many pictures of the life of the saints in heaven. Titian's 'Flaying of Marsyas' is about the death and resurrection of the soul. It is not obvious that this gallery of pictures has much truck with the declared doctrine of the 'separated soul'. And why should a picture of people in heaven, banqueting or dancing, be a less than perfect rendering of the doctrine?

In any case, making one of his key points, it is what we do with our pictures, how we use our signs as Wittgenstein says, that matters. We need not be held captive by *one* picture; we are free to turn to many other objects of comparison. In fact, if we remember the poetry and art that we have in the tradition, a heaven of bodiless souls, awaiting resurrection, has never been the only picture.[21]

SCAPEGOAT CHRISTOLOGY

The execution of Jesus of Nazareth, understandably, remains the focus of a good deal of Christian theorizing. Some recent accounts at least, while suitably high-toned, are unsatisfyingly jejune. Karl Rahner, for example, arguing that understanding the crucifixion in terms of expiatory sacrifice and such like is secondary and optional, comes out with the resounding but somewhat hollow declaration that 'we are saved because this man who is one of us has been saved by God, and God has thereby made his salvific will present in the world historically, really and irrevocably'.[22] Edward Schillebeeckx also insists that atonement need have nothing to do with propitiation, substitution, satisfaction, sacrifice and so on.[23] But if Wittgenstein's comments on *The Golden Bough* have any hold on our imagination, we may surely be allowed to consider the stories of the

[21] On Christ's resurrection see Wittgenstein's remarks: *CV*, p. 33.
[22] *Foundations of Christian Faith*, p. 284.
[23] *Jesus*, pp. 274–94, 318.

execution of Jesus in the light of Frazer's description of the sacrifice of the King of the Wood at Nemi.

What Wittgenstein argues, after all, is that the interest in what Frazer describes is not an interest in something totally remote from our own lives. On the contrary: our response to it reveals something deep and sinister in our own ways of thinking and behaving: something that, if it unites us with those who ritually slew the priest-king, surely also offers the possibility of uniting us with the adversaries of the Jewish wandering prophet.

But, if Frazer used the dispassionate objectivity of the modern scholar to conceal from himself his kinship with his savages, Christian theorists have, almost from the beginning, passed so rapidly to a level of high speculation that they leave the history of Jesus' last days far behind, and, much more importantly, they lose touch with the feelings of anger and desire in themselves that unite them with his tormentors. Preachers then come on with urgings that 'we are all sinners', etc., but this 'sin' turns out to lie, rather vacuously, in 'pride' and the like. Following Wittgenstein on Frazer, however, one might be able to root the doctrine of the atonement in brute facts about the internal dynamics of any human community.

The most interesting contribution to current discussion of the theological significance of the death of Jesus rehabilitates the language of sacrifice by drawing on considerations from social anthropology. Raymund Schwager has embarked on a series of re-readings of the literature from the Scriptures to the Middle Ages,[24] but the key idea comes from René Girard.[25]

In wide-ranging investigations of classical and modern literature, from Greek tragedy to Proust, Girard has gradually reached the conviction that the stability of any society is maintained by the periodic expulsion of an often quite arbitrarily chosen victim. Every group suffers from internal tensions; one member of the group becomes the focus of everyone else's frustration. He becomes the alien who threatens the community, but, since expelling him restores peace and harmony, apparently, for a time, he also appears as a saviour. Anger and desire are thus equally lodged in this 'scapegoat'.

For Girard, then, we are not the rational and autonomous selves of Cartesian psychology but the irascible and concupiscent animals who make fleeting appearances in the jungle of traditional moral theology. To survive, he argues, every tribe needs a supply of scapegoats. The

[24] Schwager, *Sündenbock*; see Galvin, 'Jesus as Scapegoat?'.
[25] *Violence and the Sacred, Des Choses Cachées, Le Bouc Emissaire*.

importance of religion, he goes on to say, lies in its being, at bottom, a way of securing the survival of society by (on the whole) purely ritual sacrifices which absorb the essential social-psychological need for victimizations. Knowledge of the function of the scapegoating mechanism necessarily remains hidden, for its efficacy depends on ignorance of its true nature on the part of all who benefit.

Coming very late in the day to the Judeo-Christian sacred texts, which he had supposed too boring to open, Girard has been amazed to find a history of the revelation of how communities scapegoat individuals or subgroups in order to maintain stability. When the scapegoating mechanism is *revealed*, the possibility arises of a way of life *without* victimizations. Jesus was scapegoated, willingly, to preserve the community, but in the aftermath of his execution the cycle was apparently broken: the 'sin' of his tormentors did not fall in turn upon them. His execution effected something that, granted the place of scapegoating in any human group, could not have been achieved in any other way. If we go on saying '*We* have no sin', Girard says, we shall be resisting the terrible truth about ourselves that we need scapegoats to keep ourselves at peace. It is no surprise, however, that people do not take to Christianity: the Christian tradition has frequently succumbed to bouts of anti-semitism, for example, not to mention many internal victimizations – but that only confirms Girard's thesis.

Raymund Schwager, with considerably greater knowledge of Christian literature and more sophisticated exegetical skills, is trying to work out a theory of the significance of Jesus' death which takes account of Girard's thesis. While I am not saying that it is entirely new, or that I cannot see difficulties about it, a theology of the atonement with links to the natural history of human beings seems a promising prospect. If it is only when we can say that we are sinners that we can say anything interesting about the death of Jesus we need not be surprised; but the problem is to get substantial anthropological content into our understanding of ourselves as 'sinners'. 'Christianity is not a doctrine', Wittgenstein wrote: 'not, I mean, a theory about what has happened and will happen to the human soul, but a description of something that actually takes place in human life. For "consciousness of sin" is a real event . . . ' (*CV*, p. 28).

SAVAGE RELIGION

The idea that man is a ceremonious, as well as a rational, animal surely has a great deal in it. Indeed, the exile in the flesh in the metaphysical way of thinking may well have been qualified, at least until the rise of mentalist–individualist epistemologies and the atomistic social order of capitalism, by an unnoticed sense of human life as necessarily communal and enjoyably pervaded by ceremonial. Ritual actions, which have no *purpose*, belong to the forms of our culture (cf. *RFM* I, 153). 'I know why churches are true', a four-year-old is reported to have said, 'it's because the people in them like singing and walk about in patterns'.[26]

That shows far more insight than rationalistic explanations in terms of the *Urdummheit* of people who think that if they dance it will rain, or if they light a candle at a shrine they will pass the driving test. Religious behaviour, like language, is not the product of ratiocination. Religion is not the sort of thing that people might have thought up; as David Martin shows, it is rooted in social processes.[27]

It is because people exult and lament, sing for joy, bewail their sins and so on, that they are able, eventually, to have thoughts about God. Worship is not the result but the precondition of believing in God. Theological concepts, like all concepts, are rooted in certain habitual ways of acting, responding, relating, to our natural-historical setting. The very idea of God depends on such brute facts as that, in certain circumstances, people cannot help shuddering with awe or shame, and so on. It does not follow that the idea of God has a place in the conversation simply because we enjoy singing hymns: but if we cannot imagine what it is to observe rites, enjoy singing hymns and the like, the nature of religion is bound to remain opaque.

In recent years, often in connection with Wittgenstein's remarks about Frazer, philosophers have written a good deal about ritual with which students of theology should be familiar.[28] The fundamental importance of primitive reactions in concept-formation, in religion as everywhere else, has also been brought to the fore.[29] We have been reminded of that marvellous remark by the Oxford anthropologist, R. R. Marett: 'My own view is that savage religion is something not so much thought out as danced out'.[30] He was opposing the idea that rites must be based on hypotheses about the world which, as *we* know, have turned out to be

[26] A sociologist of religion's son, admittedly: Martin, *Tracts against the Times*, p. 179.
[27] Martin, *The Breaking of the Image*.
[28] Karl Britton, 'Symbolic actions and objects'; Richard Wollheim, *The Sheep and the Ceremony*; Gareth Matthews, 'Ritual and the religious feelings'; Anthony Holiday, 'Wittgenstein's silence'.
[29] D. Z. Phillips, *Primitive Reactions and the Reactions of Primitives*.
[30] *The Threshold of Religion*, p. xxxi, cited by Phillips.

mistaken. As befitted an educated European, before 1914, he supposed that *some* sort of religion was, if not exactly 'thought out', at any rate substantially a matter of reason: the deism in his college chapel. But do we not have to say that *all* religion, at least if it has any hold on people's lives and imaginations, is 'danced out'? At any rate, when people no longer praise God there will be no need for theology.[31]

FINITUDE AS FLAW

It would be easy to prolong this list of topics in theology that should look rather different in the light of reading Wittgenstein, but let me offer only one more, which will bring us back, in conclusion, to the radical critique of the metaphysically structured self that I have tried to exhibit as *a* (if not *the*) central concern of his later writings.

Edward Schillebeeckx has argued that believing in God, far from being the result of accepting an explanation of the world's existence, is rather a repudiation of metaphysical dualism.[32] Given the distress anyone must feel at the suffering, evil and injustice in the world, it is natural to think that God cannot have willed the world to be as it is. Our condition cannot be normal but must be the result of some defect in the system. Salvation, the restoration of wholeness, must lie either in some lost paradise or in some new heaven and new earth to be imposed from above upon the ruins of this world. Perhaps God is locked in mortal conflict with the powers of darkness. Perhaps God has withdrawn from this vile scene, or is so great and exalted that he does not foul himself by contact with it. In any case, it seems that human well-being resides in our being freed from our mortal humanity and our creatureliness. Yet, so Schillebeeckx argues, this is precisely the myth that the story of Adam and Eve in the garden is directed against: human beings refuse to accept their finitude. They crave to be immortal, omniscient, omnipotent:

> The basic mistake of many conceptions about creation lies in the fact that finitude is felt to be a flaw, a hurt which as such should not really have been one of the features of this world . . . finitude is thought to be improper, an ailment, even sinfulness or apostasy, a flaw in the existence of mankind and the world. There is a feeling that . . . mortality, failure, mistakes and ignorance should not be part of the normal condition of our humanity . . .[33]

[31] On praising God see D. W. Hardy and D. F. Ford, *Jubilate*: *Theology in Praise*.
[32] *God among Us*, pp. 91–102.
[33] Ibid, p. 92.

The Genesis story is in effect a protest against this conception of the self which involves us in refusing to be subject to the conditions of humanity. 'If God is creator, then he creates that which is not-divine, that which is completely other than himself, in other words finite things'.[34] But the inclination, encouraged by the metaphysical tradition, is to say that creatures like us, as images of God, are not naturally bound to time and space, history and world – against which Schillebeeckx comments: 'To want to transcend finitude is megalomania or arrogance which alienates people from themselves, from the world and from nature'.[35]

The doctrine of creation *ex nihilo* was historically at the centre of the Church's polemic against Gnosticism.[36] For Schillebeeckx, the point of Christian belief in the world's being created from nothing is that it still rules out dualistic metaphysics. When we first reflect on the human condition – '*Was* I anywhere, or anyone?' – it remains tempting to succumb to the thought that the self *is* out of place in the world, and then bodiless and language-free experience, epistemological solitude, and so on, at once become unavoidable and even desirable possibilities. Thus we return to the ancient picture of human life as essentially exile from our true nature.

THE NEW CARTESIANISM

That Gnostic dualism should retain its grip, however covertly and residually, on Christian spirituality and discourse, may seem a far-fetched claim, at this late date. But, well away from explicitly religious concerns, it continues to hold people in thrall. The 'New Cartesianism', as it has been called,[37] is to be found rather in current debates about the prospects for 'Cognitive Science'.[38]

Roughly: the internal states of information-processing machines have become the paradigm for the psychological states of creatures of our kind. If our mental processes once seemed a deficient form of angelic intuition, they have now become an inefficient kind of mechanical

---

[34] Ibid.
[35] Ibid, p. 93.
[36] E.g. in Irenaeus.
[37] John McDowell's phrase, *The Times Literary Supplement*, 16 July 1982, p. 774.
[38] Alan Turing (1912–54), pioneer of computer theory, whose 'Machines' are mentioned in *RPP* I, 1096, attended Wittgenstein's lectures in 1939, see *WLFM*, when they disagreed fairly radically. For the state of the debate, see Geoff Simons, *Are Computers Alive?*; H. L. Dreyfus, *What Computers Can't Do*; A. Sloman, *The Computer Revolution in Philosophy*.

calculation. The ghost in the machine has given way to the clockwork in the animal. In Marvin Minsky's charming phrase, people are 'meat machines'. You do not have to read far into the writings of some of the new theorists of consciousness to meet strong feelings of dislike for the soft pulpable stuff that human brains are. You feel that some of these thinkers would much prefer bodiless minds: computers that do not run on blood.

Theologians should be the last to be surprised at the recurrence of Gnostic antipathy to the body. Cognitive science takes 'artificial' intelligence as the model for the human kind, but it might have been as well to stick with angels. Right in the middle of a thriving area of research in contemporary philosophy, that is to say, the age-old dream is repeating itself: thinking is something better done independently of bodiliness, in some clear and pure zone, beyond time and space, into which our muzzy heads rarely rise. The desire to think away our incarnate nature remains as seductive as ever in our culture. That shows the vitality of our metaphysical inheritance.

Inside philosophy itself, then, we may trace a certain reluctance to take our bodiliness seriously. Theologians, reflecting on their own metaphysical inclinations, have a place in the general conversation: paradoxically, but appropriately, it would be in helping to lay bare that persistent religious understanding of human existence from which Christian theologians should surely want to release us – that 'aspiration to rise above the merely human, to step outside the prison of the peculiarly human emotions, and to be free of the cares and the demands they make on us'.[39]

SKIN DEEP

Theologians (I hope I have shown) have great scope for philosophical work inside the practice of theology. More than this, they are in an advantageous position to take part in excavating the foundations of a religious myth about the self that continues to imprison much modern philosophy. If I am right about this, theologians have not only a great deal to learn from reading Wittgenstein, but they are well qualified to understand him.

As von Wright says, the *Tractatus* fits into a tradition in European philosophy, running from Russell and Frege back to Leibniz and beyond,

---

[39] Taylor, *Philosophical Papers*, vol. 1, p. 112.

while Wittgenstein's later writings have 'a spirit . . . unlike anything I know in Western thought and in many ways opposed to aims and methods in traditional philosophy'.[40] What he is suggesting, I think, is that, in Wittgenstein's later work, there is a radical questioning of the whole way of thinking about the self, and hence of others, of the world and of the divine, which has captivated Western Christian culture for a long time.

Christian theology has, of course, always harboured suspicions of the metaphysical regime of thinking under which it has been conducted almost from the outset. The history of theology might even be written in terms of periodic struggles with the metaphysical inheritance. Augustine practically invented Western theology in the course of his polemics against a residually Gnostic neo-Platonism, which inevitably scarred his alternative. Inheriting a Platonizing Augustinianism, Thomas Aquinas strove to revolutionize it in the light of the rediscovered works of Aristotle. Martin Luther, with his theology of the Cross, sought to end the metaphysical regime altogether. In our own day, many theologians suppose that they are free of metaphysical prejudices.

When the existence of metaphysical commitments is ignored or denied, their grip only tightens. In all traditions, Christian theologians are to be found who work with a concept of the self that needs to go to the cleaners. The awkward questions that philosophy puts to theology *inside* the discipline, when anyone is listening, range far more widely than I have registered here; but theological talk about persons, which is obviously indispensable, is certainly pervaded with metaphysically structured assumptions. My thesis is that the only way to resist, or even recognize, the sway of the metaphysical way of thinking is to learn to watch our language about ourselves. The difficulty is to listen to the things that we say about ourselves in such a way that our metaphysical inclinations are laid bare. There must be other methods besides Wittgenstein's; but, since he is the last great philosopher in our tradition who cared passionately about the Christian religion, it would be perverse of theologians to avoid his studies of what we may properly say.

Stanley Cavell writes: 'He wishes an acknowledgement of human limitation which does not leave us chafed by our own skin'.[41] The therapy is required to free us from the inclination to compare ourselves, unfavourably of course, with bodiless beings, whether angels or machines. The bodiliness that seems to keep us apart is exactly what

[40] Malcolm, *Memoir*, 1984, p. 14 footnote.
[41] *Must We Mean What We Say?*, p. 61.

makes our being together possible in the first place. According to Cavell's reading (I have said how much I owe to it), Wittgenstein's later writings are key texts in subverting the entire metaphysical tradition which is constituted by rancour against the physical and historical conditions of human life.

In this respect, it would be interesting to know how deeply read in Nietzsche's work Wittgenstein was. In the 1886 preface to *Die fröhliche Wissenschaft* Nietzsche wrote: 'I have often asked myself whether, taking a larger view, philosophy has not been merely an interpretation of the body and a *misunderstanding of the body*'.[42] With his emphasis on seeing the other's soul in his face, and on staying with the phenomena rather than assuming that we always have to penetrate to something lying behind them, Wittgenstein might have been attracted by Nietzsche's celebration of (what he took to be) the pre-Platonic Greek way of thinking:

> Oh, those Greeks! They knew how to *live*. What is required for that is to stop courageously at the surface, the fold, the skin, to adore appearance, to believe in forms, tones, words, in the whole Olympus of appearance. Those Greeks were superficial – out of profundity![43]

The depth of the world is on the surface, so to speak: but also, what is most secret about the self is public knowledge. According to the modern philosophy of the self, we have to 'infer' what other people's experiences are, but have perfect vision of our own. Scepticism about knowing other people's minds goes with complacency about knowledge of our own. But, as Cavell notes, 'those capable of the deepest personal confession' – and he heads the list with the name of Augustine – 'were most convinced they were speaking from the most hidden knowledge of others'.[44] Wittgenstein's confidence that he is speaking for us all, when he notes what we are naturally inclined to say, rests on his being free enough to own to that rancour against *life* that keeps us, in our philosophical moments, from coming into our own.

THINKING MORTAL

There cannot be much doubt that, from his return to philosophical work

[42] *The Gay Science*, p. 35.
[43] Ibid, p. 38.
[44] *Claim of Reason*, p. 109.

in 1929, Wittgenstein sought to retrieve a full sense of the bodiliness of human life – consider two remarks made in 1931:

> It is humiliating to have to appear like an empty tube which is simply inflated by a mind. (CV, p.11)

Plainly he had been reading, or remembering, Pascal's remark: 'Man is only a reed, the weakest in nature, but he is a thinking reed'.[45] This *roseau pensant* is pretty much Descartes' *res cogitans*: either way, it is a picture of the living man which makes Wittgenstein ashamed.

The remark that immediately precedes that quoted above runs as follows:

> The delightful way the various parts of a human body differ in temperature. (CV, p. 11)

That is *all*. It does not sound to me like the conclusion of a man who has been using a thermometer on his own or anyone else's body. It is not the kind of remark that you find in much metaphysical literature.

To be human, however, does not come easy: Aristotle's advice sounds much more attractive:

> We should not heed those who counsel us that, being men, we should think human, and being mortals, we should think mortal. But we ought, so far as in us lies, to make ourselves immortal, straining every nerve to live in accordance with the highest thing in us.[46]

Aristotle, here quite indistinguishable from Plato, is explicitly refusing to listen to the poets: 'Cleverness is not wisdom', Euripides says: 'And not to think mortal thoughts is to see few days'; while Sophocles, even more clearly, writes: 'Being mortal, I think mortal thoughts: I am not senseless'.[47]

The metaphysical way of thinking, which it would be useless to regret, originated in this refusal to keep within the bounds of the human condition which the poets recognized. At an early stage, a craving for a knowledge that no human being could attain drove Plato, with his theory that learning is always remembering, to speculate that every human soul existed long before birth, had gone through many previous incarnations

---

[45] *Pensées*, p. 95.
[46] *Nicomachean Ethics* 1177b 31–34.
[47] *Bacchae*, 395–7; *Trachiniae*, 473.

and has thus acquired an omniscience which the fleshly condition keeps ineffably hidden.[48] Once installed, this picture of the self has enthralled the Western imagination ever since. In our own day, if I am right, Wittgenstein set out to reveal the myth-eaten power of the idol by which, in our self-conscious moments, we are still easily captivated. It is not a matter simply of discovering where the myth started, but of detecting its continuing vitality. Even if I am wrong, however, the reader will have been immersed in an anthology of Wittgenstein's texts, many of which will surely stay in the memory, whatever is to happen, after Wittgenstein, to the practice of Christian theology.

[48] Gregory Vlastos, in his Gifford Lectures at St Andrews in 1981, devoted to the philosophy of Socrates, has clearly reopened the whole question of the origins of the metaphysical way of thinking: see 'Socrates' disavowal of knowledge', esp. pp. 28–9, from which I have taken the last three quotations, and 'The Socratic Elenchus', esp. pp. 55–6.

Bibliography

Aldrich, Virgil C., 'On what it is like to be a man', *Inquiry*, 16 (1973), pp. 355–66.

Alexander, Samuel, 'The basis of realism', *Proceedings of the British Academy*, 1913–1914, pp. 279–314.

Anscombe, G. E. M., *Ethics, Religion and Politics*, Blackwell, Oxford, 1981.

Anscombe, G. E. M., *Intention*, Blackwell, Oxford, 1957.

Anscombe, G. E. M., *An Introduction to Wittgenstein's Tractatus*, Hutchinson, London, 1959.

Anscombe, G. E. M., *Metaphysics and the Philosophy of Mind*, Blackwell, Oxford, 1981.

Anscombe, G. E. M., 'Misinformation: what Wittgenstein really said', *The Tablet*, 17 April 1954, p. 373.

Ayer, A. J., *The Central Questions of Philosophy*, Weidenfeld & Nicholson, London, 1973.

Ayer, A. J., *The Foundations of Empirical Knowledge*, Macmillan, London, 1940.

Baldwin, Thomas, 'Moore's rejection of idealism', in *Philosophy in History*, eds R. Rorty, J. B. Schneewind, Q. Skinner, Cambridge University Press, Cambridge, 1984.

Barth, Karl, *Church Dogmatics*, vol. I, part 1, T. & T. Clark, Edinburgh, 1936.

Barth, Karl, *Church Dogmatics*, vol. III, part 1, T. & T. Clark, Edinburgh, 1958.

Barth, Karl, *Church Dogmatics*, vol. III, part 2, T. & T. Clark, Edinburgh, 1960.

Bearsley, Patrick, 'Augustine and Wittgenstein on language', *Philosophy*, 58 (1983), pp. 229–36.

Beehler, Rodger, *Moral Life*, Blackwell, Oxford, 1978.

Bell, Richard H., 'Understanding the fire-festivals: Wittgenstein and theories in religion', *Religious Studies*, 14 (1978), pp. 113–24.

Bernstein, Richard J., *Beyond Objectivism and Relativism: Science, Hermeneutics, and Praxis*, Blackwell, Oxford, 1983.

Bolton, Derek, *An Approach to Wittgenstein's Philosophy*, Macmillan, London, 1979.

Bolton, Derek, 'Life-form and idealism', in *Idealism Past and Present*, ed. G. Vesey, Royal Institute of Philosophy Lecture Series 13, Cambridge University Press, Cambridge, pp. 269–84.

Britton, Karl, 'Symbolic actions and objects', *Philosophy*, 54 (1979), pp. 281–91.

Bukharin N. I., 'Theory and practice from the standpoint of dialectical materialism', in *Science at the Cross Roads*, Papers presented to the International Congress of the History of Science and Technology by the Delegates of the USSR, Kniga, London, 1931, pp. 1–23.

Burnyeat, M. F., 'Idealism and Greek philosophy: what Descartes saw and Berkeley missed', in *Idealism Past and Present*, ed. G. Vesey, Royal Institute of Philosophy Lecture Series 13, Cambridge University Press, Cambridge, 1982, pp. 19–50.

Cameron, J. M., 'Autobiography and philosophical perplexity', in *Pleasure, Preference and Value*, ed. Eva Schaper, Cambridge University Press, Cambridge, 1983, pp. 158–70.

Cavell, Stanley, *Must We Mean We Say? A Book of Essays*, Scribner's, New York, 1969.

Cavell, Stanley, *The Claim of Reason: Wittgenstein, Skepticism, Morality and Tragedy*, Clarendon Press, Oxford, 1979.

Cavell, Stanley, *Themes out of School: Effects and Causes*, North Point Press, San Francisco, 1984.

Cherry, Christopher, 'Meaning and the idol of origins', *The Philosophical Quarterly*, 35 (1985), pp. 58–69.

Chirico, Peter, *Infallibility: The Crossroads of Doctrine*, Sheed and Ward, London, 1977.

Cioffi, Frank, 'Wittgenstein and the fire-festivals', in *Perspectives on the Philosophy of Wittgenstein*, ed. Irving Block, Blackwell, Oxford, 1981, pp.212–37.

Congregation for the Doctrine of the Faith, 'Epistula de quibusdam quaestionibus ad Eschatologiam spectantibus', *Acta Apostolicae Sedis*, LXXI (1979), pp. 939–43.

Cook, John W., 'Human beings', in *Studies in the Philosophy of Wittgenstein*, ed. Peter Winch, Routledge & Kegan Paul, London, 1969, pp. 117–51.

Cupitt, Don, *The Sea of Faith*, BBC Publications, London, 1984.

Cupitt, Don, *Taking Leave of God*, SCM Press, London, 1980.

Davidson, Donald, *Inquiries into Truth and Interpretation*, Clarendon Press, Oxford, 1984.

Davie, Ian, *A Theology of Speech: An Essay in Philosophical Theology*, Sheed and Ward, London, 1973.

Descartes, R., *The Philosophical Writings*, vol. I, trans. J. Cottingham, R. Stoothoff and D. Murdoch, Cambridge University Press, Cambridge, 1985.

Dilman, Ilham, *Studies in Language and Reason*, Macmillan, London, 1981.

Doyal, Len, and Harris, Roger, 'The practical foundations of human understanding', *New Left Review*, 139 (1983), pp.59–78.

Dreyfus, H. L., *What Computers Can't Do*, Harper & Row, New York, 1979.

Drury, M. O'C., 'Letters to a student of philosophy', *Philosophical Investigations*, 6 (1983), pp. 76–102, 159–74.

Dummett, Michael, *Truth and Other Enigmas*, Duckworth, London, 1978.

Eaglcton, T. F., 'Wittgenstein's friends', *New Left Review*, 135 (1982), pp. 64–90.

Easton, Susan, M., *Humanist Marxism and Wittgensteinian Social Philosophy*, Manchester University Press, Manchester, 1983.

Edwards, J. C., *Ethics without Philosophy: Wittgenstein and the Moral Life*, University of South Florida, Tampa, 1982.

Evans, Gareth, and McDowell, John, (eds), *Truth and Meaning*, Clarendon Press, Oxford, 1976.

Feyerabend, Paul, *Problems of Empiricism*, Cambridge University Press, Cambridge, 1981.

Findlay, J. N., *Wittgenstein: a Critique*, Routledge & Kegan Paul, London, 1984.

Ford, D. F., 'Barth's interpretation of the Bible', in *Karl Barth: Studies of his Theological Method*, ed. S. W. Sykes, Clarendon Press, Oxford, 1979, pp.55–87.

Galvin, John P., 'Jesus as scapegoat? *Violence and the Sacred* in the theology of Raymund Schwager', *The Thomist*, 46 (1982), pp. 173–94.

Girard, R., *Le Bouc Emissaire*, Grasset, Paris, 1982.

Girard, R., *Des Choses Cachées depuis la Fondation du Monde*, Grasset, Paris, 1978.

Girard, R., *Violence and the Sacred*, Johns Hopkins University Press, Baltimore and London, 1977.

Goodman, Nelson, *Ways of Worldmaking*, Harvester, Hassocks, 1978.

Griffin, J., *Wittgenstein's Logical Atomism*, Clarendon Press, Oxford, 1964.

Hallett, Garth, *A Companion to Wittgenstein's 'Philosophical Investigations'*, Cornell University Press, Ithaca and London, 1977.

Hardy, D. W., and Ford, D. F., *Jubilate: Theology in Praise*, Darton, Longman and Todd, London, 1984.

Hauerwas, Stanley, *The Peaceable Kingdom: A Primer in Christian Ethics*, SCM Press, London, 1984.

Heaney, Seamus, *Preoccupations: Selected Prose 1968–1978*, Faber and Faber, London, 1980.

Hölderlin, F., *Poems and Fragments*, trans. M. Hamburger, Routledge and Kegan Paul, London, 1966.

Holiday, Anthony, 'Wittgenstein's silence: philosophy, ritual and the limits of language', *Language and Communication*, 5 (1985), pp. 133–42.

Holland, R. F., *Against Empiricism*, Blackwell, Oxford, 1980.

Hylton, Peter, 'The nature of the proposition and the revolt against idealism', in *Philosophy in History*, eds. R. Rorty, J. B. Schneewind, Q. Skinner, Cambridge University Press, Cambridge, 1984, pp. 375–97.

James, William, *Essays in Radical Empiricism and A Pluralistic Universe*, E. P. Dutton, New York, 1971.

James, William, *The Principles of Psychology*, vols 1 and 2, Macmillan, London, 1891.

James, William, *The Varieties of Religious Experience: a Study in Human Nature*, Longman, Green, London, 1902.

Janik, Allan, 'Wittgenstein, Ficker, and *Der Brenner*', in *Wittgenstein: Sources and Perspectives*, ed. by C. G. Luckhardt, Harvester, Hassocks, 1979, pp.161–89.

Jones, J. R., 'How do I know who I am?', *Proceedings of the Aristotelian Society*, *Supplementary Volume*, 1967, pp. 1–18.

Jüngel, Eberhard, *God as the Mystery of the World*, T. & T. Clark, Edinburgh, 1983.

Kaufman, G. D., *God the Problem*, Harvard University Press, Cambridge, Mass., 1972.

Kaufman, G. D., 'Is there any way from Athens to Jerusalem?', *The Journal of Religion*, 59 (1979), pp. 340–6.

Keightley, Alan, *Wittgenstein, Grammar and God*, Epworth Press, London, 1976.

Kenny, Anthony, *The Legacy of Wittgenstein*, Blackwell, Oxford, 1984.

Kerr, Fergus, 'Küng's Case for God', *Vidyajyoti*, XLIX (1985), pp. 118–23.

Kerr, Fergus, 'Language as Hermeneutic in the later Wittgenstein', *Tijdschrift voor Filosofie*, 27 (1965), pp. 491–520.

Keynes, J. M., *Two Memoirs*, Rupert Hart-Davis, London, 1949.

Kripke, Saul A., *Wittgenstein on Rules and Private Language*, Blackwell, Oxford, 1982.

Küng, Hans, *Does God Exist? An Answer for Today*, Collins, London, 1978.

Küng, Hans, *Eternal Life?*, Collins, London, 1984.

Lampe, G. W. H., 'Christian theology in the Patristic period', in *A History of Christian Doctrine*, eds H. Cunliffe-Jones and B. Drewery, T. & T. Clark, Edinburgh, 1978, pp. 21–180.

Lash, Nicholas, 'How large is a "language game"?', *Theology*, LXXXVII (1984), pp. 19–28.

Lawrence, D. H., *Collected Letters*, vol. I, Heinemann, London, 1962.

Lovibond, Sabina, *Realism and Imagination in Ethics*, Blackwell, Oxford, 1983.

Luckhardt, C. G., (ed.) *Wittgenstein: Sources and Perspectives*, Harvester, Hassocks, 1979.

McDowell, John, 'Criteria, defeasibility, and knowledge', *Proceedings of the British Academy*, 1982, pp. 455–79.

McDowell, John, 'Wittgenstein on following a rule', *Synthese*, 58 (1984), pp. 325–63.

McGinn, Colin, *Wittgenstein on Meaning*, Blackwell, Oxford, 1984.

MacKinnon, Donald, *Explorations in Theology 5*, SCM Press, London, 1979.

McLain, Michael, 'On theological models', *Harvard Theological Review*, 62 (1969), pp. 155–87.

McMillan, Carol, *Women, Reason and Nature*, Blackwell, Oxford, 1982.

Madell, Geoffrey, *The Identity of the Self*, Edinburgh University Press, Edinburgh, 1981.

Malcolm, Norman, *Knowledge and Certainty: Essays and Lectures*, Cornell University Press, Ithaca and London, 1963.

Malcolm, Norman, *Ludwig Wittgenstein: A Memoir*, with a Biographical Sketch by G. H. von Wright, Oxford University Press, 1958, second edition with Wittgenstein's letters to Malcolm, 1984.

Malcolm, Norman, *Thought and Knowledge*, Cornell University Press, Ithaca and London, 1977.

Malcolm, Norman, 'Wittgenstein: The relation of language to instinctive behaviour', *Philosophical Investigations*, 5 (1982), pp. 3–22.

Manser, Anthony, 'Language, language-games and the theory of meaning', *Proceedings of the Aristotelian Society, Supplementary Volume*, 1982, pp.1–19.

Marett, R. R., *The Threshold of Religion*, Macmillan, London, 1914.

Martin, David, *The Breaking of the Image: a Sociology of Christian Theory and Practice*, Blackwell, Oxford, 1980.

Martin, David, *Tracts against the Times*, Lutterworth Press, Guildford and London, 1973.

Marx, Karl, *A Contribution to the Critique of Political Economy*, Lawrence & Wishart, London, 1971.

Marx, Karl, and Engels, Frederick, *Collected Works*, vol. 5, Lawrence & Wishart, London, 1976.

Matthews, Gareth, 'Ritual and the religious feelings', in *Explaining Emotions*, ed. A. O. Rorty, University of California Press, London, 1980, pp. 339–53.

Mill, J. S., *An Examination of Sir William Hamilton's Philosophy*, Longman, Green, London, 1889.

Moore, G. E., *Philosophical Studies*, Kegan Paul, Trench, Trubner, London, 1922.

Mounce, H. O., *Wittgenstein's Tractatus: an Introduction*, Blackwell, Oxford, 1981.

Murdoch, Iris, *The Sovereignty of Good*, Routledge & Kegan Paul, London, 1970.

Nagel, Thomas, *Mortal Questions*, Cambridge University Press, Cambridge, 1979.

Nielsen, Kai, 'Wittgensteinian fideism', *Philosophy*, 42 (1967), pp. 191–209.

Nietzsche, F., *The Gay Science with a prelude in rhymes and an appendix of songs*, trans. W. Kaufmann, Random House, New York, 1974.

O'Connell, R. J., *Saint Augustine's Early Theory of Man*, Harvard University Press, Cambridge, Mass., 1968.

O'Connell, Timothy, *Principles for a Catholic Morality*, Seabury Press, New York, 1978.

Ogden, Schubert M., *The Reality of God and Other Essays*, SCM Press, London, 1967.

O'Neill, Aidan, 'After Warnock: the ethics of embryo experimentation', *Bulletin of the Australian Society of Legal Philosophy*, 9 (1985), pp. 3–25.

O'Shaughnessy, Brian, *The Will: a Dual Aspect Theory*, vols 1 and 2, Cambridge University Press, Cambridge, 1980.

Pascal, B., *Pensées*, trans. A. J. Krailsheimer, Penguin Books, London, 1966.

Pears, David, *Wittgenstein*, Fontana/Collins, London, 1971.

Phillips, D. Z., *Primitive Reactions and the Reactions of Primitives*, Exeter College, Oxford, 1983.

Popkin, R. H., *The History of Scepticism from Erasmus to Descartes*, Harper & Row, New York, 1968.

Quine, W. V., *The Ways of Paradox and Other Essays*, Harvard University Press, Cambridge, Mass., enlarged edition, 1976.

Quine, W. V., *Word and Object*, MIT and John Wiley, New York and London, 1960.

Rahner, Karl, *Foundations of Christian Faith: an Introduction to the Idea of Christianity*, Darton Longman & Todd, London, 1978.

Rahner, Karl, *Theological Investigations*, vol. I, Darton Longman & Todd, London, 1961.

Rahner, Karl, *Theological Investigations*, vol. IX, Darton Longman & Todd, London, 1972.

Rahner, Karl, *Theological Investigations*, vol. XI, Darton Longman & Todd, London, 1974.

Ramsey, Ian, 'The systematic elusiveness of "I" ', *The Philosophical Quarterly*, 5 (1955), pp. 193–204.

Rhees, Rush, 'Can there be a private language?', *Proceedings of the Aristotelian Society, Supplementary Volume*, 1954, pp. 77–94.

Rorty, R., *Consequences of Pragmatism*, Harvester, Brighton, 1982.

Rubinstein, David, *Marx and Wittgenstein: Social Praxis and Social Explanation*, Routledge & Kegan Paul, London, 1981.

Russell, B., *The Analysis of Mind*, George Allen & Unwin, London, 1921.

Russell, B., 'Knowledge by acquaintance and knowledge by description', in *Mysticism and Logic*, George Allen & Unwin, London, 1917.

Russell, B., *An Outline of Philosophy*, George Allen & Unwin, London, 1927.

Russell, B., 'The philosophy of logical atomism', in *Logic and Knowledge: Essays 1901–1950*, ed. R. C. Marsh, George Allen & Unwin, London, 1956.

Schillebeeckx, Edward, *God among Us: The Gospel Proclaimed*, SCM Press, London, 1983.

Schillebeeckx, Edward, *Jesus: an Experiment in Christology*, Collins, London, 1979.

Schwager, Raymund, *Brauchen wir einen Sündenbock?*, Kösel, Munich, 1978.

Sherry, Patrick, *Religion, Truth and Language Games*, Macmillan, London, 1977.

Shwayder, D. S., 'Wittgenstein on mathematics', in *Studies in the Philosophy of Wittgenstein*, ed. Peter Winch, Routledge & Kegan Paul, London, 1969, pp.66–116.

Simons, Geoff, *Are Computers Alive? Evolution and New Life Forms*, Harvester, Brighton, 1983.

Singer, Peter, *Practical Ethics*, Cambridge University Press, Cambridge, 1979.

Singer, Peter, and Wells, Deane, *The Reproduction Revolution*, Oxford University Press, Oxford, 1984.

Sloman, A., *The Computer Revolution in Philosophy: Philosophy, Science and Models of Mind*, Harvester, Brighton, 1978.

Sorabji, Richard, 'Myths about non-propositional thought', in *Language and Logos*, ed. M. Schofield and M. C. Nussbaum, Cambridge University Press, Cambridge, 1982, pp. 295–314.

Taylor, Charles, *The Explanation of Behaviour*, Routledge & Kegan Paul, London, 1964.

Taylor, Charles, *Philosophical Papers*, vols 1 and 2, Cambridge University Press, Cambridge, 1985.

Tennant, F. R., *Philosophical Theology*, vols 1 and 2, Cambridge University Press, Cambridge, 1928–30.

Thomson, George 'Wittgenstein: some personal recollections', *Revolutionary World*, 37–39 (1980), pp. 86–8.

Timpanaro, S., *On Materialism*, NLB, London, 1975.

Torrance, T. F., 'The mind of Christ in worship: the problem of Apollinarianism in the Liturgy', in *Theology in Reconciliation*, Geoffrey Chapman, London, 1975.

Trigg, Roger, *Reason and Commitment*, Cambridge University Press, Cambridge, 1973.

Velecky, L., ' "The Five Ways" – Proofs of God's existence?', *The Monist*, 58 (1974), pp. 36–51.

Velecky, L., 'Flew on Aquinas', *Philosophy*, 43 (1968), pp. 213–30.

Vetter, A., 'Ich', *Lexikon für Theologie und Kirche*, vol. 5, Herder, Freiburg, 1960.

Vlastos, Gregory, 'Socrates' disavowal of knowledge', *The Philosophical Quarterly*, 35 (1985), pp. 1–31.

Vlastos, Gregory, 'The Socratic Elenchus', *Oxford Studies in Ancient Philosophy*, vol. I, ed. Julia Annas, Clarendon Press, Oxford, 1983, pp. 27–58.

Waismann, F., *The Principles of Linguistic Philosophy*, ed. R. Harré, Macmillan, London, 1965.

Warner, Martin, 'Philosophical autobiography: St Augustine and John Stuart Mill', in *Philosophy and Literature*, ed. A. Phillips Griffiths, Royal Institute of Philosophy Lecture Series 16, Cambridge University Press, Cambridge, 1983. pp. 189–210.

Weiler, G., 'On Fritz Mauthner's critique of language', *Mind*, LXVII (1958), pp.80–7.

Williams, Bernard, *Descartes: The Project of Pure Enquiry*, Penguin Books, London, 1978.

Williams, Bernard, *Morality: an Introduction to Ethics*, Cambridge University Press, Cambridge, 1972.

Williams, Bernard, 'Philosophy', in *The Legacy of Greece*, ed. M. I. Finley, Clarendon Press, Oxford, 1981.

Williams, Bernard, 'Wittgenstein and idealism', in *Understanding Wittgenstein*, ed. G. Vesey, Royal Institute of Philosophy Lecture Series 7, Macmillan, London, 1974, reprinted in *Moral Luck: Philosophical Papers 1973–1980*, Cambridge University Press, Cambridge, pp. 144–63.

Williams, Rowan, ' "Religious realism": on not quite agreeing with Don Cupitt', *Modern Theology*, 1 (1984), pp. 3–24.

Wilson, M. D., *Descartes*, Routledge & Kegan Paul, London, 1978.

Winch, Peter, '*Eine Einstellung zur Seele*', *Proceedings of the Aristotelian Society*, 1980–81, pp. 1–15.

Winch, Peter, 'Introduction: the Unity of Wittgenstein's philosophy', in *Studies in the Philosophy of Wittgenstein*, Routledge & Kegan Paul, London, 1969, pp.1–19.

Wisdom, John, *Other Minds*, Blackwell, Oxford, 1952.

Wisdom, John, *Philosophy and Psycho-Analysis*, Blackwell, Oxford, 1953.

Wittgenstein, L., Full bibliographical details of the major works of Wittgenstein are given in the list of abbreviations at the beginning of the book (p. xi).

Wittgenstein, L., 'A lecture on ethics', *Philosophical Review*, 74 (1965), pp. 3–12.

Wittgenstein, L., *Letters*, with a memoir by Paul Engelmann, Blackwell, Oxford, 1967.

Wittgenstein, L., 'Letters to Ludwig von Ficker', trans. Bruce Gillette, ed. A. Janik, in *Wittgenstein: Sources and Perspectives*, ed. C. G. Luckhardt, Harvester, Hassocks, 1979, pp. 82–98.

Wittgenstein, L., *Letters to Russell, Keynes and Moore*, ed. G. H. von Wright, Blackwell, Oxford, 1974.

Wittgenstein, L., '*Ursache und Wirkung: Intuitives Erfassen*', *Philosophia*, 6 (1976), pp. 427–45.

Wollheim, R., *The Sheep and the Ceremony*, Cambridge University Press, Cambridge, 1979.

Index

absolute conception, 23–6
action, 67, 110, 115, 120, 158
adoptionism, 140
Alexander, S., 126, 131
angels
  how they talk, 79–80
  human beings contrasted with, 14,
    80, 168, 179, 185–7
Anscombe, G. E. M., 32, 174–5
anti-realism, 127–30
Aristotle, 4, 50, 187, 189
atomism, 24, 59–66
atonement, 180–2
Augustine, 38–42, 56–7, 70–1, 75,
    157, 166, 187, 188

Bachtin, N., 66
Bakhtin, M., 66n
Barth, K., 8–9, 152
Beethoven, L., 168
behaviour, 46, 74, 100
behaviourism, 25, 91–2, 111, 130
Berkeley, G., 36, 128
Borges, J. L., 165n
Bukharin, N., 67, 120, 134

Caramuel, J., 175n
Cartesian psychology, 4–5, 8–10, 14,
    20, 43, 94–5, 175–8

Cavell, S. L., 75–6, 110n, 187–8
ceremony, 34–5, 157–60, 183–4
Chirico, P., 20–1
cognitive science, 185–6
community, 8, 26, 65, 70, 76, 85, 118,
    132, 135, 172
conceptual frameworks, 105–8
consciousness, 4–7, 10, 178
  and community, 76
  Marx on, 68
  from the outside and as the world,
    96
  satirized, 116–17
Cupitt, D., 16–18, 129

Davidson, D., 105–9
Descartes, R., 3–5, 7–10, 15, 23–4,
    42–3, 50, 55, 82, 112, 117, 118,
    121, 178, 189
designating objects, 70–1, 85, 88, 96,
    104, 125, 133, 146–7
docetism, 140
doubt, 114
Drury, M. O'C., 32–8, 152–3, 156–9
Dummett, M., 127–30

Eddington, A. S., 123
embryo research, 176–7
empiricism, 21, 130–2

Ernst, C., 14
Euripides, 189

faith as private object, 148–50
Feyerabend, P., 24
Ficker, L., 36–7
finitude, 9, 12, 45
   as flaw, 130, 184–5
first person perspective, 3, 41, 43, 84,
   94–8, 178
flyglass, 75n
forms of life, 29–31, 64–5, 68, 69,
   109, 120, 132–4
   Cavell on, 75
   as natural *a priori*, 105, 135, 177
Frazer, J. G., 119, 159–61, 181
Frege, G., 129n, 186
Freud, S., 51

Girard, R., 181–2
Gnosticism, 140, 185–6, 187
God, existence of, 8–9, 13, 16, 128,
   151–6, 184
God's-eye view, 16, 17, 24, 44–5, 97,
   135
Goethe, J. W., 32, 38, 120, 137, 168
grammar, 145–7
Gregory the Great, 80–1

Haecker, T., 37
Hannah, 171
Heaney, S., 35
Hegel, G. W. F., 36, 61, 65
Heidegger, M., 151
Hölderlin, F., 115
Holland, R. F., 131
human body, 27
   antipathy to, 137, 140, 186, 188
   metaphysical conception of, 45–6,
      60, 93–4, 139
   natural expressiveness of, 41–2, 88–
      90, 109, 150
human nature, the sinister in, 161–2,
   181

idealism, 101–4, 121–3

Ignatius Loyola, 15, 50
incarnation, 13, 169
inner life, 11, 74–5, 77, 85, 90–2, 100,
   125, 172
   paradigm of the indescribable, 164,
inside–outside, 40–1, 43, 56
intention, 174–5
interpreting, 110–12
introspection, 69, 96, 98–9

James, H., 164
James, W., 5–7, 61, 83, 96, 157–9,
   164, 174
Johnson, S., 34, 162
Jones, J. R., 94n, 96n
Jüngel, E., 8

Kant, I., 5, 17, 36–7
Kaufman, G. D., 14n, 21–3
Kenny, A. J. P., 14n
Keynes, J. M., 60
Kierkegaard, S., 15, 37
Kripke, S., 29n, 101n
Küng, H., 14–16, 170

labour, 68
Lawrence, D. H., 59–60
laxism, 175
Leavis, F. R., 51
life, 133–6
life-philosophy, 134n, 136, 140
liturgy, 34–5, 172, 183
Lovibond, S., 132n, 137n
Luther, M., 39, 146, 148–9, 187

McDowell, J., 137n, 140n, 185n
MacKinnon, D., 123n, 129n, 130n,
   171
Malcolm, N., 30–2, 39, 74, 98
Malebranche, N., 5
Marett, R. R., 183
Martin, D., 73n, 183
Marxism, 66–8
meaning as mental activity, 42, 55–6,
   71, 72, 76

metaphysical tradition, 52, 115, 136, 140, 168–9, 186, 187, 189–90
Mill, J. S., 82–3, 123, 176
Minsky, M., 186
mistrust, 78
Molinism, 128
Moore, G. E., 5–7, 24, 59, 61, 152
Murdoch, I., 5
music, 33, 163–6

Nagel, T., 24
naming, 56–8, 69–71, 95
'New Cartesianism', 185
Nielsen, K., 28
Nietzsche, F., 15, 61, 151, 168, 188
nuclear deterrence, 175

objectivity, 24, 32–3, 169
O'Connell, T., 19–20
Ogden, S., 18–19
O'Neil, A., 176–7
Origen, 33–4, 40, 168–9
ostensive definition, 11, 70–1, 73, 104, 123, 125
other minds, 78–83, 91–3

Pascal, B., 15, 158, 175*n*, 189
Pascal, R., 66–7
Pears, D., 32
Pepler, C., 32*n*
phenomenalism, 123–4
Phillips, D. Z., 183*n*
philosophy
  data of, 38
  as misunderstanding of the body, 188
  raw material for, 48
Plato, 40, 62, 187, 189
Plotinus, 40
pluralism, 105
prejudice, 49, 58, 98, 137
presupposing, 22, 113, 115
private language, 72, 84–90, 91–2, 106, 132
psychologism, 129, 158

Quine, W. V., 81–2, 173

Rahner, K., 7–9, 10–14, 170, 180
Ramsey, F. P., 66
rationalism, 9, 92, 118, 153, 183
reactions, 65, 70, 76, 92–3, 108, 110, 112, 115, 117, 132, 183
realism, 121–40
religion
  'danced out', 183
  philosophy of, 29, 171
representing, 134–6
Ricardo, D., 67
Russell, B., 24, 44, 59–65, 139, 157, 164, 186
  and the parsons, 156

scapegoating, 181–2
Schillebeeckx, E., 180, 184–5
Schwager, R., 181–2
secret thoughts, 172–3
self
  autonomous, 7–8, 16–18
  as deity, 17–18, 23, 116
  mentalist–individualist, 14
  metaphysical conception of, 89–90, 92
  as private object, 18–21, 100
  as world viewed, 98
sense-data, 24, 123–6
Sextus Empiricus, 121
Shwayder, D. S., 129
signs, communication without, 43–5, 93, 136
Singer, P., 176–7
Skinner, F., 68*n*
Socrates, 76, 190*n*
solipsism, 26, 72, 81, 87
Sophocles, 189
Sraffa, P., 66–7
sympathy 'essential', 108

Taylor, C., 25–6, 33, 46
Teilhard de Chardin, P., 14
Tennant, F. R., 157

theology
  as grammar, 145–8
  naturalized, 163
  philosophy of, 171, 187
Thomas Aquinas, 4, 39, 79–80, 154, 178–9, 187
Thomson, G., 66
Titian, 180
Trakl, G., 37
Trigg, R., 29
Turing, A., 185n

Uhland, J. L., 166

Vetter, A., 178
Vlastos, G., 190n

Waismann, F., 47, 56
Williams, B., 23, 101–2, 162
Wisdom, J., 80
Wittgensteinian fideism, 28–31
Wright, G. H. von, 32, 39, 43n, 186